as we forgive

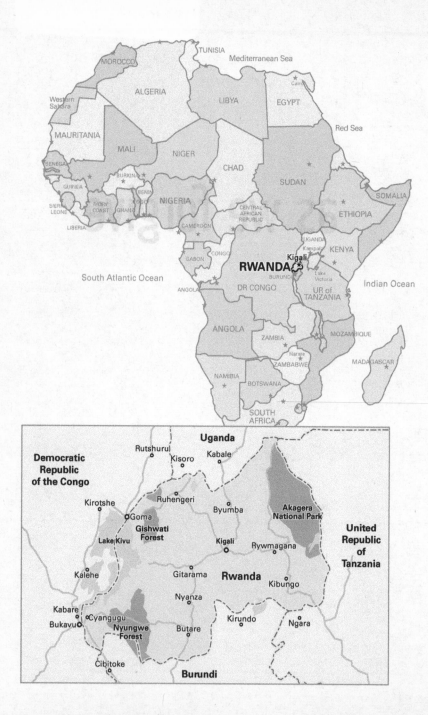

as we forgive

Stories of Reconciliation from Rwanda

catherine claire larson

ZONDERVAN®

ZONDERVAN.com/
AUTHORTRACKER
follow your favorite authors

ZONDERVAN®

As We Forgive
Copyright © 2009 by Catherine Claire Larson

Requests for information should be addressed to:
Zondervan, *Grand Rapids, Michigan* 49530

Library of Congress Cataloging-in-Publication Data

Larson, Catherine Claire.
    As we forgive : stories of reconciliation from Rwanda / Catherine Claire Larson.
    p.   cm.
    Includes bibliographical references.
    ISBN 978-0-310-28730-8 (softcover: alk. paper)
    1. War victims—Rwanda—Biography. 2. Reconciliation—Social aspects—Rwanda.
3. Genocide—Rwanda—History—20th century. 4. Rwanda—History—Civil War,
1994—Atrocities. 5. Rwanda—Ethnic relations. 6. Social change—Rwanda. 7. Social
conflict—Rwanda. 8. Rwanda—Social conditions. 9. Rwanda—Biography. I. Title.
DT450.442.L37   2008
967.57104'3—dc22   2008033462

The appendix on pages 276–77 is copyright © 2006 by John Steward and David Fullerton. Used by permission. www.rwandanstories.org

Published in association with the literary agency of Alive Communications, Inc., 7680 God-dard Street, Suite 200, Colorado Springs, CO 80920. www.alivecommunications.com

Interior design by Beth Shagene

Printed in the United States of America

---

09 10 11 12 13 14 • 24 23 22 21 20 19 18 17 16 15 14 13 12 11 10 9 8 7 6 5 4 3 2 1

as we forgive

Stories of Reconciliation from Rwanda

catherine claire larson

ZONDERVAN®

ZONDERVAN.com/
AUTHORTRACKER
follow your favorite authors

ZONDERVAN®

As We Forgive
Copyright © 2009 by Catherine Claire Larson

Requests for information should be addressed to:

Zondervan, *Grand Rapids, Michigan* 49530

Library of Congress Cataloging-in-Publication Data

Larson, Catherine Claire.
    As we forgive : stories of reconciliation from Rwanda / Catherine Claire Larson.
    p. cm.
    Includes bibliographical references.
    ISBN 978-0-310-28730-8 (softcover: alk. paper)
    1. War victims—Rwanda—Biography. 2. Reconciliation—Social aspects—Rwanda.
3. Genocide—Rwanda—History—20th century. 4. Rwanda—History—Civil War,
1994—Atrocities. 5. Rwanda—Ethnic relations. 6. Social change—Rwanda. 7. Social
conflict—Rwanda. 8. Rwanda—Social conditions. 9. Rwanda—Biography. I. Title.
DT450.442.L37   2008
967.57104'3—dc22   2008033462

Published in association with the literary agency of Alive Communications, Inc., 7680 Goddard Street, Suite 200, Colorado Springs, CO 80920. www.alivecommunications.com

Interior design by Beth Shagene

Printed in the United States of America

09 10 11 12 13 14 • 24 23 22 21 20 19 18 17 16 15 14 13 12 11 10 9 8 7 6 5 4 3 2 1

To those who had the courage and hope
to allow me to share their stories
with the world

contents

chronology of events

1885   At the Berlin Conference of European Powers, Germany received control of the area constituting present-day Rwanda.

1894   The first European explorers arrived in Rwanda.

1921   A League of Nations mandate awarded Rwanda and Burundi to Belgium. The Belgians maintained the Tutsi king to rule the country.

1926   The Belgians introduced ethnic identity cards.

1933   Identity cards became compulsory after Belgians conducted a census. What had largely been a semifluid distinction of class between Hutu and Tutsi became a distinction fixed from birth.

1957   The Hutu manifesto was published, denouncing the Tutsi-dominated political leadership of the country. The Parmehutu party (or Party for the emancipation of Hutu) was formed.

1959   The Tutsi king Mutara Rudahigwa III mysteriously died. Hutu, supported by the Belgians, rose up against the Tutsi aristocracy. Hutus killed thousands of Tutsis and thousands more fled the country.

A Hutu president, Gregoire Kayibanda, rose to power, representing the Parmehutu party. Rwanda gained independence.

Tutsis who had been forced to flee in 1959 attacked the country. Hutus attacked Tutsis in retaliation, killing an estimated 12,000. More Tutsis fled the country.

1967   More massacres against Tutsis in Rwanda occurred.

1973   In a coup d'état Major Juvénal Habyarimana took control of Rwanda. He created a one party state and established quotas that only allowed Tutsis less than 10 percent of the available jobs. More Tutsis fled the country as tensions mounted.

1978   Juvénal Habyarimana was elected president.

1986   Exiled Tutsis in neighboring Uganda formed the RPF (Rwandan Patriotic Front). Originally, the RPF was composed of those who helped overthrow the Ugandan dictator, Milton Obote.

1990   The RPF achieved its first victory in Rwanda. RPF leader Fred Rwigema was killed by a sniper. His childhood friend, Paul Kagame, took control of the RPF.

1991   The Rwandan Armed Forces (FAR) began to equip civilian militias, composed of extremist Hutus, to fight back. These militias were called *interahamwe*, or literally, "those who stand together."

1992   Local massacres of Tutsis were carried out.

1993   Hutu and RPF leaders negotiated a power-sharing agreement at Arusha, Tanzania. Extremist Hutus considered the agreement a sell-out. Under the command of Canadian General Romeo Dallaire, 2,500 UN peace-keeping forces (UNAMIR) were deployed to help ensure the Arusha Peace Agreement.

1993   Radio Milles Collines was launched as a private radio station. Family members of Hutu President Juvénal Habyarimana were shareholders. The president delayed implementation of power-sharing agreement. Interahamwe continued to be recruited and trained. Radio Milles Collines broadcasted anti-Tutsi propaganda.

January 11, 1994   Canadian General Romeo Dallaire faxed a warning to UN headquarters that preparations for a mass killing are underway.

March 1994   A prominent Hutu, Felicien Kabuga, is believed to have imported 50,000 machetes from Kenya.

April 6, 1994   On a return trip from Tanzania a mysterious plane crash killed Rwandan and Burundian presidents. Today many believe that Hutu extremists, worried that Habyarimana was about to implement the Arusha Peace Agreement, planned the attack. Word spread that the RPF had shot down the President's plane. Killings began that night as the Rwandan Armed Forces (FAR) set up roadblocks and interahamwe militias went from door to door killing. UNAMIR forces were forbidden to intervene.

April 7, 1994   Moderate Hutu leaders were tracked and killed, including Prime Minister Agathe Uwilingiyimana. Ten Belgian UNAMIR peacekeepers ordered to protect the Prime Minister were murdered in an ambush attack. Meanwhile, Hutu interahamwe forces killed thousands of Tutsis. The RPF launched a counterattack.

April 8, 1994   An interim government was established and Hutu Jean Kambanda was appointed prime minister. He supported calls over the radio for Hutus to abuse, hurt, and kill Tutsi and Hutu moderates. In 1998 he would plead guilty to charges that he incited the slaughter of over 800,000 Rwandans. General Dallaire warned Kofi Annan that the Kigali government was planning to slaughter the Tutsi. Annan's office ordered General Romeo Dallaire not to protect the informant or to confiscate arms stockpiles.

April 9 – 10, 1994   French, Belgian and American civilians were rescued by their governments. No Rwandans were rescued.

April 11, 1994   UNAMIR soldiers protecting 2,000 Tutsis at the Don Bosco School were ordered to withdraw to Kigali airport. Most Tutsi were killed after their departure. In the countryside, the interahamwe gathered local farmers and began systematic attacks.

April 14, 1994   Belgium withdrew its UN peacekeeping forces.

April 16, 1994   Pastor Elizaphan Ntakirutimana permitted an armed convoy of Hutu officials and militia to carry out a day-long massacre in Mugonero. Meanwhile about 12,000 Tutsis were murdered at a local Kibuye church and stadium and in the surrounding countryside.

April 21, 1994   The UN Security Council voted unanimously to withdraw most of the UNAMIR troops, cutting the force from 2,500 to 270. The International Red Cross estimated that tens, perhaps hundreds of thousands of Rwandans were now dead.

April 25, 1994   In the southern region of Butare, a building where 500 Tutsis were hiding was set ablaze. In 2001 Benedictine Sister Maria Kisito stood trial in Belgium for providing the gasoline.

April 28, 1994   Christine Shelley, spokeswoman for the State Department, was asked whether what was happening in Rwanda was a genocide. She responded, "... the use of the term 'genocide' has a very precise legal meaning, although it's not strictly a legal determination. There are other factors in there as well." Meanwhile, the State Department issued a secret intelligence report identifying the killings as genocide.

April 30, 1994   Hundreds of thousands of fleeing Tutsis poured into neighboring Tanzania, Burundi, and Zaire. The UN agreed to a resolution condemning the killing but omitted the word "genocide." If the word had been used, the UN would have been bound to prevent it.

May 14, 1994   RPF forces reached Nyamata area and started combing the marshes for survivors.

May 17, 1994   The UN Security Council issues another resolution, this time saying that "acts of genocide may have been committed." While the UN agreed to send 5,500 troops with new powers to defend civilians, disagreements between the US and

UN over the financing of the operation delayed deployment. Meanwhile, the International Red Cross estimated death toll rose to around 500,000 Rwandans.

May 22, 1994   The Kigali airport and Kanombe barracks fell to RPF forces, as well as the northern and eastern parts of Rwanda.

June 22, 1994   Disagreements continued over the funding and deployment of UN forces. The UN authorized emergency help through 2,500 French troops known as Operation Turquoise. They were to create a "safe" area in the government-controlled part of Rwanda, although killing continued here also.

July 4, 1994   The RPF took control of Kigali and Butare in the south. RPF leaders said they would form a government on the basis of the Arusha Accords.

July 13–14, 1994   Hutus fleeing the RPF advance flooded into Zaire along the Gitarama road. A tidal wave of approximately 10,000–12,000 refugees per hour washed across the border into the town of Goma, creating a severe humanitarian crisis.

July 18, 1994   The RPF announced that the war was over, declared a cease-fire, and named Pasteur Bizimungu, a Hutu, as president with Faustin Twagiramungu as prime minister. An estimated 800,000 to a million Tutsis and moderate Hutus were killed in the span of 100 days, some 300,000 of them were thought to be children, while another 95,000 children lost one or both parents.

October 3, 1994   The United Nations Security Council called the massacres committed in Rwanda, "a genocide."

November 1994   The UN Security Council established an International Criminal Tribunal to prosecute those responsible for the Rwandan genocide. Almost fifteen years later, only 28 people had been convicted.

November–December 1996   Rwandan forces supported rebel groups opposing Congo President Mobutu Sese Seko's regime.

Tens of thousands of Hutus were killed and thousands more were forced to return back to Rwanda. They joined the 85,000 held in prisons built for no more than 20,000. Those interahamwe who were not killed or forced back during this time continued to live in Congo and made border raids over the years to come.

April 1996 President Pasteur Bizimungu dedicated the Kigali genocide memorial.

March 15, 1998 President Clinton apologized to Rwandan genocide victims, saying, "We did not act quickly enough after the killing began ... We did not immediately call these crimes by their rightful name: genocide."

May 7, 1998 UN Secretary General Kofi Annan apologized to Rwandan parliament, saying, "What we did was not nearly enough ... to save Rwanda ... We will not deny that, in their greatest hour of need, the world failed the people of Rwanda."

March 23, 2000 President Pasteur Bizimungu resigned following a month-long debate on ethnic tensions and corruption.

April 17, 2000 Paul Kagame was elected the country's first Tutsi president.

January 2003 Rwandan President Paul Kagame issued a decree to release elderly, sick, and lower-level killers and looters from the 1994 genocide who had confessed their crimes in an effort to ease intense overcrowding in the country's prisons and foster national reconciliation. At the time of this writing, approximately 60,000 prisoners have been released, many of whom have been tried in gacaca courts.

secrets of
the Umuvumu's scars

THE GASH ACROSS THE FACE OF EMMANUEL MAHURO, A SEVENTEEN-year-old Rwandan native, is no longer an open wound. Today, like a jagged boundary line on a map, a scar juts down the plateau of his forehead, across the bridge of his nose, and up the slope of his right cheek. It is impossible to look into Emmanuel's eyes without seeing this deep cut, a mark of division etched across his face—and the face of Rwanda—fifteen years after the genocide.

My first reaction to such scars is to avert my eyes. But to look away from Emmanuel's scars is to look away from him. Strangely, as my eyes adjust to Emmanuel's face, there is an impulse, not to recoil, but to follow the line of the scar across his skin.

Emmanuel's scar testifies to two realities. It is a witness to the human capacity for evil. To look at it is to hear it scream the brutality of an April that aches in the memory of an entire people. Yet his scar testifies to another truth: the stunning capacity of humans to heal from the unthinkable. To trace that scar is to discover the hope of a people who, despite losing everything, are finding a way to forge a common future for Rwanda.

Rwanda's wounds, like Emmanuel's, are agonizingly deep. Today, they are being opened afresh as tens of thousands of killers are released from prison to return to the hills where they hunted down and killed former neighbors, friends, and classmates. In the everyday business of life—purchasing corrugated metal for roofing, burying bananas in the ground to make *urwagwa*, and hauling harvested sorghum to the market—survivors commonly meet the eyes of people who shattered their former lives. How can they live together? This is not a philosophical question, but a practical one that confronts Rwandans daily.

In some shape or form, all Rwandans ask this question. Some, like Antoine Rutayisire, himself a survivor, put the question starkly: "If they told you that a murderer was to be released into your neighborhood, how would you feel? But what if this time, they weren't just releasing one, but forty thousand?" For Antoine and his country, which has released some sixty thousand prisoners since 2003, these questions are not hypothetical.

Fatuma Ndangiza, executive secretary of the National Unity and Reconciliation Commission, began wrestling in earnest with the questions on January 10, 2003, when the president first decided to provisionally release forty thousand of the 120,000 Rwandans held in egregiously overcrowded prisons. Even with a fully functional legal system, something which had been wiped out with the slaughter of many Tutsi in 1994, the backlog of cases would have taken over two hundred years. "I was driving in the car around one o'clock, when I heard President Kagame say that these people who are going to be released have to be taken to the Reconciliation Commission for reeducation before going back to the community." At first, Fatuma thought the president was crazy. "What sort of education do you give to people who confessed that they killed? What do we tell the victims?" she wondered.

Government officials weren't the only ones who worried about the pending release. For Gahigi, a Tutsi who lost 142 family members during the genocide, the question dripped with fear: "This time, will they kill us all?" The survivors could not imagine living side by side with their tormentors. Would Rwandan society, still barely functioning, now collapse entirely?

But even as survivors were tormented with fears and questions, so also were many of the offenders themselves. Saveri, one of the killers, recalls how he felt when he heard he would be released: "I was so overjoyed, but fear lingered also. How was I going to face a survivor and squarely look her in the eyes after I had wiped out her family?" This thought terrorized him.

Similarly, John, another man who stained his own hands with blood when he killed his neighbor, remembers, "I had a mixture of fear when I learned I was going to be released from prison. After a long time in prison it was hard for me to come back to the community that I had sinned against. My biggest challenge was how I was going to meet Chantal, whose father I had killed. This was my deepest fear."

Years later, these fears and questions continue. Each day Rwandans struggle to understand how to live together. Behind prison walls, perpetrators are urged to tell the truth publicly about their crimes and to make actual or symbolic restitution. Some survivors volunteer to enter the prisons and share the stories of their shattered lives, hoping to create empathy and shared understanding. In mud-walled homes, widows and survivors gather to share and to support one another.

An ancient form of justice, known as *gacaca* (pronounced "gah-cha-cha"), unfolds on grassy fields under wild fig trees, called *umuvumu*, where trusted elders, men and women of integrity, hear cases. Unlike the Western court system, where the best strategy can be to deny guilt until the government proves it beyond a reasonable doubt, gacaca works best if there is truth telling and confession. Together, the elders, the perpetrators, and the community—including the survivors themselves—work out solutions. The solutions may involve more prison time or require the offenders to return to the place of their crime and participate in community service and reconciliation. Gacaca strives to bring justice and peace into communities that have been shattered.

Sometimes this process even paves the way for moving beyond justice to reconciliation. Some perpetrators, whose hearts are truly changed, are eager to go beyond what is required of them. Hands that once swung machetes in violence now smooth mud bricks in peace as they voluntarily build homes for their victims. Survivors, once seething with rage, are moving toward forgiveness. While there are still deep wounds—many that may never heal—there are also clear and unmistakable signs of hope, bearing witness to the possibility of reconciliation.

There's an ancient craft practiced in Rwanda, an age-old art that has been almost lost today. The Umuvumu trees that shade the Gacaca gatherings have another purpose. Once the Umuvumu tree has matured, a small strip of bark is cut away. Like our own bodies, the tree responds to the gash. The Umuvumu produces a fine red matting of slender roots to cover the wound. The ancients then treated that matting to create a cloth, commonly called bark cloth. Historically, the bark cloth was used to make royal clothing. Today, artisans fashion the reddish-brown fabric into traditional African ceremonial dress, wallets, purses, placemats, book covers, and maps of Africa, adding decorative detail through paint, print, or needlework. Strangely, mysteriously, things of beauty and usefulness sometimes come from wounds.

This is why I want to understand what is happening in Rwanda today. Because I too have scars—wounds that make me wonder if these too can become emblems not of shame but of triumph, not of rage but of restoration. I hesitate to evoke my scars in the same breath as those the Rwandans carry. Somehow I feel that I am treading on hallowed ground when I see the kind of pain these people have had to go through. Their pain makes my pain look like a paper cut in comparison. Perhaps you will feel the same as you read on. Perhaps not.

But for me, this is part of the importance of understanding. If Rwandans can find the courage to forgive, then perhaps there is hope for us in those problems that seem to pale in comparison and in those that echo the horrors of the genocide. This is why when I see a country known for radical brutality becoming, person by person, a place known for radical forgiveness, I want to understand. While this process is far from complete, every instance is so beautiful, so extraordinary, so beyond ordinary human capability, that it demands our attention and exploration.

We in the West, just as Rwandans, desperately need to understand forgiveness. We live in a violent world filled with conflicts. Political polarization, terrorist attacks, racial tensions, immigration fears, and school shootings define our national landscape. Meanwhile, privately, we struggle with broken marriages, splintered relationships, and doubts that pierce us to the core.

Could there be a common road map to reconciliation? Could there be a shared future after unthinkable evil? If forgiveness is possible after genocide, then perhaps there is hope for the comparably smaller rifts that plague our relationships, our communities, and our nation.

Rwanda looms as an uncharted case study in forgiveness. *As We Forgive* traces the route of reconciliation in the lives of Rwandans —victims, widows, orphans, and perpetrators—whose past and future intersect. We discover in these stories how suffering, memory, and identity set up roadblocks to forgiveness, while mediation, truth telling, restitution, and interdependence create bridges to healing.

But this is not a path, nor a book, for the faint of heart. For the boy whose face bears the scars of a torturous gash, for the child who witnessed her family burned alive, for the daughter who cannot blot out the picture of her father's blood-soaked face, forgiveness is one of the most excruciating journeys imaginable. Its miles wind through chasms of pain and across solitary deserts of rage. Yet, while it is perhaps the most difficult of all journeys, it is, nonetheless, a journey that is possible.

In *No Future without Forgiveness*, Bishop Desmond Tutu describes "a picture of three U.S. servicemen standing in front of the Vietnam Memorial in Washington, D.C. One asks, 'Have you forgiven those who held you prisoner of war?' 'I will never forgive them,' replies the other. His mate says, 'Then it is certain they still have you in prison, don't they?'"[1]

Scars represent a natural border between past and future. If not healed properly, these borders become mementos of rage that propel their bearers into a vindictive future. But a different story can be written. Rather than being lines of demarcation between Hutu and Tutsi, scars can become the intersection of justice and mercy, stitched by forgiveness, the only thread strong enough to bind these wounds. Through forgiveness, these scars cease to be emblems of vengeance, becoming instead evidence of supernatural hope. This is the story that Rwanda can tell the world. This is a story we need to understand.

Rosaria's litany

*"My soul is overwhelmed with sorrow
to the point of death."*
Matthew 26:38

CADEAUX'S EYES LAUGHED. A GRIN FLICKERED ACROSS HER FACE AND settled into a slight smile as she went to fetch water. Leaning over the bucket, Cadeaux splashed water on her cheeks, not noticing the dark beauty shimmering back at her. With a block of soap, she scrubbed her neck, her arms, her legs, her feet, and finally her sandals while her slender shadow bowed beneath Rwanda's fierce August sun. At the age of twelve, she was on the cusp of womanhood, but still had the frame of a child and a sheen of innocence.

Her sandaled feet skimmed along the path as she returned home. Were it not for the vividness of the yellow jacaranda trees, the seamless blue skies, and Cadeaux's swishing lavender skirt, the road, the homes, and the roofs would have seemed a still life in sepia.

Back home, Cadeaux broke a deep silence with her soft footfalls and the creak of a door latch. Inside, her mother, Rosaria, had been going about her daily chores cloaked with an air of solemn dignity, wearing her sorrow like holy garments. A crushed hand hung like prayer beads loosely at her side.

Rosaria's eyes lit on Cadeaux as she flitted past. Somehow, the saturated air felt less stifling with her there. Rosaria breathed more freely. More than bread or wine or water, Cadeaux seemed to her mother a sacrament—a visible sign of inward grace. The name Rosaria gave her had this ripeness of meaning. Born in December of 1994, nine months and four days after horror's opening night, Cadeaux is her mother's consolation, her laughter, and her hope. Her name means "gift," because, as Rosaria will tell you, "She was the only gift I had left."

In a place where each person's grief is strung together like bead upon bead, Rosaria must focus her mind on Cadeaux, on the gift before her. But sometimes, she can't help how her thoughts circle back to a painful past.

WHEN ROSARIA'S SON, ALEXIS, HAD BECOME ILL WITH A LENGTHY stomach sickness, she had taken him to the hospital in Kigali. That was three days before the fighting began. When the violence erupted, Rosaria's husband, a driver for an agricultural processing plant, gathered clothes and food and drove the three other children with him to work, hoping they would be safe there. Only months after the slaughter would Rosaria learn their fate.

On May 10, 1994, two weeks after the UN conceded "acts of genocide" had been committed and thirty-five days into the slaughter that had already consumed an estimated 500,000 people, the hospital where Rosaria and her son found refuge forced all the patients to leave. Ostensibly, the hospital had too many military soldiers who needed care. More likely, hospital officials were being pressured to turn out the Tutsi patients.

Sheltered from a month of horrors, Rosaria and her son were now thrust onto the center stage of the nightmare. Along the roadside, bodies lay in various positions of flight, glass from a smashed-in car

windshield glinted in the sunlight, and a wild dog gnawed at something resembling a human leg. While the U.S. State Department argued over whether or not to jam Rwandan radio stations, Rosaria and Alexis walked by a radio blaring, "Search houses, search the marshes, search the ditches; make sure no rebels have slipped in to hide." A few miles down the road they found temporary shelter in the Holy Family Church, the largest cathedral in Kigali.

The church teemed with the barely living: a woman without an arm trying to nurse a baby, an old man moaning with bloodied cloths wrapped around his head, a child crying inconsolably for her missing mother. As Rosaria unrolled a blanket for her son, she saw the head priest speaking angrily with one of the nuns. He was a young man with a face full of hate, dressed not in a collar, but in a flack vest with a gun. After the genocide, the tribunal would charge this man with aiding the militia and also with rape. Two nights after Rosaria arrived, the militia did, in fact, raid the church. They came with a list of men, who were promptly taken outside. Alexis and Rosaria heard the shouting, then the shots. Rosaria and Alexis would not stay to see more executions; they decided to move at first light.

From there they fled to Nyamirambo Stadium and then along the Nyabarongo River out of the city toward Nyamata. They did their best to avoid the roadblocks where their fellow Rwandans, drunk on banana beer and blood, shot or butchered anyone without a Hutu identity card and piled the bodies in ditches beside the road.

Two days into the journey, Rosaria and her son encountered three Burundian refugees who were now caught in the midst of Rwanda's genocide. Hoping that identifying with them might offer her some protection, Rosaria posed as their leader. When they reached Nyamata, however, a few of Rosaria's neighbors, who had moved farther north to continue looting, recognized her.

"They sliced us with machetes and left us to die," Rosaria said slowly as if reciting details rubbed smooth through heavy handling.

Rosaria was the only one who survived, and Cadeaux was still in her womb. She paused, rolling over the mystery in her mind. "The people who cut us with machetes were neighbors—people who knew me."

SAVERI WAS ONE OF ROSARIA'S NEIGHBORS AT THE TIME OF THE genocide. Though he is only forty, his face seems drawn and tired, as if the memories of the past find their center point where his eyes narrow and his forehead pinches down. He doesn't recall any animosity toward the Tutsi as a child. "But the government would indoctrinate us," he explained, "telling us that a Tutsi is an enemy, as a result of our bad history that took place before we were born."

That "bad history" stretches back to the time of German, then Belgian, colonization around the turn of the century. The *muzuungu*, or foreigners, noticed how the majority of the king's inner circle, the ruling class, had certain characteristics—thinner noses, lighter skin, taller frames. They theorized that this ruling class was a different race originating from Northern Africa, with common ancestral lineage to the Caucasian race. They deposed any chiefs or subchiefs who did not fit their stereotype. Like a disease, racism spread, as did the myth that the Tutsi were genetically predestined to rule over the Hutu.

When Saveri started school, he was taught this division: the Tutsi were herders, tall, with long noses, while the Hutu were farmers. Such distinctions taught him there was a sharp dichotomy between Hutu and Tutsi. But even back in school, Saveri suspected these were just fabrications geared to incite strife.

The story of those in power inciting strife in the population is one of the most grievous tales of the history of Rwanda. To divide and conquer, the Belgians incited strife by putting Tutsi in power, and relegating Hutu to lesser positions. Basically, the Belgians maintained power by propping up the Tutsi. In the midfifties when King

Mutara Rudahigwa, influenced by other African leaders, began distributing power in a more democratic fashion among Hutu and Tutsi alike, the Belgian colonialists swung the pendulum the other way. They released a prominent liberal Tutsi from prison, and aided him in the creation of his own political party. Meanwhile, disgruntled Hutu formed another party, the Parmehutu. When violence inevitably ensued, the Belgians favored the revolutionary Hutu party as a means of retaining their colonial power.

Ousted from power, Tutsi sought refuge in the neighboring countries — Uganda, Tanzania, Burundi, and Zaire (the present-day Democratic Republic of Congo). In the meantime, the legacy of strife continued under the Hutu reign. When these exiled Tutsi began to press for the right to return to their homeland, they were repelled. As this Rwandan Patriotic Force or RPF gathered to take back this right by violence, the Hutu extremists incited hatred among the Hutu against the Tutsi through radio broadcasts. Saveri was one of hundreds of thousands indoctrinated to hate the Tutsi people and told to cleanse the countryside of such "cockroaches."

"What brought us the conviction to commit genocide was the indoctrination of divisive ideas by bad government," continued Saveri.

Bad government took many forms. The government-backed newspaper *Kangura* printed the Hutu Ten Commandments, one of which stated that a Hutu man who married a Tutsi woman should be thought of as a traitor. Presidential advisor Leon Mugesera, speaking at a political rally in 1992, asked, "What are we waiting for to decimate these families?" and "The person whose neck you do not cut is the one who will cut yours." Little by little, those in authority laid the psychological foundation necessary to build genocide. In fact, between 1990 and 1994, systematic killing of Tutsi had already become widespread. And when the United Nations negotiated a treaty of peace and distribution of power between the two groups at a summit in Arusha, Tanzania, on August 4, 1993, those Hutu clinging to power made preparations for one of the worst genocides in history.

On April 6, 1994, President Juvenal Habyarimana's plane plummeted from the sky after being hit by a missile. It became the albatross around the neck of the Tutsi people when Hutu claimed that the RPF had shot it down. The most widely accepted theory today is that radical Hutu, unsatisfied with the direction of the peace talks, assassinated the Rwandan and Burundian presidents. Either way, the sudden streak of a missile and the fiery light of a falling plane were a diabolical kind of fireworks that night — evil's unseemly opening ceremonies to a hundred days of slaughter that would consume the country.

Within hours of the plane's metal shrapnel gashing Rwandan soil, Hutu sharpened their machetes to do likewise. Radios hissed a message that "the season for slaughter" had arrived. In the days to follow, Hutu killed the Tutsi and their sympathizers at a rate five times higher than the mechanized Nazi gas chambers.

Saveri originally objected to the killings. He was standing with some others, mending a fence that April day, when a community leader approached them. The leader told Saveri and the others that he had seen where some rebels, or *inkotanyi*, were hiding, and that they should follow him. But when they got there, they found what the community leader, Ngabonziza Zakayo, had known all along: these weren't rebels at all. It was a mother, hiding in a neighbor's house with her two children.

Zakayo ordered the old man who had been hiding this mother and her children to kill them. If the old man refused, he would be killed himself. The old man began pleading. Zakayo demanded ten thousand francs. But the old man begged, saying that he did not have that much money.

Zakayo had eyed the small herd of cattle as he approached the house. Greedily, he said that he would take a bull instead as a ransom for the old man's life, so that he would not be buried with the Tutsi he was hiding. The old man continued to plead, suggesting that if he gave Zakayo the bull that the mother and her children should be able to go free. But Zakayo was adamant; the bull was merely penalty for hiding the "cockroaches" and the price for the old man's own life.

"Dig a grave," Zakayo yelled in the direction of the old man. The old man and his neighbor reluctantly obeyed. When the grave was done, the mother and her two children were told to sit in it. They did not try to run, but did just as they were told.

Zakayo selected one of Saveri's friends to beat the mother and her children to death using a spiked club. He refused, was beaten severely, and was then told to sit aside. "Whoever will refuse to kill will be punished later at our discretion," Zakayo warned.

After seeing what had befallen his friend, Saveri did not resist. When given the spiked club, he pummeled the woman and her two small children until they died. Though there were many who then joined in, Saveri was the first to strike. Once they had finished, they covered the bodies with dirt and left the scene. The mother's name was Christine; she was Rosaria's sister.

After killing, Saveri was changed. "Something happened to me," he said. "I was not the same. I was void of peace in my heart from that moment."

UNLIKE SAVERI, ROSARIA DOES NOT SAY MUCH ABOUT THE PAST.

If asked, she will bare her scars. A gash across her left shoulder reminds the onlooker how she used her back as a human shield to hide two fragile lives, hers and Cadeaux's.

Those mysteries not told by her scars are spoken plainly through her eyes. In the flash of a moment, in the glint of steel, something changed her, and she would never be the same. She too became void of peace in her heart from that moment.

These are the sorrowful mysteries. But Rosaria must turn her eyes again to other mysteries — the mystery of a spared life. Cadeaux: her name is a word Rosaria is just beginning to understand.

CHAPTER 2

ripening

Men must endure their going hence,
even as their coming hither; ripeness is all.
William Shakespeare, *King Lear*

OUTSIDE HER MUD-WALLED HOME, ROSARIA WATCHED CADEAUX WIND
the narrow path that leads down the hill from their house toward the
community school. Her eyes followed the willowy silhouette past the
eucalyptus tree until she had disappeared out of view.

Rosaria then turned her attention to a tarp that covered her harvest: a pile of newly cut sorghum stalks. At their full growth, the
stalks had stood at an average man's height. Arms of wide, cornlike
leaves curled outward, deflecting attention from the plant's fragile
spine. At the stalk's head, a branched cluster of small red kernels
nodded before the harvester's blade with the weight of life. Severed
from their roots, the stalks lay limp, piled one on top of the other, a
waist-high mound shrouded with cloth.

Though Westerners tend to be unfamiliar with sorghum, one-
fifth of the world depends on it for life. Rwandans like Rosaria grind,
crack, and roast its red kernels to make porridge or unleavened bread.
Sometimes it is used to make beer or to dye leather, but sorghum is
mostly a matter of sustenance.

The process of severing the head from the stalks with machete and beating open the hard kernel with a club is labor intensive. For Rosaria—with the nerves of her right hand severed and without her husband to help—it could take two months to process a crop that should take two weeks. She didn't have that long to wait. If thieves didn't get at it, the sorghum midge, a common pest, would burrow its way to the heart of the cereal grain.

A small worm inched its way toward the plants. Rosaria flattened it with the heel of her foot, but not before the image of the tiny predator had burrowed into her memory.

WHEN ROSARIA REGAINED CONSCIOUSNESS AFTER MILITANT HUTU left her for dead in Nyamata, south of Kigali, she found herself face-down amid a pile of bodies. Her first sensation was in her hand—a searing pain. It was nothing compared to the next moment. Her back screamed a shrill announcement of its recent history. But the surge came with its own discovery; she could lift her head. While her eyes darted about in confused panic, the eyes of her oldest child and the three Burundian refugees were locked open in final, agonized expressions.

The Hutu had threshed Rosaria's back with machetes and cracked the butt of a gun to her chest. Apparently, however, she had not been worth the cost of a bullet. She was left for dead only to awaken still ripe with life.

Rosaria craned her head in the direction of her right shoulder. Her wounds had begun to attract life of their own: maggots. Her mind clamped shut like a vise at the sight. Pulling herself from atop the pile of bodies, Rosaria felt her knees hit dirt and her chest fold toward them as she heaved convulsively. She quickly straightened, her back revolting at the pain of the motion. A cry escaped her. She glanced around, frightened by her self-disclosure. She must move before full light.

Swallowing hard, she bent again, flares of pain shooting up her back. She closed her son's wide-open eyes and kissed him. Then a scan of the early-morning horizon: no one. She breathed deeply and willed a burst of concentrated energy—a lurching crawl of hand, elbow, scraping knees. Bit by bit, fear dragged her along.

She collapsed some distance into the forest, aware of the foul odor of her open wounds mixing with the heavy dampness of the air. The April rains had flattened the tall grasses, bending them low. They were near enough to reach and the blades were limp. Her fingers moved along the jagged edge. She twisted one, then another, and another, until some time later she was but one broken stalk covered among the many. Then stillness, more pain, and finally sleep.

At nightfall she made her way to an empty house. There she hid for two weeks. A frightened farmer's wife brought her water while the men were out at their gruesome work. But the Hutu woman, knowing she could not continue to hide Rosaria for long without discovery, shooed her away.

Like many Rwandans, Rosaria hid in mud of the papyrus swamps bordering the Nyabarongo River. She woke often in the night. When she did, she would pray, remembering the words of Psalm 63:6–7 she had learned from missionaries who taught her to read: "I think of you through the watches of the night because you are my help." The words were those of a soldier named David who also spent nights evading enemies. For many nights, it was Rosaria's litany and the lullaby for unborn Cadeaux.

Finally, on May 29, fifty days into the slaughter, RPF forces penetrated the country. Being in the southernmost region, Rosaria was one of the first to be rescued and one of the few to survive. She found herself transported by RPF troops to a makeshift militia hospital, where she received what little treatment was available.

Miraculously, not only did she survive, Cadeaux did too. Unable to stand or lie down, Rosaria recovered in the militia hospital, crouched on a low stool. As she regained her own strength, a small life pulsed and kicked within her.

It was only the pulsing thought of Cadeaux that jolted Rosaria back to the present and the dilemma of the ripened sorghum before her. She remembered Gahigi's words of promised help, but trust was hard to find in her heart. She wondered if Gahigi and the others would really come.

A THIRTY-MINUTE WALK AWAY FROM ROSARIA'S LANGUISHING CROP —past marshy valleys, past children carrying yellow water containers and dragging goats, past herds of long-horned cattle, past dark-red grain drying in the sun—Saveri bowed and stretched low. It was not prayers of penitence or some ancient ritual that bent him; he was folded at the waist over a pile of mud bricks, smoothing small imperfections with the flat of his fingertips.

By his side, another man worked. Mattias was stacking the large mud bricks which had already dried. His face creased with the strain of bending and lifting. A bead of perspiration formed and rolled across his brow down his cheek.

It was August, the final month of the long dry season in Rwanda. But that year, drought threatened the already poverty-stricken region near the border of Burundi. The air felt as though one were breathing through a sponge; the heat was direct and intense.

Stopping to mop his face with a cloth, Mattias surveyed the work. Not only had he made the thousand bricks before him, hauling water in his jerry can for each from his own well, miles away, but he'd also helped construct multiple dwellings in this village of thirty new homes outside Mbyo District. Several of these now stood completed, yet empty, awaiting their owners. The other houses belonged to Mattias, Saveri, and several of the other men who had worked beside them over the last year.

The sight of so much empty space was a welcome relief to Mattias and Saveri, who spent nine of the last twelve years in the cramped confines of one of Rwanda's sixteen prisons. Built to hold 40,000 people, the prisons held some 120,000 in the wake of the slaughter. Prisoners like Mattias and Saveri awaited formal trials in hellish conditions: little food, dirty drinking water, rooms sometimes so crowded that inmates slept crisscrossed on top of one another.

The decimation of the Tutsi population, and the subsequent exile of many Hutu, left the country with only the skeleton of a judicial system and a handful of lawyers, clerks, and judges. The enormity of the prison population would have taken nearly two hundred years to process, even *with* a fully functioning court system.

To address the backlog of cases, the government announced in January of 2003 that it would provisionally release selected suspects, such as Saveri and Mattias, who had already confessed to their crimes, who were not the planners of the genocide, or who had not perpetrated the more heinous acts, such as rape. These men would instead be tried in Gacaca Courts, which would attempt to mete out justice in nine thousand towns and villages, each overseen by nine locally elected men and women of integrity. Across Rwanda, billboards reading "The Truth Heals" in Kinyarwanda encouraged local villagers to attend the Gacaca Court sessions, where they participated both as witnesses and as part of the solution-making process.

As Mattias tucked his sweat rag back into his pocket and began to turn back to his labor, a thin silhouette appeared on the horizon. The man was tall, nearly six feet, a feature which the Belgians taught the Rwandan people to stereotypically associate with the Tutsi. As the rest of the man's features came into focus, Mattias recognized Gahigi.

A MILITARY TRUCK LURCHED TO A STOP THAT APRIL OF 1994. IN THE large open bed, some forty-five people huddled together, loaded in the open-caged semi like so many of Rwanda's sinewy Ankole cattle on their way to market. Hutu militia herded Gahigi and others off the truck to an open field where Mattias and some of the Hutu men of the village were gathered. Mattias and these men gathered there each morning in those days with their common work tools to go out and do the uncommon work of tracking and killing their neighbors in homes, forests, and marshes. Already, many of the men had departed for the day, but Mattias and a handful of others had straggled behind.

Gahigi and his relatives had been on their way toward Burundi. But less than six miles from the border, they were met by Hutu militia who loaded them up and brought them back to their own village where Mattias stood. The militia shouted orders.

"Here are *your* cockroaches," sneered the commander. "Kill them." The militia had brought them back to be killed by their own neighbors. "If you don't kill them, we will kill you."

Mattias did not hesitate. A machine in hand, he swiftly cut down six of them. The motions and tool were not new to him. Like many Rwandans, he had used a machete since childhood to cut sorghum, hack brush, slaughter chickens, or chop firewood. His mind contracted around the mission: kill every Tutsi, even those in the womb.

During the attacks, particularly those in the swamps or brush, Mattias and the other men from the village had a strategy: sweep in lines like a search party. Only their objective was not deliverance, it was decimation. A group of killers was composed of sometimes upward of one hundred people. To Mattias, it was like hunting. Whoever jumped out of hiding was immediately killed. This particular

killing did not have the thrill of the hunt. He felt nothing at the task. It was easier than farm work—human flesh was surprisingly soft.

MATTIAS HAD BEEN IN THE BEIGE-BRICK PENITENTIARY IN RILIMA FOR four years when Gahigi first began to visit. Mattias recognized Gahigi immediately. He had been one of three to evade them that April day their neighbors were returned from the border. Once the captives were unloaded from the truck, Mattias and the others had descended on the Tutsi. But a few of the militia dragged the women off to the bush to have their way with them before killing them also. With the militia distracted, and the rest of the men engaged in the slaughter, a few victims, Gahigi included, managed to slip unnoticed into the woods. By the time Mattias and others realized the pastor and some others were missing, the captives had escaped.

Seeing the once-hunted amid the throngs of prisoners, Mattias could think of no other reason for Gahigi to be there, except that he must be some kind of spy, sent on behalf of the RPF. It was a reasonable assumption, considering Gahigi would have reason for hatred, having lost many members of his family in what some Hutu call "the war." So Mattias hid among the throngs of pink-clad prisoners milling in the open courtyard. But even as he hid, he watched and listened to Gahigi, who now had a small huddle of prisoners gathered around him. As the weeks and months went by, and Gahigi continued to visit and teach, Mattias and the others slowly realized he was no spy.

For Gahigi's part, after the tragedy he had been filled with anger and hatred. It is little wonder. Two of his children died that day in Mbyo. Gahigi and two of his cousins managed to evade death. They hid until nightfall and then returned to scan the carnage for survivors. They found only one: Gahigi's five-year-old son, still breathing, but with a severed arm. Carrying him, Gahigi and the others made it in a few days' time to Burundi and to a refugee camp teeming with thousands of others as mangled and traumatized as they. His son died from loss of blood amid the fear, squalor, and dysentery of the camp. By the end of July, after the RPF had gained control of the country and the frenzy of killing had largely subsided, Gahigi and the other refugees were told they could return home.

But there was little to return home to: only eight out of the 150 members of Gahigi's family had survived. Still, he returned. He could not imagine, however, how he was to live again with people who murdered his family. He felt powerless. Sometimes when the grief became too overwhelming, he would think about revenge. But Gahigi's convictions would not allow him to savor these thoughts for long. Gahigi was a spiritual man, a Christian pastor. In fact, before the genocide, he had been jailed twice in 1992 for teaching people that hating is a terrible sin. The authorities saw Gahigi's Tutsi identity card and said that it wasn't God speaking through Pastor Gahigi — it was the RPF.

What would he do with his own anger and hatred? Gahigi began to pray. These were not words recited by rote at mealtime. These were hours of prayers over many weeks and months. In these prayers, Gahigi first sensed comfort, then a call to compassion. Finally, he sensed that he had work to do. He was to go and preach in the prisons, and so, with great misgivings, Gahigi went, slicing across the savannah on a seven-hour journey from Nyamata to Rilima. There the prison perched on a hill overlooking the marshes of Nyabarongo River where Rosaria and other Tutsi hid during the genocide.

On his first visits, Gahigi began by talking to the men one-on-one. By the fourth time Gahigi visited the prison, he summoned the courage to speak to a large group gathered under a tarp in the open yard, which by night slept about five hundred prisoners. After he spoke to them, a prisoner approached him, crying.

"Have mercy, have mercy."

Without thinking, Gahigi took a step back. He studied the thick face of this man, a neighbor he had known and whom he had heard demolished his house and killed his sister.

"I spent many sleepless nights over you. I searched for you so I could kill you," said the man now weeping before Gahigi. "But have mercy on me and forgive me." Gahigi embraced the man, who continued to weep bitterly and plead for forgiveness. As his sister's murderer wept in his arms, Gahigi sensed: *This is the purpose for which you are here, and you have seen it with your very own eyes.* That day Gahigi embraced not just a killer, but what he believed was his calling to be a mediator.

EVERY FEW WEEKS GAHIGI WOULD MAKE THE SEVEN-HOUR JOURNEY BY foot to the prisons to preach repentance and the possibility of forgiveness. Saveri was among the listeners. While Mattias had been without remorse or guilt after the killings, Saveri had been haunted from the moment he had killed Rosaria's sister and her children. He was bitterly grieved and had even turned himself over to the authorities. He had seen how innocently Christine died that day her neighbor was told to dig a grave and she was told to lie in it. From that moment, Saveri had vowed that as long as he should live, he would not justify his actions, but would tell anyone who needed to know what happened.

When he heard Gahigi and others preach of forgiveness, Saveri could not comprehend mercy. He believed that not even God's mercy could reach him. Hours would go by where Saveri would sit atop his makeshift prison mattress of cardboard and blankets imagining impossible penalties for himself because death was too small a punishment. Only the ultimate punishment, he thought, could make up for his crimes.

One day, as Gahigi preached on Isaiah 1:16–18, something

shifted within Saveri. The ancient words were an admonition to change: "Stop doing wrong, learn to do right! Seek justice, encourage the oppressed. Defend the cause of the fatherless, plead the case of the widow." The passage ended with a promise for those who changed: "Though your sins are like scarlet, they shall be as white as snow." At that moment, Saveri began to consider the possibility of divine forgiveness. He began to wonder if he too might have some role to play in reestablishing justice for Rwandan widows or orphans.

Mattias had also begun to draw near Gahigi on those Sundays he came to preach. During that time, Mattias's heart was finally pierced by the consequences of his brutality, yet he said nothing until the day Gahigi paid him a personal visit.

Gahigi had recognized Mattias on his first visit to the prison and knew he was one of the killers that day at Mbyo. Gahigi did not know what would come of the visit.

As Gahigi extended his hand in greeting, Mattias shook his head and looked away.

"You know that the government has a file on you, Mattias?"

Mattias nodded, keenly attuned to Gahigi, but still he didn't look up.

"I am not coming here today about that file. I am coming to you about another file—the file of the conscience. The conscience does the secretarial work for God, Mattias. I am coming to tell you that whatever is in this file, the conscience file, I am asking you to put it right today."

"But these hands ..." Mattias turned his leathered hands palms upward, fingers spread wide in front of him. The motion had become something of a ritual for him over the past few months. "These hands killed your family: your brother's wife, her sister, and her children."

Since so many of Gahigi's family were among the captives that day, this revelation did not come as a total shock. "Put it right," he said firmly.

Mattias began to weep.

Mattias began the process of putting things right that day. He asked for forgiveness. And Gahigi said, "If you are truly a changed man, no longer a murderer, but a good man, who is never returning to murder, I forgive you." For the first time in a very long time, Mattias felt that he could once again belong in the Rwandan community, if only he was given the chance.

The opportunity came a few years later. After being released from prison, Mattias and Saveri spent three months in the Kinyinya "solidarity camp" on the outskirts of Kigali, one of eighteen civic education centers around Rwanda, where around a thousand confessed genocidaires received instruction from government officials on how to be good citizens in the post-genocide society. Afterward they loaded buses back to a drop-off point near the border of Burundi.

A few weeks later, Saveri and Mattias were invited to a series of reconciliation meetings facilitated by local volunteers. Rosaria and other survivors were invited as well. Gahigi and others who had preached in the prisons were among the leaders of the mediation that would be known as the Umuvumu Tree Project. The goal of the meetings was not to force forgiveness on the part of survivors, but instead to create a place for perpetrators to offer apology, some form of restitution, and the declaration of changed behavior and attitudes. For the families, it was a chance to express their emotions, regain some sense of control and dignity, and often learn details that they had wanted to know about the crime. While forgiveness wasn't forced, it often came as a healing by-product of these encounters.

The leaders called it the Umuvumu Tree Project because of a biblical story about a money-pocketing tax collector. This man, Zacchaeus, climbed a sycamore tree to catch a glimpse of a traveling teacher named Jesus. (Had the story occurred in Rwanda, they say Zacchaeus would have climbed an Umuvumu tree.) Rather than spurn the well-known scoundrel, the teacher told Zacchaeus to come down, and that he would dine with him that day. In response to such unmerited kindness, Zacchaeus acknowledged his crimes and offered to pay back what he had stolen. Saveri explained that men like Gahigi came to them in prison when their hearts were hanging and told them to come down.

Initially, Tutsi and Hutu sat on separate sides of the aisle at the Umuvumu Tree meetings while men like Gahigi taught. Both groups were afraid: the prisoners were afraid of having to meet survivors face-to-face, and the survivors were afraid that the murderers had simply come back to finish the job. Each had different reasons for meeting their fear. Rosaria, having been far from her village during the killings, was pulled by a need to know the details surrounding the death of her loved ones and by a desire to somehow find release from the past.

At the first three meetings, Saveri approached Rosaria and begged for her forgiveness, but he did not tell her why. Since prisoners often expressed a kind of corporate guilt for their actions, it wasn't until the fourth meeting that Rosaria asked Saveri why he so desperately wanted *her* forgiveness. In that moment, as Saveri summoned the strength to confess what he had done, the weight of his guilt made it almost unbearable to speak.

"I am the one who murdered your sister and her children," he said weakly. "I am begging for you to forgive me."

SAVERI STRAIGHTENED HIS BACK AND STRETCHED AS HE SAW GAHIGI approach. It had been three years since their release and five since Gahigi first came to visit them in prison, but still the sight of Gahigi's long strides moving steadily in his direction made him remember how he had anticipated Gahigi's visits in prison. Had it not been for Gahigi, Saveri wondered how he would ever have managed to even begin building a future.

Without hesitation on either man's part, Gahigi and Mattias embraced in a traditional greeting. To see them interact, it was difficult to imagine that only a few short years ago, Mattias had made his way from prison to Gahigi's home, where he asked the other surviving members of Gahigi's family to forgive him for his crimes. In the years since then, neighbors had witnessed the unbelievable. Sometimes they would spot Mattias and Gahigi sitting on a bench outside the church talking together. Often, they would see Mattias pay Gahigi a visit at his home, and even more astonishingly, Gahigi welcome him. So as Mattias stood there before the mud bricks asking about Gahigi's health and Gahigi stood inquiring about their progress in the building, the strangest of interactions seemed almost routine.

Wiping the mud from his hands on his trousers, Saveri motioned Gahigi to follow him. Together they inspected the completed homes, Gahigi praising the progress the men had made.

Stopping at one empty home, Gahigi asked, "Is this the one, then?"

"It is," nodded Saveri somberly. "We finished it some time ago."

"But still she hasn't moved in?"

"No," said Saveri, his eyes drifting to the ground. "We are still waiting for her."

Having spent his life living off the land, Saveri knew that every seed sown required patience and faith. He viewed this act no differently, but still he couldn't help wondering if this particular field would lie fallow. His mind drifted back to the sound of the words he hoped were true.

"I FORGIVE YOU," SAID ROSARIA SOFTLY. "IF YOU HAVE SINCERELY confessed your sin before God and truly changed, then I forgive you."

Saveri searched for words, opened his mouth to speak them, but none came, only tears of relief.

"How can I refuse to forgive you when I did not make you? Your crime"—she paused, forming her thoughts carefully—"your crime was against God, who created the people you killed."

Saveri had been prepared for many things, but not this. He had been at the meetings as other victims vented their rage against the killers at their confessions. He had even seen some leave and refuse to return after meeting the ones who had harmed their families. Believing that even death was not an adequate punishment for his wrongs, Saveri had braced himself for retribution, insults, anger, even silence, but not this.

"Thank you," he stammered, wondering if he had truly heard her right or was in some strange kind of dream. "I don't deserve this. I'm so sorry. Thank you."

THERE WEREN'T MANY TREES IN THE LITTLE VILLAGE WHERE SAVERI stood showing Gahigi his work. The only trees were the few they had planted, Umuvumus. One stood a few meters from the home Saveri had built for Rosaria, casting its shade on the two men as they spoke.

It had been a few years after the initial meetings between survivors and perpetrators that the facilitators of the Umuvumu Tree Project told the men about the house-building project. They had gathered funds and materials so that penitent ex-prisoners could build homes for those whose families they killed. Although it was a symbolic act of restitution, Saveri jumped at the opportunity. During the genocide, so many Tutsi homes had been looted and destroyed, he believed the homes would be a huge blessing to the survivors. And if he could use his hands to form and lay bricks, and his time on Rosaria's behalf, perhaps somehow it could show externally the reality of his remorse.

Among the thirty new homes they had built, seventeen had been

designated for survivors, nine for ex-prisoners, and four for returning refugees. But even though Saveri had a brand new home of his
own in the village, the place he was proudest of was the home he
had built for Rosaria. But with the house having been completed and
empty for well over a month, Saveri was eager to change the subject
from Gahigi's line of questioning about the empty home. To Saveri's
relief, Gahigi changed it himself.

"There's another reason for my visit," he said, looking at the two
men. "I've come to see if you can help Rosaria with her crop."

Saveri breathed in deeply. Perhaps time had made things ripe for
reconciliation.

luminous mysteries

Life is a luminous halo,
a semi-transparent envelope surrounding us
from the beginning.
Virginia Woolf

A ROOSTER CROWED OUTSIDE ROSARIA'S WINDOW. SHE OPENED HER eyes. From a small gap in the thatched roof above, a sliver of light fell upon the mat where she lay. A few weeks more, and the shorter rainy season would begin. The roof would need patching before then, she thought, as the rooster continued its morning announcement. Standing, she wondered if the day would really unfold as Gahigi had promised, with Saveri and Mattias coming to help her winnow, hull, and bag the sorghum. If they did, perhaps there would be no need for patching the roof. Perhaps, by the time the rains came, she'd already be settled into her new home.

But would they come? Though she had forgiven Saveri, she still didn't know the extent to which she could trust him. Would he really walk the miles, abandoning his own day's labor, to do what African men considered women's work? It was even harder for her to imagine the home of which Gahigi had spoken, a home that was standing empty, even now, waiting for her and Cadeaux to come. Gahigi had said that it had a metal roof, one that wouldn't need patching with each new rainy season. It hardly seemed possible that hands that had swung a machete in violence had been the very same hands to smooth clay bricks and stack them into a home for her and her daughter.

Walking into the adjacent room, Rosaria found Cadeaux curled up on her side, sleeping peacefully. Her presence was enough to remind Rosaria that sometimes the seemingly impossible happens. She stooped to wake her. As often as Rosaria had seen them, Cadeaux's eyes fluttering open still had a way of sending a rush of joy through her. Cadeaux smiled.

Rosaria answered back with a smile of her own, "Time to ..."

"... wake up and pray," Cadeaux finished her mother's sentence, knowing it only too well. It was a well-rehearsed morning ritual. Her mother had told Cadeaux how during pregnancy when she was hiding in the marsh how often she had woken up to pray. And how when she had named her, she had named her Cadeaux, meaning "gift," and Byukusenge, her Rwandan name, meaning, "wake up and pray." She had wanted her to remember both realities, every day of her life.

"And why do we wake up and pray?" Rosaria asked her young catechumen.

"Because we are not like the cows, which just wake up and go," said Cadeaux, stretching. "God made us to talk to him."

Rosaria nodded in approval.

As Cadeaux made her way through her usual requests, Rosaria prayed silently for help to come and for hope to stay.

PEELING BACK THE BLUE TARP FROM OVER HER CROP, ROSARIA surveyed the work ahead. Over the past several weeks, she had succeeded on her own in the first step of the process, beating the stalks' panicles with a large stick to remove the red kernels. However, the most difficult work still lay ahead, and alone, with an injured hand, it would take her perhaps a month.

As she surveyed the work, she heard the sound of a group approaching. She went to the gate and peered down the alleyway. Rosaria's heart leapt at the sight of such a crowd. She saw Saveri first with his blue windbreaker, jeans, and T-shirt. It was hard to put words to the jumble of emotions she felt at seeing him. Beside Saveri stood Mattias, his thick coat jarringly out-of-place in the hot sun. Both men nodded at her. They had come with a dozen or so others from the village where Rosaria's new home stood. Among them were several men and even more women — one carrying a toddler on her back, another who looked too old to be of much help. They carried tools with them and they were ready to work. Rosaria's eyes brightened as she thanked them for coming and motioned them behind her house to the fenced-in area that held her crop.

They passed through the gate into the fenced space, setting down their tools and resting from their journey. Some curious children from the neighborhood peered inside the fence, gawking at the parade of people they had followed up the main road, and wondering what was about to happen. Rosaria disappeared into a storage shed and returned with a few tools of her own: a pestle pole about four feet long with a rounded bottom, along with a mortar, made of hollowed wood about two feet tall and tapered inside to a point where the pestle fit neatly. She also carried out a few closely woven circular baskets about two feet wide and three inches deep, and a shovel. Some of the women had carried extra baskets of their own, as well as an extra mortar and pestle.

Preparing sorghum is part of the rhythm of life for millions of Africans, so once rested, the strangers stepped easily into the familiar tasks. One man stationed himself next to the outdoor cooking fire Rosaria had already started that morning. With a shovel in hand, he scooped some of the embers and ash, dumping it on top of the ker-

nels in the mortar that Saveri brought him. Moving back out into the center of the yard, Saveri then took the long pestle pole and began pounding. Soon, between the heat and the pressure, the tough, outer coat of the sorghum kernel began to loosen. After some minutes of pounding, he poured the mixture into a circular basket held out by one of the women, and then went back to retrieve more kernels and more hot embers to start the arm-wearying process again.

Meanwhile, the woman held the basket out in front of her and began a steady cycle of tossing, then shaking, the kernels, allowing the bran to be separated from the outer chaff, and sifting out the good from the bad. Soon, all of the men and women were busily employed, stoking, pounding, shaking, tossing, bagging, and toting. Even the old woman had found a post; the loose skin of her arms encircling the plump, firm skin of the toddler whose mother had joined in the winnowing. The toddler had found the rosary the old woman carried tucked in her shirt, and the two took turns, the toddler moving it up to his mouth, the woman pulling it back from his lips. The children who had peered through the gate could be heard outside, laughing and calling as they chased a soccer ball made of tied banana leaves.

Within the gate, the work itself was monotonous and dragged on from morning into the afternoon. Yet even so, it held a strange beauty. The deep crimson of the kernels, the smell of the burning fire, the way the bodies of the men and women swayed as they tossed and shook the baskets, and of course, the percussion of labor. The scene took on a symphonic quality, as the rhythmic thud of the pestle pole marked a beat and the swish of the kernels tossed up in the baskets settled into the offbeat, survivors and perpetrators creating the point and counterpoint to reconciliation's song.

And so they worked, former murderers and survivors, pressed together inside a small yard, breaking the hard, bitter outer shell away from the sustaining grain. Such shells don't automatically fall away, but must slowly, painstakingly, be ground away, lest the life-giving grain rot away. It was easy to understand how long and laborious such a process is, even given the best of conditions.

As day moved quickly toward dusk, Saveri organized those present to help Rosaria move. With as few belongings as she had, it would not be difficult. All but about five bags of the sorghum, enough for about a week of food, were stored away in her shed, until they could return to move it. One man grabbed her small lightweight table, flipped it over, and balanced it on his head and began to walk. Another man, who had a bicycle, strapped two full bags of sorghum onto it and began to push. Some women carried baskets, and Rosaria carried a satchel, while Saveri balanced a canvas bag of the processed sorghum on his head.

With each man, woman, and child walking at his or her own pace, the party stretched out along the road. Cadeaux lagged a bit behind her mother, who walked at an eager clip, a renewed look of hope in her eyes. From the first sight of Saveri and the other ex-prisoners and survivors that morning, her trust had been reviving, and now with each step closer to her new home, it seemed to strengthen.

Saveri, knowing the way, walked a few paces ahead. He felt a strange mixture of emotions as he looked out over the familiar saffron-colored landscape. There was satisfaction in knowing that he had been of real help that day to Rosaria, and that within the hour, she would cast her eyes on the fruit of many months of labor. But his satisfaction was tinged with shame. Despite having asked Rosaria's forgiveness, deep down in his heart, he would never — in this life — forget what had been seared into his conscience. At the same time, he found a measure of comfort, knowing that with each action — from laying brick, to pounding kernels, to moving goods — he was helping to prove that he could be trusted once again. While no such actions could undo or pay the price for the past, he felt confident that they were helping to create a different future.

As they reached the cluster of new homes, the sun was just setting, turning everything before them into a shade of bronze, from the clay road, to the neatly stacked mud-brick homes, to the metal roofs reflecting the sun's warm hues. Rosaria could see the tall, lean silhouette of Gahigi coming toward them. "*Muraho*," he called to Rosaria in particular.

"*Muraho*," she called back, using the traditional Rwandan greeting.

Gahigi nodded at Saveri, giving him the nudge of encouragement that he knew he needed.

"This is it," called out Saveri just as he reached one of the homes. "It is yours."

Rosaria squeezed Cadeaux by the hand as she walked up to the home and placed her hand on the exterior wall. The clay was warm to the touch. She stepped inside and looked up at the sturdy metal roof. For the first time in nearly thirteen years, she didn't dread the rains. She knew she and Cadeaux would be sheltered here.

justice and
human flourishing

True peace is not merely the absence of tension:
it is the presence of justice.
Martin Luther King Jr.

THE HOUSE WAS SO NEW THAT THERE WAS NOT A SINGLE STAIN ON the carpet. The only dent in the wall had been left because of the Herculean effort involved in moving the solid wood armoire up to the third floor of the brand-new townhome. I'd lived in the home less than a month and between work, writing deadlines, and planning with my then-fiancé for our upcoming wedding, putting up blinds was on the low end of the priority list. Maybe it shouldn't have been.

Balancing an armload of groceries and a handful of wedding RSVPs from the mailbox, I struggled with the key to unlock the door, kicked off my shoes, and made my way up to the second floor. Chatting on the cell phone, I stirred around the kitchen fixing dinner, oblivious to that day's happenings. It wasn't until sometime later that I went downstairs and focused in on what I'd breezed past when my arms had been full of groceries. I'd been robbed.

CONFLICT IS INEVITABLE. TERRITORY DISPUTES, CONTRARY NOTIONS of leadership, differences of taste—in the world in which we live conflict, whether it is on the job, in the home, or on the international horizon, will always make up a part of our landscape. So when conflict arises, we should not be surprised—grieved, but not surprised. But before such conflict is upon us, it makes sense that we would have at least answered this fundamental question: "What's the end goal of dealing with crime or conflict?" The way we answer this question has ramifications that are as far-reaching as the conflicts we encounter.

For many of us, our answers are shaped by our society and by the homes in which we grew up. For Americans, we've seen a criminal justice system that solves crime retributively by locking away offenders, removing the sources of conflict—at least temporarily—from sight. Growing up, we may have learned to expect consequences for our misbehavior, whether it be sitting in time-out as a toddler or losing the right to go out with friends as a teenager. But perhaps we never questioned beyond this point. Law and rule breaking deserved punishment, which satisfied the immediate sense of justice. This much was understood. But what was the goal of that punishment? Perhaps the answer eluded us.

Ironically, however, we've grown up in the shadow of the answer. The peace symbol is everywhere in our world, from protest signs to bumper stickers. But for most of us, peace simply means the absence of war, conflict, or striving. Ancient conceptions of the term, however, went much further.

In ancient Israel, for example, peace, or *shalom*, was not defined by absence. Rather, it meant the sum total of human flourishing: socially, emotionally, physically, mentally, and spiritually. Shalom signified wholeness, rightness, and ultimate harmony.

When someone committed a crime, the focus of justice wasn't simply on the broken law and restoring order, but rather on broken shalom and restoring peace. Restoring peace took many forms. First and foremost, justice concerned itself with caring for the victim. If a criminal had stolen a goat, it meant restoring the goat. If a criminal had damaged a home, it meant restoring the home.

But true shalom also meant that punishing the offender had an ultimate goal: restoration of peace for the victim, restoration of the peace of the community, and finally, restoration of peace for the offender.

This idea wasn't limited to the Hebrew culture. In some of our earliest law codes, this emphasis on restoration can be seen. From the Code of Hammurabi (c. 1700 BC), to the Code of Lipit-Ishtar (1875 BC), to the Sumerian Code of Ur-Nammu, to the Code of Eshnunna (c. 1700 BC), to the Roman Law of the Twelve Tables (449 BC)—all required some kind of restitution. This focus showed a concern that the end goal in dealing with conflict, at the very least, included restoration for the victim. Similarly, "many pre-colonial African societies aimed less at punishing criminal offenders than at resolving the consequences to their victims."[1]

In the United States today, the primary focus of the legal system is the broken law. We see this clearly in the way cases are identified: State vs. Defendant. While law breaking is certainly an important part of the equation, victim harming is an equally

important emphasis. And when we neglect this consequence of crime, it is the victim who suffers.

Dr. Howard Zehr, professor of sociology at Eastern Mennonite University, first coined the term *restorative justice*. According to Zehr, in dealing with wrong, society most often chooses between three typical responses: revenge, retribution, and restoration.

Whether from rage or from an incomplete understanding of justice, men and women who are wronged will often take justice into their own hands. Revenge is a response to evil. Unfortunately, the response often creates a deadly spiral of retaliation. Revenge can escalate the violence, leading not to justice but to further revenge.

More commonly, societies, including ours, have responded to crime with policies of retribution. Zehr would not discount the strengths of this kind of criminal justice system with its encouragement of human rights and the promotion of the rule of law. But, he explains: "As a system of justice, however, it has its flaws. Criminal justice tends to be punitive, impersonal, and authoritarian. With its focus on guilt and blame, it discourages responsibility and empathy on the part of offenders. The harm done *by* the offender is balanced by harm done *to* the offender. In spite of all this attention to crime, criminal justice basically leaves victims out of the picture, ignoring their needs. Rather than promoting healing, it exacerbates wounds. Retributive justice often assumes the justice and healing are separate — even incompatible — issues."[2]

The third way focuses on a more reparative approach to justice where healing and justice are not separated. Crime is seen as a violation of people and relationships. Therefore, according to Zehr, restorative justice aims at identifying responsibilities, meeting needs, and promoting healing. Restorative justice is a process in which victim, offender, and community are involved in dialogue, mutual agreement, empathy, and the taking of responsibility. In contrast to retributive justice, restorative justice focuses on balancing harm done *by* the offender with making things right *to* the victim, and on restoring human flourishing.

Obviously, in the cases of violent crime, restoration has its limits. No price can be put on human life. The violation that a rape victim endures cannot be undone. However, restorative justice looks, in every case, toward the future, and toward whatever healing and restoration may be possible, regardless of its difficulty. Restorative systems still call for elements of punishment or for isolating the offender to protect others. But the goal is qualitatively different than a simple system of retribution.

After the genocide, Rwanda revived an ancient form of justice known as *gacaca*, in which the village elders, who are known for their wisdom, maturity, and fairness, preside over the disagreements of the village. The job of the elders is to facilitate the dialogue, to help parties work toward mutual agreements and reconciliation that emphasizes forgiveness, amends, and restitution. In times past, gacaca was never used for such extreme grievances as murder; the current implementation of this system is clearly flawed. Yet even with its weaknesses, gacaca does succeed in focusing on the true nature of crime as victim- and society-harming rather than simply law breaking. As it seeks to include the community both in dialogue about the crime which has occurred and the way forward to peace, it involves all participants in a way that helps all affected parties take ownership of the road forward.[3]

Justice systems are often so deeply entrenched within a society that changing them may seem impossibly slow and cumbersome. But the principles of restorative justice need not be limited to the official workings of a country's legal system. Thankfully, there are ways to infuse restorative elements into already established systems or to offer such programs on a voluntary community-wide level.

In the United States, Zehr pioneered the creation of VORPs (Victim Offender Reconciliation Programs), helping to bring restorative elements to communities across the nation through victim-offender dialogue. Likewise, nongovernment organizations or NGOs like Prison Fellowship, VOMA (Victim Offender Mediation Association), and the Restorative Justice Consortium have come alongside legal systems across the world to create programs focusing on facilitating healing between victims and offenders, helping offenders take responsibility for their crimes, and whenever possible offering amends and restitution. In Rwanda, the Umuvumu Tree Project started by Prison Fellowship is one example of this, but many other mediation programs exist to deal with the gritty reality of integrating offenders back into society.

Restoring shalom is intimately tied to the work of doing justice. As the Israelites said, "Righteousness and peace will kiss each other" (Psalm 85:10b), or as Nicholas Wolterstorff, former professor of philosophical theology at Yale translates it, "Justice and shalom will kiss each other." Seeking justice means seeking the shalom of a society. A society that focuses on restoring shalom will also focus on the needs of its weakest members. As Wolterstorff explains:

> There is something incomplete, disunified, fractured, [and] broken about the unjust society—in particular, about the society in which widows, orphans, and aliens do not enjoy the conditions of flourishing. And it's obvious what this is: The unjust society is one whose *shalom* is fractured, partial, incomplete, and thus incapable of reflecting the holiness of the divine.[4]

This is not some kind of utopian ideal. As Daniel Philpott points out in *The Politics of Past Evil*, "The purpose of a concept such as *shalom* ... is to set forth a standard, an essence, whose presence, absence, or partial realization we can then assess. It tells us not how much we may achieve, but what kind of ideal we are moving toward."[5]

NGOs and churches across Rwanda have risen to the challenge of caring for the needs of orphans, widows, and the alienated—prisoners released into society. Such programs and relationships are living, breathing paradigms for a peace that goes way beyond the symbols on protest signs and bumper stickers. Shalom is a peace that does not ignore the demands of justice or the cries of the broken.

But this is a paradigm shift, necessary not only globally and nationally, but personally as well.

Biologically, the human body responds to conflict in one of two ways: fight or flight. When it comes to personal conflict, we generally gravitate toward one of these two responses as well. Somewhere between running away or attacking is a middle way—one that is much more difficult, but that also offers much greater rewards: peacemaking.

Like the aims of restorative justice, peacemaking also works toward restoring human flourishing for all those involved. Ken Sande, the president of Peacemakers Ministries, describes the various responses toward conflict as the slope of a hill. On the one end of the slope are the escape responses; on the other end are the attack responses; in the middle are the peacemaking responses. At both ends are the extremes of violence: suicide—the ultimate escape response—and murder, the ultimate attack response. In between are many choices: fleeing, denying, overlooking, reconciling, negotiating, mediating, arbitrating, litigating, and assaulting. The responses move from one extreme to the other with the peacemaking tactics in the middle.

Sande notes something interesting about this continuum. In an escape response, the primary focus is on oneself. He writes, "I am generally focusing on 'me.' I am looking for what is easy, convenient, or non-threatening for myself." The attack responses, on the other hand, are "generally focusing on 'you,' blaming you and expecting you to solve my problem." What is noteworthy is that when using a peacemaking response, the focus shifts to "us" and toward "mutual responsibility in solving a problem." Going hand in hand with this is the fact that of all the responses, the peacemaking ones are the ones that have the best chance of a relationship surviving intact. At the extremes of both escape and fight, we find what Sande humorously labels the "KYRG" responses, or "Kiss Your Relationship Goodbye."[6]

Principles of peacemaking are not simply for ivory tower philosophers and international diplomats. They are tools we need to recover for our daily lives. And the paradigm shift from punishment to promoting peace is one that could change our relationships, our churches, our communities, and our world for the better.

I WAS A FORTUNATE VICTIM. THANKFULLY, I WASN'T HOME AT THE time of the crime, and the property stolen from the house was replaceable. The house itself had not been damaged in any way. In fact, all the doors and windows were still locked when I came home. That was the eerie part.

When closing on the house, I had been told that the keys that construction workers had been given in the months preceeding to finish the home would no longer work after I used my key.

When I put my key in, ball bearings would drop in the lock mechanism, making it impossible for the old keys to work.

When I called the locksmith to get the locks changed after the robbery, after examining the lock he told me this wasn't true. Multiple shears, or shapes of a key, would have fit my lock, he said. It seems obvious to me that whoever entered my house simply used a key.

I would love to get back what was taken from me: the property, the peace of mind, the certain feeling of joy that comes with being a first-time home owner. I doubt if I'll ever get those back in quite the same way. But as I heard the news about the locks, my thoughts went to the other people in the neighborhood, their peace, their safety.

Going door to door to tell the neighbors what had happened and encouraging them to get their own locks changed, contacting the builder, bringing the situation to light, and asking for their help — these efforts on my part were an outgrowth of a paradigm shift. And if I could meet the man or woman who broke into the house, I'd hope that the same principles would guide me. Whoever the thief is, that person is in need of a change of heart and mind — of restoration. Solving this conflict is not just about seeking my peace and safety, but about seeking the flourishing of my neighbors, my community, and ultimately the person who wronged us.

From unfathomably violent crimes to minor personal insults, I believe that if we could think differently about the goal after crime or conflict, it would revolutionize our world. Each day, as we confront shattered shalom, we have an opportunity to choose not to act out of retaliation or retribution, but to pursue the restoration of human flourishing.

Questions for Reflection and Discussion

How does the ancient concept of shalom change your view of the aims of peace?

Is the distinction between revenge, retribution, and restoration as paradigms of justice a new concept for you? If so, what aspects of each appeal to you? Why? What aspects of each concern you? Why?

Who are the weakest members of your community? Are there ways that you could help seek justice in your community by caring for their needs? Does your understanding of justice include the flourishing of the weak?

What do you naturally gravitate toward in a conflict situation: escape responses or attack responses?

How could an end goal of restoration change the way you look at shattered peace in your own life and relationships?

hide and seek

You, God, who live next door—
If at times, through the long night, I trouble you
With my urgent knocking—this is why:
I hear you breathe so seldom.
Rainier Marie Rilke, *Book of Hours*

JOY SPOKE SOFTLY. WITH THE RAIN FALLING ON THE CORRUGATED metal roof of Sonrise School and Orphanage, her voice was nearly drowned out. It was the cusp of the second rainy season, and the small homes and farms in the valleys of Ruhengeri below where Sonrise perches were still neatly tucked in by the morning's blanket of mist. That coverlet would make it nearly impossible to tell from indoors if it were raining at all but for the late August rain turning the roof into a timpani.

In the gym adjacent to the schoolroom where Joy sat, sounds of playing children echoed off the walls. The buoyant energy of childhood stubbornly refused to be held down by a little rain, especially on a Saturday. Jump ropes and volleyballs worked just as well indoors, and the children relished the swish and thump of the ropes and even the thudding sting of a ball on their outstretched arms before it lifted their eyes and chins upward.

Outside, the waxbills were obstinate, twittering from the branches of the eucalyptus trees as the vapors rose from the ground. Like the children next door, the rain only made them call more loudly to one another.

So to hear Joy's quiet, broken English, one had to concentrate, to lean in toward Joy, to watch her lips move.

It was a pleasant task concentrating on her so. Joy, an unassuming beauty, had short-cropped hair, tender brown eyes, high cheekbones, and a shy smile—a smile that dawns infrequently, but all the more gloriously for its rare appearances. Even sitting, she was a tall seventeen-year-old. As she spoke, she planted her elbows on her knees, laced her fingers together, and bowed her head in a posture resembling prayer.

SHE WAS ONLY FOUR YEARS OLD WHEN THE GENOCIDE RAVAGED HER world. At such a tender age, her memory is, at best, like tattered shreds of a nightmare. She has no fond memories of a time when she, her mom, her dad, and her six siblings lived peacefully in a mud-walled hut near her grandparents in Gisenyi, a border city in the Rubavu District in Rwanda's western province. She cannot remember the hopefulness that filled her mother's heart when she named her baby girl Joy, or the loving way her father would pat her head as he returned from the fields where they grew sorghum, beans, and potatoes beneath the towering profile of the volcanic mountains. In her mind's eye she can't see their small herd of cattle balanced on sloping hills as they gnawed the grass or the footpath plunging down toward the city. These are things she must be told later by her mother and her sisters. It is not there that the reel of her life begins.

Her memory begins in the forest. It is dark and warm, but even so she is huddling with her sisters. She is quiet, but the night is not. In the distance, she hears gunshots and shouts—some commanding, some pleading, and some wailing in tones she has never heard before. Up close, she hears breathing, hers and that of her sisters, Mulisa, Muhoza, and Ingabire. She feels the pressure of Mulisa's tight hold, and the scratchiness of the saw grass around her. Peeking her eyes out from beneath a smothering arm, she sees the sky streaked orange, not with the familiar glows of sunset on the mountains, but with fire. The smoke from the thatched roof of her burning house now chokes her, and she stifles a cough.

They are too far for her to see the neighbors wielding machetes or calling out "Matenga," her father's name, searching for him. Blessedly, it is too far for her to see the fear in her father's eyes as he is caught and butchered. It is too far for her, hiding out in the bush, but not too far for her sister Wana, who is hiding closer to their burning home.

For a week they lived in huddled terror, cowering in the bush, her mother out of her mind with fear. Alone in the forest with seven children, her mother tried desperately to keep Joy's youngest sister, Ingabire, just two, from alerting others to their location with her cries. The others, including Joy, were too numb to cry, too frightened. They were just still, as still as they could be in the grass. If it were some other time, some other place, their stillness might have been a normal childhood game of hide-and-seek. A cough, a cracking branch, might result in a game of tag, a running chase to home base, and a chorus of girlish giggles. But Joy's memory would never recall any such period of normalcy.

Only at night did they dare move, her older siblings making forays into abandoned houses to search for food while the family— walking, and sometimes crawling low to the ground—inched their way northwest to the Congo. Joy doesn't remember the Congolese friend of her father's who hid them at his own peril, while neighbors continued to make raids across the border searching to kill her mother. She doesn't remember the back room in which they continued to hide for long months.

Her memory jolts awake again in December of 1994. It was again dark and warm, and still she was huddling, this time rattling back over the border in a large flatbed truck. She again felt her sister's tight hold and the weight and scratchiness, but this time from burlap sacks of potatoes stacked on top of her and some twenty-five other men, women, and children who were once again lying very still. It was not a game.

The truck came to a halt. She could hear voices. A man was asking the driver's business. "Potatoes," he said, "hauling back another load."

She heard the low rumbles of men's voices as they backed away to let the truck pass through the roadblock, oblivious to the precious cargo hidden below the sacks. A hundred yards later, Joy breathed.

For the next four months Joy and her family lived in a camp of thousands of displaced and returning Tutsi, protected by a ring of RPF soldiers. They subsisted on maize and beans and slept on mats beneath tarps. The camp reeked of human waste and sometimes the dying or the dead. Occasionally they would meet among the hollow eyes and sunken cheeks a face that seemed distantly familiar, a friend or former neighbor. Almost always that person would be the sole survivor of a large family, all of whom had been killed in the preceding months.

Joy's mother, Nelly, searched for surviving family members. But the unspeakable evils of genocide corroded even the delight of reunions, such as the time they found Joy's cousin, Irene. The Interahamwe, or Hutu paramilitary, had raped Irene's mother and then, after cutting her with machetes, had tossed her and seven-year-old Irene into a pit of bodies. When the RPF soldiers liberated the area soon afterward, they came across the reeking open grave, and scanning for any signs of life, they saw movement.

Irene spent seven months in the hospital recovering from her wounds and waiting for someone to claim her. When the soldiers asked if there was anyone related to her, she mouthed, "Auntie Nelly." By some miracle, they located Joy's mother.

In the early spring of 1995, Joy, her mother, her siblings, and Irene moved from the camp into a home. Since the Interahamwe had burned her home and much of her village to the ground, they found another home, one that, in a manner of speaking, had been abandoned. Joy's mother and older sibling carried out the bodies of the previous owners. They scrubbed blood from the walls as best they could, but several spots could not be purged despite their best efforts.

If Joy can recall any normal period of life, it was the next year and a half. She helped around their new house with cleaning, washing her clothes, cooking, or walking to fill the yellow jerry can with water. With the buildings demolished, they went to school outside, and if it rained they would have to go back home. People began to weave together the shreds of their lives after the war; they tilled fields and rummaged for necessities like cooking pots or farm tools. They found tarps to cover their homes, since the fleeing population had stolen or carried off the corrugated metal roofs.

But many nights whatever they had woven back together would be ripped from them as a raiding party of Hutu rebels from the Congo would sneak back over the border and steal and wreak havoc, or worse, kill, burn, and loot an entire village before evading capture in the forest. When one area would become unsafe, Joy's family would have to move to a different village and repeat the exercise of making a home. Or sometimes a Tutsi family returning from hiding would seek out a Hutu neighbor and take revenge. In the morning, fresh corpses would line the street as Joy made her way to fill the water jug in the town center.

It was a Tuesday in October of 1997 when the rebels came again.

Joy's family was living near where the RPF soldiers had a base. Joy's mother found her brother and told him to go tell the soldiers. Meanwhile, she and the younger children went and hid in a cave behind the house. Soldiers went from house to house warning the inhabitants. But the places nearest the forest were attacked and scores of peoples were killed. While the soldiers were off warning others, those raiding the village sniffed out the cave where Joy and her mother were hiding and threw a grenade in that direction. Thankfully, the rocks were a sturdy enough protection, though a large stone did fall on Joy's mother, leaving her hobbled for years to come. Outside the cave, the house they had most recently called home burned with petrol-fed flames. Inside the house were two of Joy's uncles and their wives who had not fled in time.

Another world up in flames, another devastating loss: this was enough to send Nelly searching for some way to protect her two youngest daughters, Joy and Ingabire, who had the most difficult time with the nightly running and hiding. One of Nelly's brothers lived a good distance from the turbulent northwestern region of Rwanda in the city of Gakoni in the northeast. Close by was a school for orphans. By Thursday, Joy and Ingabire were on their way, accompanied by an older cousin.

While the school was Nelly's last-ditch effort to keep her daughters from harm, in actuality, it was any child's worst nightmare. Away from home, plagued with continual fears about the safety of her mother and other siblings, Joy spent her days alternately agonizing in fear for her family and developing the best plans a seven-year-old could concoct as to how she would survive with her sister if her worst fears materialized. At this orphanage there was never enough food to feed all the children, and sometimes the staff would beat them for seemingly no reason at all. Joy would sometimes see her small sister being attacked by other students or workers and she would step in front to shield her. She'd also frequently save her own food to give to

Ingabire or sing her to sleep, patting her baby sister rhythmically as other girls her age might pat a baby doll.

As months blurred together and still no word came from home, Joy's mind fixated upon one of the many scenarios she had imagined of her mother's death. When she closed her eyes, she saw only a cold waxen face, eyes rolled back, hand cupped loosely above her head, a terrible final sleep that she could not rouse her mother from.

Meanwhile, Joy barely slept. Her nights opened up before her like long corridors with doors. Terrified, she would open one door after another looking for some warm room to enter, but each door held something more fearful than the one before and left her alone, shivering in the dark.

Joy's sounds

Not only is another world possible, she is on her way.
On a quiet day, I can hear her breathing.
Arundhati Roy

JOY SAT IN THE DINING HALL AT THE ORPHANAGE IN GAKONI STARING
blankly at an empty plate. The smoke from the kitchen wafted toward her and filled her mind — as it often did — with memories. She
did not have to close her eyes to see the night sky burning orange
or to feel the strong grasp of her sister clutching her in the grass.
Nor did she have to strain to remember the smoldering rubble of
another home just two years later — a home that contained within it
the charred remains of two uncles and their wives. Like smoke, the
memories wafted easily across her consciousness.

As Joy relived these memories of death, day after day, she began
to focus on the idea of revenge. Like scratching an itch, her hatred
brought a small measure of satisfaction to her days. And so Joy's
mind was occupied when the headmistress of the orphanage approached her. Joy looked up. She could see this woman's lips moving,
shaping sounds, but somehow the words felt impossibly distant.

"Your mother is here."

Joy cocked her head slightly and blinked, but her eyes remained blank and her hunched-over position on the bench unchanged.

"I said your mother is here."

Soon after a loved one dies, your eyes continue to search for the missing form. When a familiar voice calls from behind, you turn in expectation. When you catch a glimpse of a certain curve of a neck, the hair on your own neck stands up. But after your senses have uncoiled so frequently, only to find they have been falsely charmed, eventually they coil back tightly and calcify. So it was for Joy. The phantom hope of her mother surviving, let alone coming for her, had long since ceased to rouse her.

As the headmistress repeated herself, with growing agitation, the words came closer. This time Joy's sleeping senses unfurled, but the words filled her with rage. Clenching her fists and tightening her jaw, Joy stood to her feet. Had she grown up in a more generous place, perhaps her clutched hands would have loosened; perhaps her mind would have raced ahead down the road of possibility and her legs would have followed. But two years had plodded past without any word from home. And now, as the headmistress stood there telling her that her mother had come, Joy would not let hope toy with her. She threw back her head, narrowed her eyes, and said in a low resolute tone, "My mother is dead."

ON A HILL NOT FAR FROM THE CENTER OF RUHENGERI, A HILL THAT could be seen by everyone around it, lines of people climbed the mountain, and the people carried stones on their heads. With the exception of a bulldozer to level the land, all the work on the school they were building was being done by hand. Nearby, men fired bricks and others sanded them in preparation for the walls. Almost three hundred community members worked, shaping a dream that had cast its light in the bishop's imagination.

Joy's sounds

With nearly 300,000 orphaned children in Rwanda, Bishop John could hardly turn anywhere without seeing the need. He had returned some months after the genocide from Uganda where he'd lived since being expelled from Rwanda in 1959 during the first wave of Tutsi persecution. At the time of his return, the ground still swelled with mounds of bodies in shallow graves. In other places, bones bleached white by the African sun were strewn along his path. And in many homes he passed, a little huddle of children would watch him from a safe distance before padding up behind him with hands outstretched, begging. These children, more often than not, lived alone, sometimes with an older sibling—perhaps aged ten or eleven—as their lone guardian.

During his years of exile from Rwanda, John had made a home for himself and his family in Uganda, but after the genocide, something tugged at him to return to his homeland. The pull came from both an external and an internal source.

In 1997, some men and women from northwest Rwanda wrote him, saying, "John, we know you. You are the son of John Baptist Kabango, and he was the son of Ntampuhwe," and so on, tracing his story into the far reaches of Rwanda's past. "You are Rwandan. We need you. Rwanda needs you."

The letter, an invitation to come to that region and to be their bishop, at first fell on deaf ears. After all, John had a thriving ministry in Uganda and things in Rwanda were still terribly tumultuous, especially for a man with a family. But internally, something nudged him as well. John knew God was telling him that he could not leave the fate of his homeland in the hands of those who carry guns. It was as if a fierce current were pulling him back. On June 8, 1997, John was consecrated the bishop of the Shyira diocese. And John made Rwanda his permanent home.

Shortly after John's consecration, his niece Madu paid him a visit. Sixteen, pretty, and terrified, Madu came to tell her uncle that she feared for her life and those in her family with the raids still happening in her area. John gave her some money and told her to bring the family to live near him. And he reassured her that there the family would be safe.

Two days later, John was preaching in prison to a group of genocidaires when the news came. The evening before, rebels had infiltrated Madu's home. They stripped her naked, used machetes to peal the skin off her arms from shoulder to wrist, gang-raped her, and cut off her head. They then raped her mother before killing her and her brother too. John fell on his face in the prison yard and wept bitterly. His mind replayed the horrible images and rehearsed a thousand if-onlys.

In the days and weeks that followed, John wondered how he could go on preaching in the prisons to men like those who had killed his niece. In the midst of this, a clear picture came into John's mind. He could see Jesus hanging on the cross: stripped, beaten, mocked, despised, nails tearing through his flesh, and a crown of thorns on his head. And John could hear Jesus cry, from within the pain, "Forgive!" John realized this message was for him and for his fellow Rwandans. He understood that neither he, nor they, could wait until the pain was over in order to forgive. Jesus had cried out for the forgiveness of his killers when he was still in the midst of the pain. John knew, even as the loss of his niece was such a fresh wound, that it was *then* he needed to forgive and preach hope, because they didn't have time to waste.

So John did. He continued preaching repentance in the prisons, and the message of forgiveness to victims. And soon another idea about how to achieve practical reconciliation came to him. He decided he and those from his diocese could build a world-class school for orphans, a place where they could be healed from their trauma and taught the history of their country. The school would help build

the children in character and develop them as citizens. It would be a place where Hutu and Tutsi children would live and grow together.

From the beginning, the dream seemed almost impossible. John barely scraped together enough money to have the architectural plans drawn up. When he did, he decided to show them to the executive secretary of the Unity and Reconciliation Commission, hoping the government might offer some grants or resources. Instead, she looked at them and said, simply, "You are too ambitious. You will never achieve this. Besides, you can't afford it."

Driving back from his meeting across the dangerous roads, John felt a wave of disappointment and doubt sweep over him. He had hoped the secretary might offer support, perhaps even some financial backing, but instead she had openly questioned his abilities. He contemplated giving up on the idea, but something wouldn't let him.

Only a few months later, John sat with some friends on a veranda in America, the country where he had gone to seminary. Each year, with the support of American friends, he traveled to the United States to preach in various churches there. As he sat with these longtime friends, John told them of his vision for the orphanage and of all the doubts that now plagued his mind about its feasibility. But then his American friend, who'd caught the vision, looked at him. He said in a confident, sure tone, "That school will be called Sonrise. The Son of God must rise into this problem."

From that point onward, through a sponsorship program, the needed funds for building the school began to come in. Soon, on a hill in Ruhengeri, a foundation was laid.

Joy was angrily pacing the room where she and the other girls slept when the headmistress appeared again. Joy had slammed the door only moments before, saying nothing to her sister about what just happened. But now, as the headmistress appeared in the doorway, she wasn't alone.

A slender woman in her midthirties stepped across the threshold of the room. Ingabire looked up and gasped. "Mama!"

Joy scanned this face, a face she had seen only in dreams for the past two years. As Joy's mind leapt in recognition, her body crumpled to the floor.

Ingabire flew to her mother as her mother swooped forward, dropped to her knees, and embraced both girls. "Mama, Mama!" exclaimed Ingabire. Nelly, in turn, cooed her babies' names. Joy's sounds were softer. Somewhere, at the horizon of her senses, the meaning of her own name was dawning.

from torn
to tapestry

*Joy is where the whole being is pointed in one direction,
and it is something by its nature a man never hoards
but always wants to share ... Joy is a mystery
because it can happen anywhere, anytime,
even under the most unpromising circumstances,
even in the midst of suffering. Even nailed to a tree.*
Frederick Buechner

FOURTEEN-YEAR-OLD JOY WOKE THAT MORNING, AS SHE HAD FOR THE past four years, at 5:30 a.m. Grabbing her towel, she shuffled in the dark through the outdoor corridors of Sonrise School to the bathroom, where she bathed under a weak trickle of running water, dressed, and then returned to the room she shared with a dozen other girls. She pulled the spread tight up over her bed and tucked it neatly under the mattress, straightened her pillow, snatched up her schoolbooks, and stepped out to go wrestle with math problems for an hour or so before breakfast. This general routine hadn't changed in the four years since Joy's arrival in the hills of Ruhengeri.

As Joy walked the open-air corridor to the classroom where she and others studied before breakfast, she surveyed the valley below. A woman stepped out of her small home into the just-breaking sunlight and began to sweep the dirt yard with a stiff broom. Joy pictured her mother doing the same thing. Waves of relief had flooded Joy when she first saw her mom that day four years ago in Gakoni. For her mother also, it had been like receiving her children back from the dead. She'd heard of many children dying from unclean water in that part of the country, and she feared the worst. Both mother and children wept unashamedly at their reunion, feasting their eyes on those they had feared dead. Her mother had taken the girls back home then, and the year that Joy and her sister spent in Gisenyi had passed by faster than any of the days yet in Joy's life.

As that year at home drew to a close, an invitation to enroll in the new Sonrise School came unexpectedly. The invitation, which had come from Bishop John to her and other children who had lost parents in the genocide, was a turning point for Joy. In one way it felt like dying to leave her mother behind again, especially after such a brief reunion, but the day Joy entered the school seemed like the first day of a new life.

The contrast between the orphanage in Gakoni and Sonrise School astounded Joy from the beginning. She had plenty to eat, the buildings were new and well cared for, the teachers were kind, and even though there were both Hutu and Tutsi orphans at the school, they were taught to treat each other with respect and love.

Classes were challenging. Joy had to work hard to keep up, but she found that she loved math and science—especially the satisfaction of working an equation to its solution using dependable numbers.

From the time Joy came to Sonrise, she had also begun to learn about God. Joy remembered the pastor's words in chapel that he repeated so often, "Jesus knows your problems. He knows; he sees; he cares. You are children of God, and God wants you to love each other as brothers and sisters."

But the injunctions to love didn't stop there. Joy had learned that the Bible calls people to forgive—even their enemies, even the people who had wronged them.

This put a lump in Joy's throat when she thought about it. She knew the call to forgive included the people who had killed her father. And even though so many parts of Joy's life were better now that she was at Sonrise, she was still haunted by the past. The sight of strangers could still make her skin prick in fear. A sudden commotion could undo her for hours. But mostly she found herself reliving the fear and the hatred in her past, and that past bled into her future. Even now, as Joy settled into her desk for her morning studies, she felt a sharp pain in her stomach. She gasped, held her breath for several moments, then slowly exhaled through clenched teeth. The pains had been coming more and more frequently lately. And it somehow felt like the past was reaching into her future and gnawing at her from the inside.

JOY LAY ON HER BED FLIPPING THROUGH HER HANDMADE CHEMISTRY flashcards. The morning sun had climbed high into the sky by that time, and the room she shared with the other girls, while not a particularly quiet study spot, shielded her from the afternoon heat.

She heard the latch lift on the outer door and the sound of the residence mother's heavy steps in the hallway. As she opened the door to their room, Joy looked up.

Their eyes met as the residence mother said, "A letter for you."

Joy smiled and scrambled up to retrieve the prize, a letter from home.

The familiar scrawl of her mother's handwriting comforted Joy. But her mother's letters were infrequent enough that it also sent a small chill of fear through her. "God, please let everyone be okay," she asked as she ran her finger under the envelope's fold, loosening the adhesive.

Joy's eyes scanned the plain paper quickly to make sure all was well ... a good market day recently, her sister Ingabire progressing in her studies, her brother-in-law joining the army ... and yes, there it was, saved for last: "A week ago," her mother wrote, "a letter came. It is the third like it and I haven't told you until now because I didn't know how I would respond. But I have decided and I think it is fair to give you the chance to decide also."

Joy's eyes skipped ahead, and she tried to make sense of what she was reading. Two men—former neighbors who had been a part of the group responsible for burning her house and killing her father —were writing from prison to ask for forgiveness. Soon they would be released from prison, and they were writing in hopes that Joy's mother would be willing to meet with them face-to-face, so that they could personally ask for forgiveness.

Joy put the letter down. She felt suddenly flushed. The room was stifling. Two of her friends who had been talking animatedly on the adjacent bed watched Joy's face cloud over, and one asked if everything was all right.

"I just need some air," Joy said as she slipped on her sandals and stepped out of the room, down the hallway, and into the hot African sun.

The warmth and light that had fallen softly on the valley just that morning now seemed oppressive. Joy moved toward the shade of a tree to escape the scorching heat. She collapsed in a heap. But while her body was still, her stomach turned somersaults and a lump rose in her throat like a thermometer's mercury in a room on fire. A wincing pain shot through her, several inches below her breastbone. Joy couldn't fathom the thought of forgiving these men, much less seeing them face-to-face.

THE DRIVER HONKED AS A BOY WITH GOATS STRAYED INTO THE highway. The van's handler took the curves too fast, especially for

a main road where so many people walked along the shoulder or sometimes brazenly in the middle of the street. And as it rounded the curve, the van lurched left suddenly to avoid a collision with the goat herder. Joy's mother, Nelly, didn't even seem to notice as inertia flung her into the window. Her two daughters, Mulisa and Muhoza, pressed like dominoes against her on the bench seat. A man in the backseat of the crowded taxi muttered a curse as the driver hit a pothole and careened around another corner.

Nelly didn't feel the impact. Nor did she notice the smell of too many bodies pressed too closely together. With less than thirty minutes left in her three-hour journey from Gisenyi to Kigali, Nelly's mind worked through the scenario she soon would face. She still didn't know if she had the strength to give the thing these men had asked of her. But she had decided to at least see them.

"God, help me," she breathed, and closed her eyes.

She opened them again at the main bus and taxi terminal in Kigali. There, the three women folded out of the van, stretching their sore limbs and scanning for a van to the Kigali Memorial Centre. A threesome of American backpackers stood waiting at the stop. The two men wore packs and had faces that had not seen a razor in some time, and the woman leaned against the taller of the two men looking intently into a gorilla-covered guidebook as a cigarette smoldered between her fingers. The men eyed Nelly and her daughters carefully as they approached. It wasn't a lustful gaze, but it was nevertheless unnerving. Perhaps they were searching their faces for tell-tale features they'd heard distinguished the Hutu and Tutsi. In any case, they stared unapologetically.

Soon a crowd had gathered at the stop and the van arrived. Pressing francs into the driver's hand, each passenger squeezed into the vehicle. All too soon the van reached the newly finished memorial. The building's clean vanilla stucco and grey stone exterior, white fence, and manicured drive were at odds with what lay within and below. The center was built on a site where over 250,000 people are buried, a quarter of those lost in the 1994 genocide. It had only been open a few months in 2004 and there were still streams of survivors —more than a thousand per day—visiting.

Childlike, Muhoza reached for her mother's hand as they neared the steps. But instead of finding warm reassurance, Muhoza found her mother's hands ice cold.

Once inside the memorial, their eyes adjusted to the dark walls and soft yellow light. Along the walls, metal wires ran from floor to ceiling with metal clips like a modern artist's rendition of a clothes-line. On each clip hung a different picture of a loved one lost in the genocide.

Nelly's eyes fell on a picture of a young woman. She wore a black and white flowered dress and stared unsmilingly into the camera. She couldn't have been any older than twenty-five, about the same age as her sister had been when killed in the genocide. In the picture adjacent, another woman posed outside her home with a hand on her hip, a smile, and eyes speaking a playful disapproval to the picture taker. She stood in the shadow, but the sun fell just behind her as if evening was slowly swallowing the daylight. Next to her was a picture of a man in a white dress shirt and dark slacks posing casually in his home. In the home, behind him on the wall, was a lone decoration, a picture of the Virgin Mary, her eyes full of sadness.

Pulling her mind away from the photographs, Nelly turned to an attendant and asked, "How do we get to the memorial gardens?"

The woman motioned to a set of doors behind her. It took Nelly some moments before she could force her body to obey her mind. Her thoughts fluttered about like startled birds, disorienting her. After a few moments, she managed to take several labored steps. Once out-doors, her eyes had to readjust again to the harsh daylight. There she could see, on a lower tier, eight mass graves, covered over in concrete, each holding the remains of tens of thousands of people. Nearby, stone walls wound around manicured garden terraces. There, beside a fountain, two men in civilian clothes sat hunched slightly, hands clasped in front of them. Nelly recognized them; before the war they had been neighbors in Gisenyi, though not close ones. And as the men saw the three women approach, they stood to their feet.

As they stood, fear fell heavily on Nelly. She was suddenly glad there were so many people milling about. One of the men looked only a handful of years older than Mulisa. The other had a peppering of gray on his head. Though Rwandans usually greet with an embrace or a handshake with one arm extended and another grasping the left forearm, the two men respected a careful distance and only bowed their heads in greeting. The older man motioned to a long bench, where the women took their seats, while the two men resumed their seats once more on the low stone wall.

The older one spoke first.

"Thank you for coming," he said, his voice frailer than his frame. He cleared his throat. The space between them a bit too wide for easy conversation, the man struggled to speak louder without speaking so loud that others would hear. "I have ... I ... hoped God would give me this chance." He choked on a cough and then continued. "I was leading the group of men who set your house on fire. I'm responsible. Your husband's death and the deaths of his brothers. Their deaths are my doing.

"We searched for you and for your children to kill you too. We searched day and night for you, and I know in my heart that had we found you, we would have killed you too.

"My son," he said, putting his hands on the shoulders of the younger man, "he obeyed me and took the torch to the house along with others who fled to the Congo. He is guilty also, but I am responsible. And so, I want to be the one to ask you for mercy.

"We believed the lies of the Interahamwe. We believed that the Tutsi were the enemy. It was far too late when I knew the truth in my own heart. In the prison, some men of God came and preached to us. They helped us to see the evil of what we had done, and helped us to find hope again in God's forgiveness. I know I don't deserve your mercy, or the mercy of your daughters, but I am today—I want—I am asking your forgiveness."

Nelly looked beyond the two men. The soft sound of a fountain filled the silence.

Only after some time did Nelly speak, continuing to look past the men before her.

"Wawa was my third-born. A girl like all the rest. When she was a child she used to love to lie on the hillside and watch the clouds. Matenga, her father, would sometimes sit down next to her when he came in from tending the cattle. He'd point to the clouds and say, 'Wawa, I see a lion in the sky. He looks angry.' Then, just as she saw it too, he'd roar in her ear and send her squealing and laughing in the house. I didn't understand their little game. Sometimes I would scold her for lying about watching the sky, as if there were no chores to do. I'm sorry now I scolded her for that.

"The night you came for us, Wawa lagged behind. I didn't know she wasn't with us. But she couldn't bear to leave her father's side and so she stayed close to the house in the grass as Matenga gathered a few things for us and boarded the door.

"She saw everything that night. Everything.

"She was eight years old and watched her papa die."

The old man bowed his head and covered his face with his hands. The young man too dropped his gaze and looked away.

"I am so sorry," said the father.

"For years, we have been running, hiding, running. I have no husband. My girls have no father. They are orphans. Often we have lacked for food. Wawa will go weeks without speaking. She falls ill frequently. But not just her, it is all the girls who suffer. We are all still suffering."

"Forgive me," said the old man.

"Forgive us," added the son, speaking softly and slowly raising his eyes.

After a long pause, Nelly looked the father in the eyes and said, "It is enough. It is enough for you to know what you have done."

They raised their eyes.

"I have forgiven you," said Nelly, returning their gaze.

JOY KNELT ON THE FLOOR OF THE GIRLS' BATHROOM AT SONRISE. She had slept fitfully that night, having received a letter from her mother with the news of her encounter with her father's killers. Internally, Joy had been wrestling with the whole situation, turning it over in her head as if it were an algebra equation to be solved. She kept substituting different responses to the dilemma of forgiveness that faced her, and when her mind would reach a conclusion, memory would encroach with a fresh image from the past. Joy had finally drifted to sleep when violent stomach pains jolted her awake.

She had made her way through the dark to the bathroom. And now as she coughed into the toilet, she found herself vomiting bile and blood. The sight of her own blood scared her. She didn't know what it meant.

Inside, her mind screamed out that she must be dying. Having seen so many others die in her young life, it was a reasonable conclusion.

Frightened, she gathered her strength enough to make her way down the corridors to the room where the residence mother slept. Her fist made only a soft rap on the door. When there was no answer, she knocked again with a firmer hand.

Soon, she heard some shuffling and then the sound of the locks on the door sliding loose. Mama Nadine, as they called her, answered, her hair wrapped in an orange print cloth, and her face

registering the alarm that Rwandans know only too well from midnight terrors.

"What's wrong, Joy?"

"I'm sorry to wake you, Mama Nadine."

"Well, what is it? Is everyone alright?"

"It's just me, ma'am. I'm sick. I'm vomiting blood. I'm scared."

"Stay there, child. I'm coming."

Mama Nadine disappeared into the room and came back in a few
moments dressed. "We'll see about you. Don't you worry."

MAMA NADINE AND JOY WAITED UNTIL FIRST LIGHT TO TAXI UP THE
hills to Shyira Hospital. The small, one-story brick hospital had only
opened a year before. It had been ten years since the area had had a
hospital of any sort. During the genocide, the regional hospital had
been looted and what equipment wasn't stolen was destroyed.

The young Rwandan who admitted Joy asked her several questions as he took her temperature, listened to her heart, and made
notes on a pad. His face was businesslike, but his touch was gentle.
Joy found out later that he was one of about five staff at the hospital, a mission run by the Anglican Church. The staff was a mixture
of Rwandans, Americans, and German doctors. With the hospital
serving a population of about 200,000, Joy found the doctors often
looking weary, but nonetheless treating her with a kindness and a
dignity that wasn't always afforded to the poor.

After running a few tests, they confirmed that Joy was suffering
from ulcers. The blood had indeed been a dangerous sign. The next
several days continued to be grueling as Joy's body convulsed in pain
and the nausea and vomiting continued to come in waves. Her body
felt limp, her throat ached, and the suddenness of the pain kept her
tensing her body until her muscles ached as well. In the midst of the
pain and the fear, Joy cried out to God. She remembered the lessons

the teachers and her pastor had been teaching her since she came to Sonrise: that God knows, he sees, and he cares. And in her pain, she asked God simply to show her that this was true.

Joy saw God do just that. In a place where they sometimes even ran out of aspirin, it was a minor miracle that the doctors had in house the antibiotics to treat the ulcers. Little by little, the pain and the vomiting subsided, and Joy began to get her strength back.

Over the next two weeks, each day one of the residence mothers, or matrons, from Sonrise would come to visit her. Mama Nadine came most frequently, but so did others, including a few of Joy's teachers. Often they would stay by her bedside reading or singing to her. Frequently, they would bring a card made and signed by her classmates. And more often than not, something would prompt them to hold Joy's hand as she lay in the bed recovering. To Joy, these hands felt like God's hands and fingers taking hold of her.

Soon, Joy had recovered enough to return to Sonrise. Weakened though she was, Joy asked Mama Nadine to take her by the chapel before taking her back to her room. When Mama Nadine saw the earnestness in Joy's eyes, she obliged her, even though her better instincts told her the child should rest.

Inside the chapel, Joy found a pew toward the front, one that was bathed in the midafternoon sunlight. Kneeling on the cement floor, she let her forehead rest on the well-sanded wooden back of the pew in front of her. Mama Nadine sat in the back keeping a protective eye on her ward, who was now bathed in the blue light of the sun filtered through stained glass.

Joy closed her eyes and began to pray. Though the words came easily to her, she prayed slowly, pausing after each sentence as if to soak in the gravity of the moment.

"Father God, you know that I had no confidence that you would heal me. But, God, you have. Thank you, Father. Thank you for making me well. Thank you for the matrons who came to visit me, for their kindness, for the kindness of the doctors, for the kindness of my friends. Oh, God, forgive me for dwelling so much on the past, for pushing others away and feeling lonely, when I didn't have to feel that way. And most of all forgive me for not thinking of you, or what you have given me today. Help me, God, to start living and to start being truly thankful for the ways you are working in my life."

As Joy stood up, the blue light of the stained glass pooled at her feet. And like the newly baptized, Joy drew in a deep breath. She steadied her body by gripping the pew. But inside, somehow, she felt stronger than she had in a very long time. Joy smiled at Mama Nadine, nodding that she was ready to go. Taking Joy's hand in hers, Mama Nadine gave her a squeeze.

FIFTEEN-YEAR-OLD JOY WOKE THAT MORNING, AS SHE HAD FOR THE past five years, at 5:30 a.m. Grabbing her towel, she shuffled in the dark through the outdoor corridors of Sonrise School to the bathroom, where she bathed under a weak trickle of running water, dressed, and then returned to the room she shared with a dozen other girls. She pulled the spread tight up over her bed and tucked it neatly under the mattress, straightened her pillow, snatched up her schoolbooks and her Bible, and stepped outside. This general routine hadn't changed much in the five years since Joy had come to Sonrise School — until that day.

On that particular morning, as she left her room, something was different. She came to a complete stop.

The sun had been stretching out its fingers over the valley below. And at just the moment Joy had closed the door behind her, the earth had rolled fully into the wide-armed embrace of the light. Joy stood blinking at the sun, which commanded her attention with the forcefulness only such a stunning beauty can summon. Responding,

Joy took her books to a hilltop, where she sat down and pulled her knees up to her chest, encircling them with her arms.

Warmth and light cloaked her now as Joy sat surveying the patchwork of farms below. There were patches of green, patches of dark brown-black soil, patches where the sunlight fell and turned everything golden, and there above it all was a brilliant blue swath of sky. As Joy sat on the hilltop, surveying the beauty of the sunrise and of the countryside, she couldn't help thinking how much her life had changed in the past year.

She had joined the girls' choir. She found that she loved to sing, almost as much as she loved math. Soon the other girls recognized that she was a natural leader and a quick study when it came to learning the traditional Rwandan dances that they incorporated into their songs. Later that year, she'd become the choir director, and she loved picking out the songs and teaching the dances to the younger girls.

Just a few months ago, the girls had also voted her head girl. It was an honor and also a responsibility. As the head girl, she checked on the other girls to make sure they were doing okay, whether in their studies or in their health. One part peer counselor, one part resident assistant, the role pulled on strengths Joy didn't know she had.

Joy had also started to play volleyball. Now already pushing 5'10", her height came in handy as a spiker. But even though it was fun drilling the ball over the net, she enjoyed more the company and camaraderie of her teammates.

A dream had also begun to grow in her heart. Since the days she'd spent at the hospital, she'd begun to wonder about becoming a doctor. She continued to excel in science and math, and as she talked with her teachers, they encouraged her that medicine would suit her well. And slowly her thoughts shifted from thoughts occupied in the past to ones occupied in the present, and in the hope of the future.

Other changes began as well. Before she had felt such rage in her heart, and she couldn't imagine forgiving the men who had killed her father. Now, not from a self-determined effort to forgive, but from some strange peace that had settled in her heart, she felt able to offer the forgiveness that had before seemed so elusive.

And the more she had come to understand the significance of the Bible's teachings on Jesus Christ's death, the more forgiveness seemed possible. She learned how Christ had been executed in a horrible manner, more horrible than some of the things she had seen in the war. And she learned how he willingly died to pay the penalty for her wrongdoing and for anyone else who would give up their bad ways and look to him. If Christ could forgive her, if he could forgive the people who tortured him, then Joy knew she could forgive too.

There were still difficulties. That year, the week of mourning in April, the first week of the one hundred days of slaughter that Rwandans commemorate, had hit her hard. Her mind again was filled with images of the past. And the sadness laid so heavily on her that she had difficulty getting out of bed. But she asked her friends to pray for her, and to sing to her, and she wrestled to forgive again as the memories came back fresh. And she did. And the days passed.

And now as she sat there, she felt strangely at peace. The pain of the past was still there. It would never be gone completely. But as Joy had given God the shreds of her past, he had begun to weave those dark brown-black shreds of pain into something much bigger. There were large green swatches of growth, deep golden swatches of loving friendship, and bright blue swatches of hope. It was a patchwork quilt that looked something like the beautiful Rwandan countryside that now stretched out in front of her. Joy could feel God's love for her in the warmth of the morning sun, and in the beauty of the tapestry he was weaving from her life.

wrestling
with forgiveness

If only there were evil people somewhere committing evil deeds
and it were necessary only to separate them from the rest of us
and destroy them. But the line dividing good and evil
cuts through the heart of every human being.
And who is willing to destroy a piece of their own heart.
Aleksandr Solzhenitsyn

WHEN I INTERVIEWED JOY AMID THE HARSH PATTER OF RAIN ON
a metal roof, she told me a secret. Her voice was so low and gentle and the rain so loud that I had to bend close to hear it. With
a calm voice and a faraway look in her eye, Joy told me, "Forgiveness is a gift one gives to change the heart of the offender." At
the time, I had little idea how much philosophical and theological punch was packed into that one simple statement.

As I dug deeper into the stories of Rwandan atrocities,
the notion that began this book—the power of forgiveness—

became not only more intriguing, but also more disturbing, more incomprehensible, and more miraculous than it had been when I first started.

Looking at some of the monsters of the Rwandan genocide —men who sliced open the abdomens of pregnant women, who peeled the skin of their victim's back with machetes, or who smashed the heads of babies against the walls of churches—the notion of forgiveness became nearly impossible for me to imagine. How could anyone forgive such acts and such people?

Like everyone who wrestles with forgiveness, I had to first understand what forgiveness is not. Forgiveness does not mean that what happened didn't matter. It isn't sweeping a crime under the rug. It isn't saying the crime was a misunderstanding. It isn't saying that the crime did little harm or that it left no loss in its wake. Forgiveness isn't forgetting. It doesn't have to mean forgoing the established criminal justice system. Forgiveness isn't usually a one-time act, but more commonly a lifetime commitment. Finally, and most important, forgiveness is excruciatingly difficult.

In popular thought today, forgiveness is most often associated with release of resentment; it is almost exclusively seen as a personal, internal act that helps the wronged move forward. Perhaps the best expression of this comes from Dr. Phil: "Forgiveness is a choice you make to release yourself from anger, bitterness, and resentment."[1]

While it is true—and I have certainly seen it in the faces of my interviewees—that forgiveness often offers release, this definition misses a fundamental aspect of what forgiveness is. Any definition of forgiveness must get at the fact that forgiveness is, fundamentally, a social action with social ramifications.

But what if the offender is not repentant? What if the offender is incapacitated, dead, or otherwise inaccessible—can forgiveness still occur?

This is where Joy became a guiding light for me. The notion of forgiveness as a gift is extremely helpful on a number of levels. Joy's simple metaphor is echoed in the words of Yale professor Miroslav Volf, who personally wrestled with forgiveness after his experience of interrogation under the Communist Yugoslavian regime. In his book *Free of Charge*, Volf elaborates further on this metaphor:

> Imagine that I tell my sister that I am sending her a large gift, say an expensive bracelet. For whatever reason, however, she's not sure she wants to accept it—maybe she thinks that I may be trying to bribe her to do something she doesn't want to do, that the gift is too large to be received without undue obligation, or that I can't afford it. Have I given her a gift? In one sense, I have. I bought it, I sent it, and the postal service has delivered it. But in another sense, I haven't. The gift is at her home, but she hasn't decided whether she wants to keep it. She hasn't yet received it. Given but not received, the gift is stuck somewhere in the middle between us. Forgiveness works the same way.[2]

Volf goes on to explain that implicit in the act of forgiveness is an accusation, a condemnation of wrong. Even as the forgiver offers the gift of release to the offender, in order for the offender to accept the gift he or she must accept the condemnation for the offense. If the offender fails to repent, he or she has failed to receive the gift. The gift transaction has been stopped midway.

This is helpful. But still, my deepest question, and perhaps yours too, is how does someone come to the point of being able and willing to offer such a peculiar gift—a gift that costs the giver such a high sum and is given to the person in our life who we may believe least deserves it? How does someone find the strength to extend this gift?

Like you and like the people in these real-life stories, I have wounds that have needed forgiving. These wounds have taken years of my life in the forming and taken me years from which to recover. So as good as it is to understand what forgiveness is and what it isn't, when it's accomplished and when it's incomplete, my most fundamental question and probably yours as well is: How do we forgive?

Dr. Everett Worthington has spent his professional career studying forgiveness. As professor and chair of psychology at Virginia Commonwealth University and as the executive director of A Campaign for Forgiveness Research funded by the John Templeton Foundation, Dr. Worthington, perhaps more than most, is deeply acquainted with the psychological process of forgiveness. In 1995, when burglars broke into his mother's home in Tennessee and brutally murdered Dr. Worthington's elderly mother, beating her to death with a crowbar and violating her with a broken bottle, he also came to know the process of forgiveness on a much more raw and personal level.

For a man whose life's work had been in studying and teaching forgiveness, this murder came as the ultimate test. His mind whirled with the reasons he had heard over the years that people should not forgive, that righteous anger can motivate good, that forgiveness is cowardly, or that forgiveness wasn't his to give. Each argument, his mind shot down. He also thought of the reasons that he had heard for forgiveness over the years: that unforgiveness can't hurt a perpetrator but forgiveness can set the sufferer free, or that he would be healthier if he could forgive. Ultimately though, it wasn't any of these reasons which pushed him to offer the gift. He writes, "I merely became weary of struggling against hatred ... *If only I could forgive*, I thought, *I could have peace in my heart*."[3]

As Dr. Worthington paced the floor debating himself after

his mother's murder, he began to apply the principles he himself had taught. **REACH** was the acrostic he had used to teach forgiveness: **R**ecall the hurt, **E**mpathize, **A**ltruistic gift of forgiveness, **C**ommit publicly to forgive, and **H**old on to forgiveness.

First, he recalled the hurt. With the psychological wound still fresh, this was not difficult. So as he remembered, he tried to see the events unfold from the offender's point of view, so as to somehow come to empathize with him. As vividly as Dr. Worthington could imagine, he recreated the scene of the young men entering into his mother's house, imagining their surprise to find someone inside after seeing the dark house and the empty carport. Dr. Worthington followed the emotions, as surprise turned to fear of being caught, and fear to unbridled anger. As he did this, he could begin to understand—not condone—what had happened the night his mother was killed.

From recalling the hurt to empathizing with the offender, Dr. Worthington's mind went to a conversation he had had earlier with his siblings as they each had wished for a few hours with the murderer and the crowbar so that they could exact revenge. Contemplating his own lust for revenge, Dr. Worthington suddenly saw with keen insight the darkness in his own heart. While the youth had killed his mother in a sudden moment of rage, he had wished death on the youth with premeditation. He had enjoyed the thought of bludgeoning his mother's killer. As a Christian, this drove Dr. Worthington to ask for God's forgiveness.

Feeling the relief of being forgiven, he was moved to not only look with new humility at the young man who had killed his mother, but also to want to extend the altruistic gift of forgiveness to him. This also happened to be the third step in the method of forgiveness he had taught others. Though for those who are not of a particular faith, he encouraged them to remember a time when someone had forgiven them and to use that memory of how good forgiveness had felt as a motivator to extend compassion.

In the days and months which passed, Dr. Worthington shared his commitment to forgive with others, so that when doubts inevitably came about whether forgiveness had been real, he would not doubt, but continue to hold on to the forgiveness by going back and repeating the steps as necessary.

I wouldn't go so far as to say Dr. Worthington's method of forgiveness is the only or the best way to forgive. But as I've researched experiences in Rwanda of forgiveness and thought of times in my own life that I've extended forgiveness, these principles do seem to resonate. Other methods of forgiveness focus on coming to understand the benefits of forgiveness and then releasing the hurt.[4] Still others like Christian speaker Nancy Leigh DeMoss advocate that forgiveness is "not so much a method to be taught as a truth to be lived."[5]

Perhaps forgiveness is really a confluence of these things. It is a growing empathy for the shared humanity of the offender, a growing understanding that the decision itself will also release us, and a growing enlightenment as to the power and need of forgiveness in the world and in our hearts.

Like any gift, forgiveness can bring joy to both the giver and the receiver, and the one who gives pays the highest price. But perhaps the extreme costliness of this particular gift imbues forgiveness, of all human actions, with the greatest potential to image forth the divine.

Questions for Reflection and Discussion

As you think about the concept of forgiveness, what are your biggest emotional or intellectual objections to it?

Putting those objections aside for a moment, what about forgiveness draws you or moves you?

Can you remember a time when someone forgave you for something that you had felt guilty about? How did forgiveness feel then?

Make a list of ways you are holding on to unforgiveness. Pick out one of the smaller offenses in your life and walk through Dr. Everett's steps before trying to tackle the more grievous offenses.

envy's aftertaste

Envy is thin because it bites but never eats.
Spanish Proverb

CHANTAL THREW HER HEAD BACK, STRETCHED HER ARMS WIDE, AND twirled. Her white dress swirled around her. She'd been confirmed in the church that morning and received her first communion. The dress had been a gift from her father, and she couldn't remember ever having a dress half as pretty or nearly so spin-worthy.

Sometimes, when Chantal sat on the hillside with her father watching their lean Ankole cattle graze, she would pick a wildflower and twirl the stem between her fingers. She felt like that wildflower now, twisting, her shining dress in full bloom, petals open to the sun.

She liked how the skirt seemed to stand up on its own when she spun. What made it float, she wondered, and twisted again the other way. She opened her eyes wide this time. The blue sky spun about her like the swirling waters of the River Nyabarongo where she and her mother took their clothes to wash each week. The sun was centered in the sky now and stood still even as the clouds and sky whirled. Chantal drank it in, her eyes brimming with wonder.

When she came to a staggering stop, the world did not. Bright colors spun: yellows, oranges, limes, reds, browns, and blues. But slowly the colors solidified into the rightful shapes of her brightly clad uncles, aunts, cousins, neighbors, and friends moving about the dirt yard surrounding her small mud house. They were having a good time, smiling, laughing, and tossing back bottles of banana beer and Fanta.

She decided to spin again. The white cotton was taking flight about her like a flock of "Go-away Birds," as her mother called them. Just as Chantal's skirt was in full flutter, she heard her father call her name.

"Ukubereyinfura," he called. That was her first name, but not the one she went by. Mama had told her that it meant firstborn, and her father used it when he wanted to remind her that she was not such a little girl anymore. He used it especially when he wanted her to behave like a lady. Chantal tried to walk straight to him, but she couldn't help it that the ground would not stay still in front of her.

"Yes, Papa." As Chantal got closer she could see that he was talking to their neighbor, John. The two men seemed to be laughing at her, though her father's eyes also held a look of rebuke.

"Ukubereyinfura, don't you have something to say to John?"

Chantal cocked her head to the right as she looked at her father. Her father's eyes widened. He drew his chin to his broad chest, and his eyebrows gathered like storm clouds. That look jogged her still-whirling memory.

"Thank you, Mr. John, for my confirmation party. I—I'm having a very nice time."

"I can see that. You're quite welcome," said John with a smile. He was a good ten years older than her father, old in a child's eyes, but still in his prime. Chantal looked back up at her father. The storm clouds had passed. He nodded to her with a look that said, "Good girl," and she knew she was dismissed. Chantal dashed through the crowd to catch up to her younger brother who was chasing the rooster and chickens away from the feet of their guests. She had just joined him in an impromptu stomp as her father turned back to John.

"I'm pleased," he said with a nod, turning back to the brochette in his hand. The skewered beef was still hot, and he held it for a minute with his front teeth before tossing it back into his mouth and chewing.

"Thank you, Nambaje," said John, "It has been my pleasure to play the host on such a special day for your firstborn." John eyed Nambaje carefully.

"I would like to make you a gift," said Nambaje, tearing another piece of meat from the skewer. "One of my cows," he said, motioning with his head in the direction of his herd.

"That is too generous," said the older neighbor, shaking his head.

"But you won't deny me the pleasure, will you?"

"No," he said, laughing uneasily. John took a deep swig of the banana beer, rolling the sweet smoky liquid in his mouth a moment before swallowing.

John and Nambaje had both moved to the Kivugiza area around 1972. Chantal had been just toddling about then. There was more open land in that region than in Butare. Nambaje had chosen a spot with soil that looked rich for planting and with space enough for his cattle to roam. Even at that time, he had a small herd, a badge of wealth in a community as poor as that one. John had chosen a parcel of land next to his. They got on well. John too had moved from Butare, and they both bemoaned the loss of conveniences in moving from a good-sized city back to the country. Yet both men were pleased to have the space to cultivate, to grow their crops, and to grow their families. Nambaje had more education than John, and more wealth. It sometimes grated on John that, though he was older, he was still the lesser. But usually he pushed it from his mind. They'd share a beer at his table and forget the things that divided them.

Today, as pleased as John was about the cow, something still chafed him. He did not like the feeling that somehow Nambaje was his benefactor. He swallowed his pride with another sip of the banana beer. "I certainly won't deny you that pleasure," he said, twisting his mouth as if he'd finally reached a bittersweet conclusion.

FABRICE WAS PANTING WITH EXERTION WHEN HE FINALLY REACHED his father's house. Nambaje had just come in from the fields for lunch when his youngest padded up to him. Fabrice could feel his heart beating wildly. He drew a deep breath and then managed to get out the words, "She's had the baby." Fabrice filled his six-year-old lungs again. "It's a boy."

A smile broke over Nambaje's face. He dropped his bag of seed and headed for the house. "Yvette!" he yelled. "Did you hear that?" There was no answer. Nambaje disappeared in the house.

"She's already there," called Fabrice after him. "Mama and Ange and I walked there this morning while you were in the fields. I just ran back to tell you the baby has come."

In a moment, Nambaje had returned back outside bare-chested and grinning like a king. He grabbed the yellow jerry can and a basin and poured a bit of water and then began splashing it happily on his chest, his face, and his arms. He slipped on a clean shirt.

"A boy, huh?" he asked Fabrice.

"Yes, and they've named him, but they made me promise not to tell."

"I see," said Nambaje, buttoning his shirt. "Well, let's get going then before you break that promise."

He took Fabrice's hand, but before turning down the road to the village, he turned left, walked a few paces, and yelled up to John's house, "I'm a grandfather."

He didn't wait for a reply but pulled Fabrice back the other direction and set to walking. On a normal day, Fabrice had to take two good steps to his father's one. Today, Nambaje walked even faster than usual, and so Fabrice had to concentrate hard just to keep pace.

Nambaje hardly felt his sandaled feet touch the ground. At each house they passed, he'd wave to a woman hanging out the wash, or a child playing in the dirt, or a man putting his back into flattening tea leaves. He'd wave and yell, "I'm a grandfather!"

By the time Nambaje had reached Chantal and Placide's house, the village had heard the news.

Nambaje found Chantal propped up in her bed cradling his first grandchild. He beamed. Chantal had long since outgrown the confirmation dress. She'd worn white for a second time only a year ago when Nambaje had given her away to Placide. And now, as Chantal lay adoring the little one in her arms, the world around her was again a blur.

"His name is Nambaje too," she said with a smile. Her finger stroked his cheek. "He looks like his grandpa."

Chantal's father swallowed hard; she'd never seen him quite so happy.

Nambaje walked around to get a closer look. "Oh no, Chantal," he said with a chuckle, "he is much more handsome than his grandfather."

Chantal smiled. "He's nodding off."

"You should get some rest too." He turned to leave, but before he did, he called back over his shoulder, "Ukubereyinfura."

"Yes, Papa?"

"You've made me proud today."

THE SUN WAS ALREADY STARTING TO SLIP FROM THE HIGH SKY WHEN Nambaje, Fabrice, and his daughter Ange set out for home. Nambaje happily surrendered his wife for the evening to allow Yvette to care for Chantal. But his stomach growled and he thought twice about going home with it empty. He decide to take Fabrice and Ange in to the town center and get a bite for them before they set out again for home. The rest of his five children had already either moved out, or were of the age to be boarding at the secondary school. Nambaje wasn't much for preparing his own meals. Besides, he thought, he wouldn't mind seeing folks in town and telling them his news.

Ange held her father's hand, but Fabrice ran ahead. He stopped at the flagpole in front of the district headquarters. The door was open, and inside he could see a group of men gathered. The voice drifting out now was speaking with some forcefulness. Each time the voice reached its crescendo, Fabrice could make out what was being said. The words he heard didn't make much sense to him. "*Inkotanyi*," "Tutsi," and "conspirators" were a few of the words that drifted out to him. Nambaje could hear the men too. And when he reached Fabrice, he took his hand and pulled him rather brusquely along.

"What is *inkotanyi*, Papa?" asked Fabrice when they walked well past the government building.

"It means 'rebel,' Son."

"Why were they calling Tutsi rebels?"

"Because they are afraid someone will take their power."

"Well, what were they doing in there?"

"I don't know, but I'm sure it's nothing that will turn out well for us."

"I could see our neighbor, John, in there."

"I'm sure you're mistaken. John is a good man. He is our friend."

"The teacher at school made the Tutsi stand up yesterday."

"Is that so?"

"Yes, Papa. She said that we think we are better than everyone else."

"Hmmm …"

"Are we?"

"No, Fabrice. But we aren't less than everybody else, either. I want you to remember that, okay?"

"Yes, Papa."

Blessed little could have disturbed Nambaje's high spirits that day. But the sight of that meeting unsettled him. He was old enough to remember the bloodshed in 1959 when the Hutu had seized power, and then again in 1972 when Hutu flooded into Butare from Burundi. And he was perceptive enough to have noticed formerly friendly relationships eroding. Some of his Hutu neighbors would stop whatever they had been discussing when he entered the local cabaret. They hardly spoke to him now, when before they would have shared a beer together freely.

By the time Nambaje and Fabrice had reached the small public restaurant in town, the new grandfather had lost his appetite.

NAMBAJE AWOKE SUDDENLY. SOMEONE WAS SHAKING HIM. AS HIS EYES adjusted to the dark he saw his old friend, Sebugabo, standing over him, his face covered in fear.

"They have plans to kill you."

"Who?" said Nambaje, grabbing his friend's forearm to stop him from shaking him.

"Your Hutu neighbors," he said. "We've got to go."

"Yvette? Chantal?"

"I stopped by Chantal's house on the way here. I told them to get to the Catholic church in Ruhuha as fast as they could. They've gone. Placide's with them. They should be safe. But we must hurry."

"Fabrice is here. Ange too. I'll get them."

Nambaje shook his son. "Fabrice. Get up! We must hurry. Ange, wake up. Get dressed."

In a moment, they were out the door. Ange was crying.

"Ange, you must stop. We've got to be quiet," Nambaje whispered.

She somehow managed to stifle her tears.

It was still dark—about two in the morning, Nambaje judged.

"They've accused you of collaborating with the RPF," said Sebugabo breathlessly as they ran. "They say you've got family in Burundi and have crossed the border to collaborate with the enemy."

"That's nonsense."

"Of course it is."

"But your name is on the top of a list. My brother-in-law was at the meeting yesterday. I overheard him talking late last night to my sister. When they had gone to bed, I crept out and went to Chantal's house. I figured that they'd come for your family also. Then I came here."

"Is Chantal alright to be walking so soon?"

"She has to be."

The children had begun to tire. So Nambaje picked up Ange, and Sebugabo put Fabrice on his back. They continued running. They stayed off the main road and kept to the footpaths. The darkness still provided a measure of protection, but they felt safer keeping to paths close to the bush—ones that could provide thick cover should someone suddenly come upon them.

Half an hour had passed by the time they neared Ruhuha. But first they had to pass through the coffee plantation owned by old man Remeri. Remeri was a quiet and stubborn fellow whom Nambaje knew vaguely. His two youngest sons, Jean and Jerome, were well known as troublemakers. Aside from the main road, the only way into town was to pass through Remeri's land. Nambaje and Sebugabo had begun to relax. They were almost there. They'd put the children down and they were walking silently at a quick pace. Just then they heard voices.

Nambaje froze in midstride, and in an instant the others did too.

Nambaje could see Jean and Jerome. He couldn't tell why they were outside in the middle of the night, but there was no time to speculate. Those teenagers were not ones you wanted to meet in the daylight, much less in the dark. Nambaje, Sebugabo, and the children turned around and stepped softly and slowly back the way they had come. As soon as they crossed through the last of the coffee bushes and stepped into the thicker grasses of the wild lands, they grabbed the children and continued running.

"Emile's house," whispered Nambaje. "He will hide us."

"But it is almost back where we started."

"Yes, but we will be closer there to the border. And Emile will hide us. He is Hutu, but he is family."

After that, they said nothing more. The sky was beginning to lighten and the ground moved quickly under their sandaled feet. Breathless and aching, they reached Emile's house. Sebugabo was to hide off to the side with the children in case the old man didn't receive him, so Nambaje approached the door alone. He knocked. There was no answer. He'd have to knock louder to rouse the man from a dead sleep.

Finally, the old man appeared. His eyelids drooped and his forehead was creased with confusion. Sebugabo could see him speaking animatedly with his hands and the old man shaking his head, sometimes leaning in close to him, pointing down the road, or turning and walking from him. In a little while, Nambaje came back over to Sebugabo. "The old man has agreed to hide me. He says, though, that you should take the children along the high road to his mother's house. He says they will be safer there. I tried to reason with him on this, but he is adamant. I'm not sure what we should do."

"I think it's best if you stay here. Perhaps they are just looking for you. If so, the children are safer if they aren't with you. I don't think they would hurt the children. I will take them and then come back again tonight when it is dark again to check on you. If it is safe, we will leave then and I'll help you make your way to the border. You can wait this out in Burundi."

"If you think it best, I'll stay."

"I do."

Nambaje bent down and kissed the children. "You mind Sebugabo. I'll see you at next nightfall."

The children clung to him tightly. Nambaje pried their fingers from his neck and handed them to Sebugabo. He watched as the three took to the footpath again. When they had disappeared from sight, Nambaje went inside the house.

Fabrice held his sister's hand tightly and Ange held tightly on to Sebugabo. The sky was growing lighter. They were exhausted and hungry, but they knew better than to complain. They had gotten only as far as the widow Solange's house when they saw two boys heading toward them. Sebugabo recognized them as Remeri's sons. They froze.

It was Jean, the older, who called out to Sebugabo, "You were escorting someone this morning. We can see the children. Where is the man?" Sebugabo stepped forward to shield the children, but he said nothing. Jean raised the machete in his hand and whipped the flat side of it across his face. Sebugabo put a hand to his cheek. As he pulled it away he could see that it was stained with blood.

"Where is that traitor?" demanded Jean, raising the machete. The children wailed. "Where is he?"

"Enough," pleaded Segugabo. "He is hiding in Emile's house. Just don't harm us."

The boys turned and walked away. They had what they needed. Nambaje's wealth and education had marked him. His death would serve as a warning to other collaborators.

IT WAS JUST AROUND SUNRISE WHEN JOHN HEARD THE SHOUTING. HE was at home preparing to go out to the fields. He grabbed his club and headed in the direction of the commotion. It was coming from Emile's house, where a small mob had assembled: Remeri's boy Jerome and another neighbor named Karoli were dragging a man from the house by the arms. As John got closer, the man whose head was bowed and whose knees were being scraped across the rocks moaned. John recognized him, though he still hadn't seen the man's face. It was his neighbor, Nambaje.

By the time John reached the crowd, they had already dragged him out to the main road. Jerome began pounding him with a club as he shouted, "Traitor." John did not stop to ponder the accusations, but raised his club and began pounding as well, joining in the work as if it were some wild animal they would soon feast upon. Beating Nambaje gave John a sickening satisfaction, but at the same time, he also felt a strange relief that Nambaje did not lift his head. Eliyabo, Silasi, Karoli, and Jean joined in working on the crumpled man before them, hacking him with their machetes until their clothes were wet from the labor. It did not take long for them to decide that Nambaje was dead, or if not, that he soon would be.

Eliyabo plunged a hand into a bloody trouser pocket. With eighteen hundred francs in hand, the men decided, the day's work was done. They headed to the local cabaret to slake their thirst. John lagged behind the rest. He felt nauseous and light-headed. He was already beginning to realize that blood had a bitter aftertaste.

buried in stones

I've known rivers ancient as the world
and older than the flow of human blood in human veins.
My soul has grown deep like the rivers.
Langston Hughes

CHANTAL AND HER HUSBAND, PLACIDE, COWERED IN A SMALL BACK room of a Hutu friend's home. Chantal clutched baby Nambaje to her, but he kept struggling to free himself from his mother's arms. Already nearly two years had passed since Chantal's father was murdered, and, for the second time, violence had erupted in their small village of Kivugiza. Oblivious to the danger outside, Nambaje kept wanting to toddle about and Chantal kept pulling him to herself.

Even in the shadows, she could see her father's resemblance in the child: his chin, his stormy eyes, and his moods. She kissed his forehead tenderly and closed her eyes. But when she did she saw the blood-soaked ground where her father had been killed when violence broke out in 1992. At that time, they had fled to the Catholic church in Ruhuha. When they returned to Kivugiza her husband buried her father, but the ground near where Chantal had grown up still told the brutal story of his death. The Hutu in that village murdered a handful of the most influential Tutsi—including her father—stole a few cows, and burned some fields. The madness soon subsided, but the grief did not.

This time was different though, and Chantal could sense it. Bodies lined the streets. The president's assassination had meant a free-for-all, and now Tutsi and their sympathizers were being killed indiscriminately. Chantal had a sick feeling that the killers would not be satisfied until they had wiped out the Tutsi completely. Something told her that it was only just a matter of time.

Chantal had finally nodded off to sleep when the sound of men shouting near the house startled her awake. She opened her eyes to see Placide listening intently, his body tensed as if he were a treed animal.

Pulling her face close to his, Placide whispered into Chantal's ear. "Our only chance is to run. Do you understand?"

Chantal nodded.

"I will go first and distract them long enough for you and Nambaje to make it down to the river. Don't wait for me there. Just go. I will find you."

Placide crouched low and moved toward the back door. He looked back in Chantal's direction once more, but it was too dark for her to see his face. A moment later, he sprang out the door.

Chantal could hear a man yell. Another responded, and soon there was more shouting and the sound of men running.

Pressing Nambaje tightly to her chest, Chantal charged into the open air, running as fast as she could. In the periphery, she could see men bringing clubs down violently on her husband. Pushing through the fear and the brush, Chantal sprinted into the valley below. The sound of her own footsteps and breathing came steadily. But soon the sounds mingled with those of men behind her.

"Over there! Quickly, she is getting away."

She ran faster, dodging bushes and trees in the moonlight, branches tearing at her arms and legs. She strained ahead. The brush grew thicker, and the terrain steeper as she neared the river. She could hear the water rushing and the sound of machetes hacking a path through the brush behind her. Nambaje grew heavy in her arms and it was difficult to navigate the overgrown drop-off in front of her with the weight of the toddler and without a free hand to steady her. The men's footsteps and heavy breathing drew closer. A moment more and the river opened up in front of her, rushing rapidly past, as if it too were fleeing for its life.

Chantal waded in. The waters were cold, and as they hit Nambaje, he began to cry. She muffled him in her breast, but the waters were now reaching above her waist. With some effort she lifted the baby above her head, her feet grappling for the river bottom. She didn't know how to swim, but she didn't hesitate. She knew the waters would be more merciful than the men who were now reaching the water's edge.

A moment more and she could no longer feel the bottom. Her arms began to ache from lifting Nambaje. She shuffled her feet and struggled to keep her head above the waterline. Her senses focused keenly on survival.

After some minutes the waters slowed. She could feel her feet glancing off the bottom once more, while the waters whirled her and Nambaje in slow circles. It was a gentle current that carried her along now and set her feet solidly in the shallower waters of the river's bank. Chantal labored up the hill, collapsing breathlessly with Nambaje in the tall grasses. The moonlit shoreline seemed to spin and Chantal lay still, willing the world to still itself also.

NAMBAJE WOKE CHANTAL BEFORE THE ROOSTER WITH AN ANGRY wailing. His skin was hot to the touch. Using a bit of cloth she tore from her skirt, Chantal tipped a water can against the fabric until it was moist. She squeezed the water over his head and mopped his face. He cried the louder for it, but it did cool him some. A woman next to her opened her eyes, shot a disgusted look in her direction, and turned over to try to get a bit more sleep. Picking up Nambaje, Chantal began to try to pace with him. But there was a hardly a place to step without rousing someone.

So Chantal stood and swayed with the toddler, examining the mass of humanity packed tightly into the refugee camp just on the other side of the border in Burundi. An old man moaned. She could see a stub wrapped tightly where an arm had been. She turned a different direction, and she could see a clump of children sleeping. She wondered how many of them had lost a mother or a father. A sudden pain shot through her. Several weeks had already passed since she had escaped by fording the river, but still there had been no word from Placide. She wondered if Nambaje would be an orphan.

It was nearing nightfall the next day when Chantal heard a woman call her name.

She was coming from the south side and breathing heavily. "My boy says there's a man looking for you. He's down at the entrance of the camp."

Chantal felt her heart race. "Placide," she said.

Leaving Nambaje in another woman's care, she headed through the swarms of people to the camp's entrance. People were already bent over their cooking pots, preparing what food they had, and the smoke from the small, scattered fires stung her eyes. Finally she reached the entrance. Several RPF soldiers stood about, their guns slung across their shoulders, their eyes scanning the horizon. Close by lay a man so badly swollen and bloodied that she hardly recognized him as her husband.

"Placide," she said, dropping to her knees beside him.

He lifted his eyes to her. She noticed that they seemed to be full of shame, as if he had somehow let her down.

"You survived?" she asked, needing some word from him to know that the broken body she saw was still living.

"Nambaje," he said in a hoarse whisper.

"He is here. He is sleeping."

Satisfied, Placide shut his eyes.

"I will wait with you until you have the strength to move."

Placide did not respond.

IN THE WEEKS THAT FOLLOWED, PLACIDE'S RECOVERY WAS GRADUAL and incomplete; Nambaje's decline was rapid and final. Chantal buried the child alone under a tree outside the camp. Placide was too weak to dig the grave, so Chantal dug the shallow pit with a shovel borrowed from the soldiers, prying past tree roots and large stones until her fingers were bloody. It felt as if she had buried both her only child and the last living piece of her father. Covering Nambaje over with the rocky earth, Chantal felt smothered, as if her heart too had been buried in stones.

JOHN'S FIELDS WERE OVERGROWN. HIDING IN HIS HOME IN KIVUGIZA, John felt restless as he thought about the crops that would not be planted or harvested this season. His Hutu neighbors called this harvest season, although for a more sinister reason. They were out morning to night with their machetes and clubs. But it was a harvest for which John had no taste, not since two years prior when he'd pummeled his friend and neighbor, Nambaje, to a premature death. Washing the blood from his clothes and club that day, he vowed that he would never again kill another human being.

For a year after Nambaje's death, John had hidden in Butare in the home of relatives, fearing that he might be punished for his crime. But two months ago, in April of 1994, when the killing erupted across Rwanda, he'd made his way back to his family and his home in Kivugiza. He was still lying low, though. Not because he thought he'd be caught and punished now, but because he thought he'd be pressed into service as a murderer. Several times already, gangs of his Hutu neighbors had descended on his home and tried to bully him into joining them in cleansing the land. Even the chief of the sector had come, but each time, John had found some excuse, pretending to be ill or dismissing himself as an old man, unfit for such work.

He'd managed to evade the pressure thus far, but still he knew he had to stay out of sight. If his neighbors saw him working his own fields while they went out, morning to night, cutting down the "tall stalks," as they called them, he knew their jealousy would lead them either to kill him or force him to join. So he fidgeted in his home and brooded.

It wasn't long, though, before the tables were turned. The hunters became the hunted as the RPF pushed back the Hutu militias and fought their way into the country in late June and early July of 1994. John and his wife, children, and grandchildren gathered what they could carry—a bit of harvested sorghum and rice, some clothes and cooking pots—and walked to Tanzania. The roads were teeming with people who likewise carried their lives—corrugated metal roofing, bags of potatoes, baskets of clothing, babies, bananas, and the sick and the dying. The roads were clogged with human traffic.

For three years they would bide their time in an international refugee camp where they had food and clean water. But finally, John's land and livelihood beckoned him to return. It was the beginning of July 1997 when they found their way back to Kivugiza. It was hard to recognize the place. So many homes and buildings had been burned, looted, or simply overgrown and decayed that it seemed another world entirely. His neighbor Nambaje's house had all but fallen to the ground. The roof was missing, the clay bricks had crumbled, the fields were grown over, and yet still John could see it all in his mind's eye as it had once been, teeming with life. And when the wind rustled through the grass his mind replayed the sound of men dragging Nambaje to the main road; his ears rang with their shouts and with the sick thud of clubs against the crumpled frame of a man.

John returned to his fields, but the family tried to keep to themselves. It was only a matter of weeks, however, before the authorities came to his house and arrested him. Nambaje's daughter, Chantal, had accused him of participating in the 1992 killing of her father. Silasi, Jean, and Eliyabo also were rounded up with him and taken to the prison nearby. That prison held some ten thousand men. Rooms were crammed with nine bunks of three, each room no bigger than three by three meters. Infection, disease, and dysentery abounded. John's ankles swelled from the lack of movement. Eliyabo and Jean both died there, but John survived to face year upon year of confinement.

He worried for his family, left to make it on their own. He wondered if his wife would remain faithful to him, if he would live to see his children or grandchildren again, and what would become of them; would they be executed, or simply left to waste away?

Several years into his imprisonment, preachers began visiting the prisons to call the inmates to repentance. While John had battled with guilt for years, it wasn't until then that he began to grasp the full measure of the evil he had done. He wondered about Chantal for the first time. John feared having to face her. In his guilt and despair, he cried out to God for forgiveness. He found a measure of peace, but did not dare to imagine that a day would ever come when Nambaje's family could forgive him also.

the still point

At the still point of the turning world. Neither flesh nor fleshless;
Neither from nor towards; at the still point, there the dance is.
T. S. Eliot

WHEN THE WAR ENDED, CHANTAL AND PLACIDE TRAVELED BACK TO Kivugiza, the only area they had ever considered home. Their own home had been burned to the ground, and for Chantal there were too many memories to return to her father's land. Plus, it would be better to stay close to the other survivors than near the border where raiding parties could attack. So Chantal and Placide built a tiny mud home with a thatched roof some kilometers outside of Ruhuha, tightly wedged between those of many other survivors.

They had nothing. Their cattle, their crops, and their possessions had all been stolen or demolished in the orgy of violence. And so they planted and tilled the fields, working each day from first light to setting sun.

The toll of the work hit Placide the hardest. He had never fully recovered from the attack he suffered in the genocide. When he finally found a doctor, the physician could only speculate that Placide might have severe internal damage, since the hospital equipment had also been demolished in the genocide. In the two years before he died, Placide provided Chantal with a roof for her head and her only comfort: two children.

For the next ten years, Chantal eked out an existence on the land with two small children to care for. Out of her entire family—her mother, father, grandparents, aunts and uncles, and six brothers and sisters—only one brother had survived the genocide, and now Chantal blamed the Hutu also for the death of her firstborn and her husband as well.

Such poverty and such grief could cause anyone's heart to turn bitter, but when that kind of pain has such a clear cause, the bitterness becomes concentrated. Like some venomous serum, Chantal's rage was being stored up for anyone who could be called Hutu, but especially anyone directly involved in the deaths of her family.

When Chantal found out, in 1997, that John had returned from exile in Tanzania, it was a great pleasure to see him put in prison, along with Eliyabo, Silasi, and Jean. But this satisfaction only distilled more bitterness inside of her—while her own parents and siblings had been slaughtered, John had his wife, his children, his grandchildren, his land, and his home. So she savored every evil thing she could imagine befalling them: a terrible sickness wiping out the entire family, a revenge attack, a slow and painful death in prison, a poisoning.

This was the Chantal that Pascal met when he first came to visit her in August of 2005, the year the authorities released John from prison.

Pascal too survived the genocide, but lost his new bride, eight months pregnant at the time with what would have been his first child, to killers with no conscience. He also lost nearly every member of his extended family. In a courageous evasion, Pascal had managed to survive by fleeing toward the enemy camp while the Hutu militias were moving out to attack a certain village. When he later circled back to check on a church where hundreds of others had fled for refuge, he found some three hundred of his neighbors dead. Pascal finally reached the RPF camp, where he joined the ranks and returned to Rwanda as a liberator.

After the war, Pascal was put in charge of punishing any soldiers who participated in revenge killings against the Hutu. It was an ironic assignment for the RPF to give him, since he frequently contemplated revenge himself, and had he been given the opportunity to seize it with impunity, he certainly would have. But he fulfilled his duty fairly and with honor, in spite of the memories that haunted him.

In 1997, when he had turned to heavy drinking to relieve the ache of his memory, he heard an internal voice telling him he must stop. Not long after that, a friend shared with him the Christian gospel, and when he understood that he could receive God's forgiveness, Pascal did not hesitate. He accepted this gift from God and immediately began living out the reality of that forgiveness.

To begin, he used the strength he found in God to forgive the men who killed his family. But God prompted Pascal that this was not all he wanted from him. Pascal could sense God leading him to serve as a mediator between Hutu and Tutsi across Rwanda.

By the time Pascal knocked on Chantal's door in August of 2005, he had been mediating for almost five years. While living in Butare in the South, he was trained by African Evangelistic Enterprises, or AEE, in healing and reconciliation. When he returned to the Bugesera region where Kivugiza and Ruhuha were located, he began simply. He would seek out offenders and survivors and encourage them to visit one another and request or offer forgiveness.

In 2003, he gathered seventeen Hutu and Tutsi together in that area to train in reconciliation. Their first meeting was on a weekend. By the next weekend, attendance had risen to forty participants. By the time he reached fifty participants, Pascal decided to start an organization devoted to reconciliation. He traveled then to

AEE headquarters in Kigali to receive more formal training and met with others involved in Nyamata's reconciliation efforts. AEE backed the formation of the reconciliation organization that Pascal and four others would begin in Bugesera and Kigali. They decided to call it CARSA, which stood for Christian Action in Reconciliation and Social Assistance, and which emphasized meeting both the physical and emotional needs of the participants.

So it was that only a few days after John's release, Pascal invited him to share a drink with him. John feared him at first, knowing that Pascal was not only a Tutsi, but a former RPF soldier. But he also remembered Pascal from when he was just a boy. And others in the community told him that Pascal only sought to bring peace.

Over a couple of bottles of Fanta, Pascal asked John about his attitude toward his crime. John shared how in prison he had come to see the evil of his actions and how he had asked for God's forgiveness. Pascal inquired whether John would be ready to ask for Chantal's forgiveness as Nambaje's only surviving child in the area. It was a difficult question for John. He certainly desired Chantal's forgiveness, and was more than willing to confess his actions and his sorrow over them, but the idea of seeing Chantal face-to-face and personally asking her—this was more than he could yet imagine.

"Do you think she would agree to meet me?" asked John.

"Perhaps," said Pascal. "I have seen it happen before."

"I fear seeing her," admitted John.

"But would you be willing?" pressed Pascal.

"Yes, if she would meet with me, I would ask her."

That was enough for Pascal. He would visit Chantal right away.

WHEN CHANTAL OPENED HER DOOR, SHE SAW A FAMILIAR FACE. Pascal had grown up in that village with her and they had played together when they were just children. She had seen him over the years since returning from Burundi, but this was the first time he had come to visit her at home.

Chantal came outside to talk with him, and they took their seats on a wooden bench out in the open. Pascal inquired about her health, her children, and her crops—the usual small talk. And she asked about him in return. She sensed that there was more he wanted to talk about, but that was the extent of their conversation that day. Pascal shook her hand and told her he would come again soon.

Over the weeks that followed Pascal dropped by frequently, and little by little they exchanged stories of survival and loss. Even having someone simply to ask about her story was a comfort to Chantal. After all, everyone had a tragedy to tell, and because of this, often people did not ask, nor did they listen. Because of this reticence, many carried their stories of pain silently and alone. When Pascal would share the stories of his loss, he would often talk about the comfort he had received in God. For Chantal's part she had not returned to the church after the war. She believed God had forgotten her.

After several visits, Pascal asked Chantal if she might be willing to meet with John. He told her simply that John wanted to ask her forgiveness. Chantal grew incensed. She didn't want anything to do with that man. It was awful enough for him to be out of prison, resuming his life with his family and children and his land. She did not want to see him. "I have not one iota of mercy for that man," she said, her eyes filling with tears and anger. "I will not see him."

PASCAL VISITED CHANTAL MANY TIMES OVER THE NEXT SEVERAL months, listening, pointing Chantal toward God for healing, and encouraging her to consider meeting with John. A year after his first visit, in August of 2006, Chantal agreed to see John. "I can go there and discuss," she told Pascal, "because I respect you as a brother. But don't talk to me about reconciliation."

Pascal knew that this would be better than no meeting at all. If Chantal and John met, she would be able to see John's true repentance and, if nothing else, find out details about her father's death that would help bring her closure. Pascal hoped for more, but was satisfied that Chantal had, at least, agreed to an initial meeting. He encouraged Chantal to spend the day leading up to the meeting in prayer.

Meanwhile, Pascal visited John again. John feared meeting Chantal, but he was willing to do it. He wanted the opportunity to ask her forgiveness in person. Pascal arranged a meeting place at the new Catholic church in Ruhuha. Since many Hutu lived near John's home, and many Tutsi lived near Chantal's home, this would be a safe and neutral third place.

Chantal slept fitfully the night before the meeting. She had followed Pascal's advice and spent the previous day in prayer, as best she knew how for someone who had not prayed in twelve years. She could sense that because of this she was far more at peace than she would have been otherwise, but still she wasn't ready to forgive.

John arrived first but waited at a nearby spot until Chantal and Pascal were settled into the church. When they were ready, another CARSA worker, Christophe, came and brought him into the small room where the meeting would be held.

When Chantal saw John, the sight of him flooded her mind with memories of her father. She could hear her father asking her if she had something to tell John, she could remember his smile when she had named her son for her father, and she could see the blood-soaked ground where her father had been killed by John.

John burned with shame in Chantal's gaze. He wished he could cover himself, or somehow make himself disappear. Stiffly, he shook

Chantal's hand and then took a seat. His hands reached reflexively to cover his head.

Christophe began the meeting by opening in prayer. "Father, we come before you now asking for mercy. The devil invaded us to a point where human hearts turned into animal hearts, and neighbors turned against neighbors, but Jesus, we thank you so much that you came so that we may have life and life more abundantly. You are a God who is rich in mercy. Personally, we have no mercy, but your mercies are new each morning. That's why we call upon you right now, Father, that your mercy may rain down on us here and your Holy Spirit guide us. Father, you desire to see the unusual take place right here. Be kind to John, Pascal, and Chantal. Father, let us all feel your presence with us. It's you alone that we desire in this place, Father. The honor and the glory be yours alone, for we've prayed believing in the name of Jesus Christ. Amen."

When Christophe reached the conclusion of his prayer, he nodded to John that he could begin his confession. John shifted in his chair uncomfortably and then spoke, letting his eyes only have fleeting contact with Chantal's own before settling his gaze on the ground again.

"Chantal, thank you for this moment. I sinned against you terribly by killing your father, a man I lived beside and even shared drinks with. I even prepared the feast when you received the sacrament of confirmation in the church. But the archenemy of good, the Evil One, embedded in my life, and I committed this horrible sin of killing your father. I'm falling before you begging for mercy for the sin I committed."

"How did you kill my father?" asked Chantal.

"A gentleman by the name of Sebugabo took your father with a young boy and girl early in the morning."

"You're lying," said Chantal. "Fabrice was not there. It was only Ange."

John looked unsettled. He shifted his weight in his chair and continued again more slowly. "There were two children, Fabrice and Ange. As I understand, when they got to the coffee plantation, Remeri's two sons Jean and Jerome prevented your father from proceeding. He came back and hid himself in Emile's house. The gentleman who was helping your father to escape was asked, 'You were escorting someone; we can see the children, but where is the man?' They slapped him with the machete, and he told them that he was hiding in Emile's house. They went to Emile's house at 5 a.m. in the morning. Shouting began. I was alone at home but heard the shouting that morning and went to Emile's house. When I found him, others had brought him outside.

"We took the money he had in his pocket: eighteen hundred francs. We took him to the main road and we killed him — six of us: me, Eliyabo, Silasi, Jean, Jerome, and Karoli. We killed him and left him there. This is why I'm asking for forgiveness."

"How come you only took eighteen hundred francs? He had only just sold his cow," demanded Chantal.

"That's the only amount he had left."

"Since you were working together, who took the money?"

"The money was taken by Eliyabo, but I was there. That's why I'm asking for forgiveness. I was a part of it."

"Do you think eighteen hundred francs was all the price for this cow?" continued Chantal, adamant on this issue.

"That is the only amount he had left on him."

"Do you have an idea where he could have gone first that he might have left the other amount?"

"I have no idea. Eliyabo got the money from his pocket and counted it. I remember we used it for alcohol."

"How long has it been since you came out of prison?"

"About nine months since I came out."

"And all these nine months you had no clue where I live?"

-119-

"I knew where you lived, but I was afraid."

"Fear?"

"Fear of one's crime."

"You could have tried to see whether I would have sent you back or welcomed you or called these people around to hear what you had to say."

"Forgive me."

"I will not forgive you on the account that you didn't counsel yourself to come and it had to take this mediator for you to come. You knew us well. I can't forgive you, because all this time you never thought to come. I won't forgive you."

"To come before you has been the most difficult thing for me, the most shameful."

"How come we live with others who killed, but you have never come?"

"It's true, but have mercy upon me."

"It's painful for someone like me who had a big family, but today I'm alone. I can't even go back to where we used to live. Why do you think I can't go back? It's because I knew I was going to see your face again. You were not able to come and even ask me for forgiveness. Did you think I was crazy—that as soon as I would see you I would stone you? Even if I would do that, people would stop me!" Chantal leaned forward in her seat as she said this while John covered his face with his hands.

"To kill someone is the most terrible sin someone can do. Even for someone to confess and ask for forgiveness is a result of many years of teachings to a point where your heart is set free." John managed to look at Chantal as he said this.

"It's so painful to see someone you shared together with, your neighbor. You shared drinks with my father; he would come to your house. But when the time came, you were the first one to kill him.

In the whole community he was the first one to die. I'm not going to forgive you."

"I'm begging you, be merciful."

"It's painful for an old man with gray hair like you. You never even bothered to come and ask for forgiveness."

LEAVING THEIR MEETING THAT DAY, JOHN FELT DISCOURAGED. HE entreated Pascal to continue talking to Chantal. At the same time, he sensed an important first step had been taken. The encounter had relieved a lot of fear. He knew afterward that he could meet Chantal on the street and bear to see her, and that a door of communication had been opened. He knew that he could visit her and offer to help her with her chores, and that he could begin to show her that his repentance was real.

Immediately after the encounter, Chantal seemed worse off than before. Nightmares tormented her sleep. And her days were haunted again by memories of the past. But on the Sunday after she met with John, she also went to church again for the first time since the genocide. She could not explain what had drawn her there, but in church one day, she found herself thinking, "Maybe if God forgives, he can help me also to forgive."

From that day forward, gradually, the venom in her heart toward John began to dissipate. A few weeks later, with Chantal's permission, John visited Chantal at her home. John brought with him, as was the custom, traditional Rwandan drinks. Sharing these was a symbol of peace and free-flowing relationship. The meeting was awkward and Chantal's emotions ranged from hatred to rage to sadness to peace, but it was another step.

Pascal too continued to visit. One day as they were talking, Chantal told Pascal that she had begun to pray again. Sitting on the stoop in front of her house, Pascal commended her. "Chantal, that's a great step. The saddest thing was for you to lose hope. Once you find hope again all things are possible. God didn't leave you. His love endures forever, you know. His love is everlasting. Maybe God protected you for such a time as this. God will always help you."

"I'm still not ready to forgive," said Chantal matter-of-factly.

"We cannot force you, or pressure you to," said Pascal. "No. This is still a process. The journey is still on. But I want to commend you for even going to see John. Some other people do totally refuse to even see their killer's face. This is the first step."

"I know," said Chantal. "I do feel as if I'm moving closer to it. But still sometimes I feel helpless, especially when I think about the past."

"I understand, of course," said Pascal. "But I want you to know, forgiveness has a source. You can honestly say to God, 'I have no strength in me to forgive John. But you, O Lord, have the power to forgive. Give me the power to forgive him.' And God will help you. I believe he will help you."

Chantal thought deeply about Pascal's words. And when he left that day, she began to pray, just as he said. "God, I have no strength in me to forgive John. But you, O Lord, have the power to forgive. Give me the power to forgive him."

AT THE END OF THE SHORT RAINY SEASON, CHANTAL JOINED ONE of the eight work groups that Pascal had begun through CARSA. These were groups of survivors, ex-offenders, and their respective family members who had been through the reconciliation training. Having been taught about forgiveness, restitution, and the importance of seeking peace, these men and women were working toward shalom together. They worked building homes, repairing them, tilling fields, and harvesting them for the survivors or returning prisoners among them who needed such tangible help to restore their lives. It was a way for both parties to regain trust and tear down the barriers between them.

One day, as Chantal bent over gathering mud in her hands and placing it in the brick mold, one of her neighbors asked her a question.

"Do you think forgiveness is really even possible?" This woman had recently been through one of the workshops with CARSA, but still had nothing but skepticism for the process.

Almost reflexively Chantal replied, "If you think it's impossible, come and see."

For months, little by little, as Chantal had prayed, she had felt her heart opening to the possibility of forgiveness. That day she invited the woman, John, and several of her neighbors to her home. There, with her neighbors gathered around in a circle, she said in front of them all, "John, from now, I have forgiven you."

John shed his reserve and clapped his hands at the news. Lifting his gaze toward the sky in thankfulness, he shouted, *"Imana ishimwe,"* or "God be praised!" His usual somber eyes filled with tears of joy.

As John clapped and praised God, the neighbors also joined in. In a few moments the scene had erupted into a spontaneous chorus of praise, as friends and neighbors shouted, clapped, danced, and sang, moving around Chantal in the circle they had formed. For the fourth time in her life, Chantal felt the world spinning around her. But this time it was a wave of relief that washed over her. She felt a sense of deep peace as she remembered her confirmation in the church, the birth of her first child, her deliverance from her persecutors, and now this forgiveness she felt toward John. At the center of her turning world, God had been with her. He was the still, unchanging center.

John, Pascal, her neighbors, her children — they seemed to spin about her once more. But this time, Chantal stood still. Her heart, for the first time in what seemed forever, was at peace.

journeying toward reconciliation

*I am not persuaded that reconciliation
should be pursued only after injustices have been removed,
but rather believe that the struggle against injustice is part
of the more fundamental pursuit of reconciliation.*
Miroslav Volf

CONFESSION: THE WORD ITSELF TURNS MOUTHS DRY, MAKES PALMS grow wet, and makes hearts race. Few things in life are more difficult than admitting wrong. When simply admitting our faults to ourselves can exact such a toll, is it any wonder that prostrating before another and accepting the consequences of our actions is so difficult?

As a rising sophomore in college, I had a troubled conscience over a friend I had wronged in high school. Too cowardly to pick up a phone, I remember that summer sitting down to write a letter of apology. Before I could even admit the wrong to another, I had to admit it to myself. I had to quit justifying, quit recasting the story in my memory, and quit shifting the blame. From forming the sentences, to sending the letter, to waiting for a response, not one aspect of the process proved easy. Let me take that back. Committing the wrong was easy. Gravity helped it. But trying to make things right was an uphill climb.

In the award-winning film *Schindler's List*, one of the most moving scenes comes near the end as the protagonist, Oskar Schindler, expresses remorse over not having saved more people. Though others would not condemn him, Schindler's own heart knows the truth: he could have saved more people. He looks at his car in disgust: "Why did I keep the car? Ten people right there. Ten people. Ten more people." He looks at his Nazi lapel pin. "This pin. Two people. This is gold. Two more people," he sobs. "I could have gotten one more person ... and I didn't! And I ... I didn't!"

We feel pity for Schindler. He saved some eleven hundred Jewish men and women. But even so, the weight of his guilt feels crushing. How much harder then is it to accept the apology of someone who has no such heroism to balance out his misdeeds? How much harder is it to admit inexcusable guilt and accept its consequences?

While forgiveness doesn't require another's confession for the gift to be extended, reconciliation is an act that requires two willing participants. It is a journey of risk and trust. Both parties must make themselves vulnerable to even take the first steps toward each other.[1]

And as if the obvious roadblocks of the offense itself and the fear of being wounded again were not enough, there are landmines hidden along reconciliation's path.

For instance, researchers Stillwell and Baumeister conducted a study where they read a story of a wrongdoing to three groups.

One group they asked to remember the events and recall them as if they were the wronged, another group as if they were the offender, and the third as people uninvolved in the conflict. The study showed both the group playing the victim role and those playing the perpetrator role distorted the facts of what happened.[2]

Not surprisingly, "victims tend to see the act as possessing severe consequences as part of an ongoing pattern of misbehavior as inexcusable and immoral and as gratuitous (i.e., having no valid reason other than meanness or cruelty.)"[3] Obviously, in some cases, this is an accurate description of events, but in less grievous offenses it may not be. The perpetrators, on the other hand, "perceive the transgression as involving mitigating circumstances, tend to downplay the consequences, divide blame among many parties, and describe their actions as arising from motives that are understandable and sometimes legitimate."[4] Again, sometimes there will be mitigating circumstances involved in a wrongdoing. What the study shows, however, is the tendency to act in these ways even when there are not.

Sometimes distortion of events may come out of the unreliable nature of memory itself. Especially in cases where post-traumatic stress syndrome may have played a role, memory may be clouded or distorted. But even in cases where trauma is not a factor, our memories are often unreliable and incomplete.

Not only is there the possibility of both sides distorting events, but also there is the reality of different values placed on the events themselves and their consequences. Researchers explain, "It is as if a debt were created by one person lending $100, but somehow the borrower received only $50. What amount should be repaid?"[5] Such are the different perceptions of the wrong and its consequences.

With such a large chasm separating victim and offender, we

must understand the planks that make up the bridge of reconciliation. These steps include: deciding to seek reconciliation, discussing the conflict, detoxifying the relationship, and devoting to rebuild the bond.[6] At some point within the discussion of the events, for a successful reconciliation to occur, there needs to be apology.

It's important to distinguish apology from two often substituted, but false means of reconciliation: appeasement and account. An account, according to David Augsburger, professor of pastoral care at Fuller Theological Seminary, "is a request for recognition of extenuating circumstances, unquestionable intentions, or unfortunate misunderstandings." An account "presents a disclaimer, offers a justifiable case for being excused, and requests recognition of innocence and release from consequences."[7]

Meanwhile an appeasement can be anything from groveling to seduction to a kind of self-flagellation to placate the wronged. Both appeasement and account miss the mark when there is real wrongdoing. Only in an apology do we have someone taking responsibility for his or her actions, expressing sorrow over those actions, and promising not to repeat the deed again. Only in apology does the request for forgiveness come on the heels of accepting the guilt.

What then makes a good confession? First, the guilty person should admit the wrong without any excuses. Next, a specific apology should be offered, being careful to express remorse over how the transgression affected the other person. The more aware the one confessing can be of the pain the other has experienced as a result of the wrong, and the more an acknowledgment of that pain can be expressed, the better. An offer to make some kind of restitution also shows that the guilty party is serious about the apology. In some cases, the restitution may specifically help redress the wrong. In other cases, no restitution will be sufficient, but some restitution should still help to show the reality of remorse. Finally, the one confessing the wrong promises the offense will not happen again. After confession, apology, remorse, and an offer of restitution, at that point the offender may request forgiveness.[8]

In most cases, at this point the offender is much more ready to receive forgiveness than the offended is able to offer it. Psychologists Baumeister, Exline, and Sommer explain: "The words, 'I forgive you,' may mark only the beginning of the process to the victim, whereas to the perpetrator they signify the matter is ended."[9] If the victim is still working through the hurts and resentments, this creates a tension. For the one who has asked forgiveness considers the matter settled, and may, therefore, bristle if the subject is brought up again. This breaks the trust that is so tenuous. It is much better then, if the victim is not ready to forgive, but is open to trying, for him or her to say something like, "I am going to begin to try to forgive you,"[10] or still better, "Can you accept my appreciation for your apology and give me time to work through these hard feelings?"[11] This creates a space in time for the victim to work through the internal forgiveness process.

Before leaving the discussion of confession and forgiveness in the process of reconciliation, it is helpful to note that there may be value in an encounter and discussion even when one party is not willing to move toward reconciliation. Many restorative justice programs emphasize the importance of victim-offender dialogue without any expectation put on either party to forgive or be reconciled. For crime victims, the opportunity to vent their anger and to ask questions regarding the crime can help as they try to recover.

For the offender, even if the victim is unwilling to forgive or be reconciled, the opportunity to acknowledge the harm of their actions, make apology, and seek amends can be critical aspects of seeing the damage of their crime and taking responsibility for repairing that damage. As Van Ness and Strong point out in *Restoring Justice*, "the encounter tends to humanize [victims and offenders] to one another and permits them substantial creativity in constructing a response that deals not only with the injustice that occurred, but with the futures of both parties as well."[12] (Unfortunately, in many places in the United States such encounters are not permitted by law even when both parties desire such a meeting.)

Returning to those cases where forgiveness is requested and accepted, and where there is desire on the part of both parties to continue moving toward reconciliation, it should be understood that even after the parties have taken these important steps toward reconciliation, there is still work to be done for the reconciliation to be made complete. As Augsburger notes, reconciliation proceeds through risk and trust: "With each risk when one is honored by reciprocal risking, there is an increase in trust."[13] This begins with the process of confessing and asking forgiveness, but the process proceeds as both parties risk moving closer to each other in relationship. Trust, goodwill, and care must all be practiced and rebuilt as harmful interactions are replaced by positive actions.

As Rabbi Elliot Dorff describes, forgiveness only brings the parties to neutral ground. After that there is still the need for "both parties [to] take positive steps to rebuild the relationship and restore genuinely good feelings."[14]

One of the most famous accounts of reconciliation in all of literature is a parable found in Luke 15:11–31. It is the story of a son who requested his inheritance before his father was even dead. He then turned his back on his family and squandered the money. When he finds himself in a faraway land, living in a pig sty, eating the swine's castoffs, he suddenly comes to his senses. He realizes that the hired hands on his father's land live better than he does. So he returns, hoping not for readmittance to his father's table, but for the privilege of perhaps being one of his servants.

Few things have the potential to so overwhelm the senses and so forge devotion than expecting thundering wrath and receiving a flash flood of grace. The father weeps over the return of his wandering son and embraces him.

I wonder sometimes what it must have felt like to feel those aged arms clasping so tightly, to feel the warmth of the father's breath and the coolness of his tears fall on the bare skin of an exposed neck bowed in shame.

The father then turns and calls out. He could call together friends to berate the foolishness of such a son, to mock him, or to bemoan the financial loss and heartache he has caused his aged father. Instead the father restores him. He calls for his best robe and ring to be given to the son, and for a welcome party to be prepared for the young man's return. This luxurious robe wrapped around the undeserving shoulders of an errant son—this is the texture of grace, a fabric all of us long to find ourselves wrapped in. Perhaps it is only the understanding of our common need to be wrapped in such grace that can move us to take the first faltering steps toward reconciliation.

Questions for Reflection and Discussion

Can you recall a time when you have exaggerated an offense, either in your own mind or in relating it to another person? Can you recall a time when you minimized the consequences of a wrong you committed?

What does it feel like to receive an apology that is really not an apology (i.e., an appeasement or an account)?

Think of a wrong you have committed someone in the past. Practice writing out a full confession of it, according to the description of what makes a good confession.

What might the process of confession and forgiveness look like when both parties share levels of blame in the broken relationship?

prey

Once in my life, I knew a grief so hard
I could actually hear it inside,
scraping at the lining of my stomach, an audible ache,
dredging with hooks as rivers are dredged
when someone's been missing too long.
Leif Enger

IN MARCH 1992, IN THE VILLAGE OF KIVUGIZA WHERE CHANTAL lived, a pretty young woman near her age was sleeping peacefully. Her husband, Auguste, a cattle owner and shopkeeper, snored next to her. Monique had just drifted off to sleep after putting the baby down and was enjoying a bit of that rare repose that a young mother of two hardly ever seems to find. Her sleep was of the deep and dreamless kind that comes easily to those who do not yet know fear.

At that time Monique had not yet read the story of Cain and Abel. It would be many years in the future that she would open a Bible to Genesis and appropriately name her newborn son Seth. At this time, Monique knew nothing of that baby boy who would come or that she was living in a story that resembled Cain and Abel's in both its jealousy and its violence.

Like Cain and Abel, Hutu and Tutsi made their living, for the most part, in two different ways, the former off the land, the latter tending flocks. And like Cain, the Hutu farmers had grown jealous of the wealthier Tutsi herders. Rather than taming the beast of jealousy, the Hutu had provoked it. The more they spurred their jealousy, the larger the beast grew. In the end, the Hutu, who had so desired to become masters, would become prey to their own worst emotions. And in so doing their Tutsi brothers would become like that very first victim, Abel, who saw a killer's eyes in the eyes of his own brother.

It was a violent thud that woke Monique and Auguste. A band of angry Hutu had crept through the dark cover of the night toward their door, crouching and waiting until their victims slept. When it grew quiet at last, they sprang, using a large log to batter open the front door. Before Auguste and Monique understood what was happening, their home was filled with five or six men. The baby cried in the next room at the commotion as two men dragged Auguste from bed, holding him with a machete to his neck. Meanwhile another man grabbed Monique's wrists with rough hands and pinned her to the bed. She could taste the foul reek of banana beer on his breath as he pressed his body against hers. Turning her face away from the monster on top of her, she caught the eyes of her husband. His look, so full of rage and shame and helplessness, would never leave her.

AUGUSTE'S LEFT EYE HAD ALREADY BEGUN TO SWELL SHUT BY FIRST light. His body was bruised from the beating he had received before that night's visitors finally took what plunder they could carry and left, threatening they would finish the job if he tried to retaliate. Auguste couldn't look his bride in the eyes as he lumbered to bring in the water can so she could rid herself of the stench of violence. But even had he been able to lift his gaze to hers, he would not have seen the dancing eyes he loved, the eyes that sometimes sparkled with mischief and sometimes warmed him with love. Perhaps it was better that his head was too heavy with shame, and his eyes were too swollen shut to meet her hollow stare.

"I'm going to the shop," he called in to Monique as she dipped a cloth into a basin and wrung it out. "I will call Isaiah to come and take us and the children some place safer. With his car, he can be here before nightfall."

Monique didn't respond and Auguste did not wait for her to do so. She lifted the cloth to her skin and rubbed it back and forth. She dipped the cloth again and again and scoured her body as if she could peel away the skin that had been touched. By the time she finished, her skin was raw. Letting her eyes fall on her curving figure, she suddenly gasped for breath as a wave of violent sobs hit her. It would be some time before she again had the luxury of time for tears. Some minutes later, she dried her eyes, dressed, and took the clothes she had been wearing to a pit behind the house. Striking a match, she let it burn until the flame reached her fingertips. She watched the match tumble through the air and ignite the yellow fabric, turning it orange and brown with flame.

Smoke was still wafting into the house when Auguste arrived home to find Monique cradling the baby and staring blankly at the wall, while three year-old Patrick sat at her feet, pushing a tiny toy truck across the dirt floor.

"Isaiah's waiting outside."

AUGUSTE, MONIQUE, AND THE CHILDREN ARRIVED AT THE CATHOLIC church in Ruhuha only to find a stream of other Tutsi also pouring in. In a matter of two weeks, as violence spread across the region, the church filled with some four thousand people. Uncomfortable with the close quarters, Auguste paid off a Hutu friend near the town center to house them until the violence passed. They stayed indoors for several weeks, relying on their good friend Isaiah to bring them food and water as needed. Though also a Hutu, Isaiah had been Auguste's friend since childhood, and recently he'd stood beside Auguste as he married his bride, Monique.

Two months later, the military had stabilized the region enough for Auguste and Monique to return home. Doors, windows, food stores, and a few valuables they had left behind were gone. But their neighbors, many of them Hutu, brought food and lent strong arms to replace those things broken or stolen.

For nearly eleven months things seemed as stable as they had been before. Slowly, Auguste found the courage to lift his eyes to meet Monique's again, but he did not see the same woman staring back at him. Monique mistook Auguste's own shame that he had not been able to protect her for a sign that he was ashamed *of* her. Without words, his shame only intensified her own.

Monique and Auguste were inhabiting the same wordless space at the shop when Patrick and Irene padded up breathlessly that April morning in 1994. Between gasps, Patrick explained that there were men in the house, stealing from them. Auguste thrust some francs into Monique's hands and told her to go and find a place for her and the two children to hide. He would return home and get the other two children and meet up with her soon.

Monique lost no time. A child clinging to each hand, she ran through the center to the clump of homes closest to the market. She knocked on the door and Yvette, a woman she had often seen at the shop over the years, answered. The woman's eyes met Monique's with a haughtiness she had not seen in them before. Holding out the cash, Monique explained the situation, pleading with her to let the children hide there until she and Auguste could make a plan to get out of town. Yvette took the money and counted it.

"I can hide the children," she said with a toss of her head, "but I can't hide you. You must go." Monique thanked her and then knelt down to the children's level, speaking to them in firm, soft tones. "You must go with this woman and stay inside. Do what she tells you and be very quiet. Papa and I will be back for you soon. Promise me to be very good and very quiet."

The children nodded their heads and wrapped their arms around her as she kissed them each on the cheeks. "I'll be back soon."

Not wanting to be far from the children, Monique made her way into the thick of the bush closest to that cluster of homes. Already the rainy season had begun, and the rain beat violently against her that night as she passed sleepless hours amid the tall stalks of sorghum. She wondered if Auguste made it safely to find Francine and Ariane. She wondered if the intruders had hurt them. Her mind churned through scenarios fitfully until she finally fell into a shallow sleep.

Monique hid for two days before venturing back to the house where she had left the children. Auguste must have discovered via word-of-mouth where the children were because Francine and Ariane had also joined them. Monique exhaled to see her babies safe, though she worried that if Auguste had been able to find them so easily, others might also know her children were hiding there.

Yvette greeted her with the same look of proud irritation that she had seen before. This time she explained that another man would help her to hide the children in a safer place, but that she would need the keys to the shop to make sure the children had the food and supplies they needed. And she said, holding out her palm, "I will also need more money."

Monique gave her everything she had left along with the shop key. She didn't know what other choice she had. She kissed the children once more, and after receiving a bit of food from Yvette's scowling teenage daughter, she made her way back into the dark, through stalks of sorghum, the rain pelting her ferociously.

Auguste had made his way to Isaiah's home near Ruhuha. Even on his way there, he had seen men dragging neighbors out into their yards and beating them mercilessly with clubs and machetes. He had heard a woman's scream from the bush, and had seen knots of men gathered together swigging beer as if it were a holiday. Isaiah quickly filled him in on the news: that the president's plane had been shot down. In hushed tones in a back room they speculated what would happen and what Auguste's best chance of finding Monique and fleeing would be. In the room next door, Isaiah's own children giggled. They had found a turtle near the river and were trying, albeit unsuccessfully, to goad the frightened animal to stick its head out from its shell.

"You can bet on blockades along the main roads," Isaiah was saying when the sound of men's voices very near the house filled Auguste's ears. Both men were immediately still, tensed with the effort of listening.

A firm pounding came at the front door. As he rose, Isaiah motioned Auguste to get down low. Carefully, Isaiah shut the door behind him and walked calmly to the front door.

A young man in military dress stood in front of him, gun slung across his narrow shoulders. What he lacked in age, he made up for in arrogance. The young man spoke with a look of disdain, "I understand that you are a cockroach lover." He pushed his way inside. "We cannot have our own collaborating with those rebels."

Auguste could hear his words clearly and he swallowed hard, hoping that the man would merely issue a warning, or that Isaiah could pay him off.

"The colonel has asked me to make a lesson of you," said the young man. A staccato of gunshots reached Auguste's ears. "Listen to me, you hiding cockroach," the man shouted. "Tell your filthy friends what happens when Hutu collaborate with the enemy." Auguste heard him fire another shot.

"Drag their bodies into the street," he ordered. "I want everyone to understand the cost of conspiring with the enemy."

WORD OF THE DEATHS OF ISAIAH AND THAT OF HIS FAMILY TRAVELED quickly; more quickly, in fact, than Auguste could reach his children. Isaiah was both wealthy and influential in the community, and on hearing his fate, Yvette did not hesitate. She sent word by her daughter to tell the killers that they had found a nest of cockroaches that needed exterminating. All four children were dead by the time Auguste could get anywhere near the house.

In his haste, Auguste betrayed himself. His heavy footsteps were easily heard by a nearby Hutu hunting party. They recognized Auguste immediately and sprinted after him, knowing that whoever brought him down would receive the colonel's praise and whatever tidy sum of money he found in the victim's pocket. Both thoughts invigorated the killers, already worn out from a day of searching for Tutsi to kill. On reaching him, one young man swung his machete down with full force, striking Auguste on the back of his skull.

MONIQUE MOVED SLOWLY AND NEAR TO THE GROUND. HER HANDS and knees were bleeding by the time she reached the garden where she expected to find a few vegetables that would appease the gnawing hunger pains. Her fingers stretched into the dark soil, following a maze of wispy roots until she felt the solid round lump of a potato. She pried it loose and tried to smooth the ground back over so her raid might not be detected.

Crawling on all fours she moved back toward the sorghum stalks. Tucked inside the high rows, she rubbed the potato against her clothes to shed the outer layer of dirt. She was opening her mouth to take a bite when a hand clamped a handful of her hair and began to drag her back toward the dirt field. She screamed in pain and grasped the hand that grabbed her while using her legs to try to push herself up and ease the strain of the pulling. A few moments later, she was in the open soil where she had just dug up the potato. The hand loosened its grasp on her hair, but grabbed her arms, twisting them behind her so that she was soon facedown in the dirt.

She could feel the burn of rope as it was looped tightly around her wrists. She screamed in pain and fear. A moment later, a young man in military dress turned her over. She had seen that look in a man's eyes before. She knew what he wanted.

"Stop," she screamed, "don't do it. My husband is a wealthy man. He owns a shop and seventy head of cattle. He will give you whatever you want if you don't harm me."

The man laughed, looking down on her as he removed his gun and loosened his belt. "Yes, I've heard of this Tutsi. I understand that he fell in just one blow. We have already helped ourselves to what we could find in your store. Your husband had good taste."

Monique closed her eyes. She longed for death to come quickly.

longing for death

Hell is empty and all the devils are here.
Shakespeare, *The Tempest*

THE RAIN STARTED SOON AFTER THE SOLDIER LEFT MONIQUE LYING naked, her wrists still bound tightly behind her back. He told her that he couldn't kill her, but maybe someone else would come along and finish the job.

As the rain fell it cut rivulets in the soil of the potato field, making hundreds of miniature streams flowing down the naturally sloped farmland. Monique turned her body on her side, her cheek pressing into the softening mud, the tiny tributaries flowing down toward her. The ground itself felt increasingly soft beneath her, as if soon nature itself would finish the job and take her into its bosom. Her chin quivered. She closed her eyes and opened them, falling in and out of consciousness.

As the sky began to lighten, the rain fell more softly. Monique knew that she would somehow need to make it to the tall stalks of sorghum if she were to avoid being spotted, but she had lost her will to hide. She lay stunned in the mud field, wishing for death.

Soon, the sounds of a small herd of cattle reached her ears. The lowing was soothing to her and she closed her eyes more tightly, assuming she was dreaming of the days of her youth when she would graze her father's herds.

A few moments later she heard footsteps and sensed someone near her. She looked up, and for a moment the rising sun blinded her. She blinked and soon saw the shape of a boy of about fifteen years old. She recognized his face, but it took her mind longer than usual to retrieve his name from her memory. Finally, she remembered: Serge. She had welcomed him into her house before. His younger brother was a playmate of her son.

"What happened to you?" asked the boy.

Monique searched for words, suddenly becoming conscious again of her nakedness. She breathed in deeply and licked the corners of her lips, tasting mud on them. "I am like the dead," she said finally, her voice a hoarse whisper.

The boy reached for a knife. Monique winced, shutting her eyes tightly. Then she felt his hands on her wrists and the gentle sawing of the knife against the ropes. Her mouth and forehead pressed into the mud as he did so. It took several minutes, but at last she felt the rope loosen. She moved her hands to wipe the mud and water from her face and then sat up, pulling her knees up to her chest and rubbing her wrists.

"You can't stay here," the boy said in a whisper. "And it is not safe for me to bring you to our house. You must get away from here."

Monique tried to stand but found herself too weak.

The boy hesitated a moment, but then awkwardly slipped her arm over his shoulder and his arm around her waist and helped her to her feet. They did not stand fully upright but kept their heads low, using the herd of cattle as a barrier in case anyone suddenly came upon them. They weren't far from the tall stalks, and the boy helped her to push through them for several hundred feet until she was in a safer, more protected spot.

"I will come find you tonight when the sun goes down," he

whispered. "I will bring you some clothes and some food if I can manage it. Rest and regain your strength. You need to move on from here."

Monique nodded her head. "Thank you, Serge."

AT NIGHTFALL, SERGE KEPT HIS PROMISE AND RETURNED WITH SOME food and a coat for Monique. He also told her that he had heard that an old man named Fidele was hiding some Tutsi in his house. Monique knew the man and set out in the night to find his home. The place was not far from her home, and she remembered Fidele to be a good man—in fact, he had been one of the Hutu who had helped them repair their home after the damage done to it in 1992.

She arrived at his doorstep wrapped in a knee-length coat and still caked in mud. She knocked softly and waited. She heard nothing, so she knocked again, whispering, "I need some place to hide. Please, answer the door!" A few minutes later the door cracked open slightly. She could see Fidele's graying head of hair reflect in the moonlight. His eyes focused on her and then his brow knotted. "Come in," he said.

Stepping into the small house, she followed him closely because it was so dark that it made it difficult to see. "Sleep here until morning," he said, motioning to the ground before them. "We'll talk then."

It wasn't until morning that Monique saw that she was not alone in the room. There were six other Tutsi crowded into the small living room of Fidele's home: three men and three women. Fidele's wife, Agathe, a woman stooped with arthritis, was the first to rise, stepping through the people and shaking her head with disgust when she saw Monique. When Agathe reached the door she carefully cracked it open, stepped outside, and then firmly closed it behind her as she went to go get water.

When Fidele emerged from the bedroom, he made eye contact

with Monique. She thanked him for letting her stay the night and then asked if he knew anything concerning her children who were staying in Yvette's house near the shop. He dropped his eyes. Monique could tell he knew something. "What is it?"

"The children are dead," he said, still not raising his eyes. "I understand that Yvette called the killers. But everyone has been panicked since they killed Isaiah for housing Tutsi and dragged him and his family into the street. None of us are safe," he said, swallowing hard. "None of us."

THREE WEEKS PASSED WITH MONIQUE LIVING IN THE TINY FRONT room of Fidele's house. Each day, Agathe seemed to grow increasingly agitated with their presence. Finally, she demanded that Fidele make them leave. "I can't live with them anymore," she said, hands lifted in disgust. Reluctantly, Fidele told the three other women whose husbands were Hutu that they must return home to their husbands for protection. He promised to find an abandoned house for the others the next morning. Two of the women left in the night; Monique and the other woman stayed behind, along with the men. But before sunrise, Hutu militiamen surrounded the house.

Four or five men in their early twenties entered the room, leading with their rifles extended. Behind them, a well-built man, perhaps in his midforties, entered the room in military dress, gun at his side. He looked at Fidele and said with a wry smile, "Your wife says that you have captured some cockroaches for us that need extermination." Fidele scowled, but he said nothing.

"Colonel," said an eager soldier, pointing his gun toward the Tutsi on the ground. "Should we take them outside first?"

The colonel surveyed the lot of them. "Take the men," he said.

Fidele stepped forward and pointed to the other woman. "That one has a Hutu husband."

"Send her home to him then," said the colonel coldly. "Let him deal with her. And that one?" he asked, motioning to Monique.

"Her husband is already dead," said Fidele.

"Very well, then, put that one in my car," the colonel barked.

As THE JEEP PULLED UP TO THE DISTRICT HEADQUARTERS, MONIQUE could see several large bonfires outside, where militia lay sleeping on mats nearby. A Rwandan flag whipped in the breeze. Before the colonel could get out of the jeep, one young soldier approached. "I think you'll be pleased with our work today, sir," he said with a smile.

"Bring them out," the colonel shouted back in the direction of the building. Immediately, a line of half-naked men stumbled out in the direction of the headlights, their wrists bound behind them.

"All these today?" asked the colonel.

"Yes, sir," said the young soldier.

"Our work is close to done then," responded the colonel. "You know what to do with them?"

"Yes, sir," said the man, saluting and pivoting back to the lineup.

Monique buried her face in her lap and pressed her fingers to her ears. Perhaps a minute passed before the short, crisp sound of gunfire pierced the night. She heard several gunshots at a time, then a pause, then several more, then a pause, as if listening to the steady beating of the heart of evil. She felt hot and light-headed, her forehead still touching her knees in the backseat of the jeep.

A moment later, she heard the door open. Raising her head, Monique saw the colonel extend his hand. She took it, and he steadied her as she stepped to the ground. "Follow me," said the colonel, heading toward the front door of the headquarters. Monique tried to keep her eyes on her own feet as they walked. She knew that no good would come of glancing to her right or her left.

As they passed through a long corridor, the young soldier followed along behind them, his gun ensuring Monique's obedience.

In a few moments, they reached the colonel's living quarters. He motioned Monique to go ahead in.

"Will you be needing me any longer?" asked the soldier.

"You're dismissed," the colonel said as he closed the door behind him.

The colonel began to unbutton his coat.

"Please sir," said Monique, raising her eyes to the man. "Please, can you kill me too?"

"I can't kill you, my dear," said the colonel, stroking her cheek. "You are my wife."

LESS THAN A WEEK PASSED BEFORE COLONEL NAENGEYINKA TOLD Monique that the RPF were nearby and that his men would be moving on to a safer area.

"I can't take you with me," he said, "because the other Hutu will certainly kill you."

Monique wondered if the colonel really thought that such news would sadden her.

"You should stay here and seek out a place to hide. Perhaps the RPF will find you and you will be safe. But even so, you must be careful—there are many Interahamwe still searching to kill."

For Monique, there was no getting used to her captor. It had been a week of living with him, and somehow evil wrapped in the guise of kindness was even more revolting to the psyche than being raped in the mud while bound at the wrist or in the plain sight of her husband. How could this man speak with concern for her, yet not bat an eye at ordering a massacre of scores of people or feel remorse for violating her night after night?

He pressed his lips against hers, grabbed his gun, and moved out with the rest of the men, leaving Monique, shaking, alone in the back room of the district headquarters.

It was still dark, so Monique waited before making her way back into the bush. She began to move in what she hoped was the direction of the RPF, but she had only gone about a kilometer when she collapsed, exhausted, in the thick, tall grass.

For three days, she continued to move by night and hide by day. One morning, however, a Hutu man spotted her as he was taking a shortcut into town. She recognized him vaguely as a man named Hakizimana, and he recognized her as well.

He raised a hand and motioned her to follow him. "I know a place for you to hide," he said softly.

Deciding to trust him, Monique followed the man to an abandoned house.

"Stay here," he said. "I will bring you food at night and will make sure that no one comes near the house."

Monique nodded. "Are the RPF really close by?"

"They are getting closer," said the man, "but they still have not reached this village. I must go now. Stay inside."

Three weeks passed this way. Hakizimana would bring food at night. At first, he only stayed to watch her eat it and then left. But soon, like the men before him, he too raped Monique. He considered it a fair exchange, and Monique understood that her protection depended upon her cooperation. But at the end of those three weeks, sometime in late May, the man told her that the RPF were indeed near and that he was leaving with his family while he still could.

Monique ventured back into the bush the next evening, only this time she encountered a Tutsi man who was also fleeing. Together they made their way into one village that looked to be empty. A dog barked and the two fled in opposite directions: the man toward the bush and Monique into an abandoned house. In the distance, Monique could hear men yelling and the sound of machetes hacking out a path. A few minutes later she heard a scream and then the dog barking once more. Monique pulled an old mattress on top of her and lay as still as she could. Soon everything was quiet once more.

THE NEXT DAY, MONIQUE HEARD THE SOUNDS OF THE INTERAHAMWE in the village. From what she could gather, hunger must have drawn them back out into the open and they were risking being seen by the RPF to loot the empty village for what food they could find. Having already swept the village of people, now they were scavenging for a forgotten bag of rice or the odd cow still tied to a post.

Two days later, Monique, still hiding in the abandoned house, heard the sound of gunfire and yelling. There was a skirmish going on outside. Peeking out a window, she caught sight of men in RPF uniforms. It looked as if they were rooting the Interahamwe out of the village. For the first time in months, Monique began to weep. Perhaps, she thought, she would survive. She didn't know if she cried from relief or sorrow. She would not be joining her husband or children yet.

Seth

"God has granted me another."
Genesis 4:25

TWO YEARS HAD PASSED SINCE THAT JUNE DAY IN 1994 WHEN MONIQUE emerged from beneath an old mattress into a shattered new life. The RPF had gone door-to-door, looking for survivors. Coaxing her out with food, they finally convinced Monique to emerge from the empty house like some sort of frightened animal.

For the first time since fifteen-year-old Serge cut her ropes, men proved trustworthy. The rations weren't the freshest, but they were more than she had had in a while. Soon the RPF soldiers settled her near the town center in Ruhuha, where they had established camp and secured the area. They showed her an empty house and told her that she could live there.

Survivors and soldiers alike helped move the dead to mass graves and carried cans of water so they could scrub walls and floors that bore silent testimony to the atrocities. One day at a time, Monique began to build a life again.

Existence was a day-to-day battle for survival. She tried to farm, but it was difficult without money for seed and without a previous harvest to get her through the long months of waiting. The work itself also felt harder than ever before. She tired easily. Fevers, headaches, and nausea plagued her incessantly. Even at night, rest eluded her. In its place, grief or terror paid nightly visits as the months of horror continued to haunt her.

So it was that when Ruzindana Aloys began stopping by offering her help with the farm or bringing the occasional bag of rice, she seldom turned him away. He had joined the RPF when he was just fourteen, living in exile in Uganda, and, like almost all RPF soldiers, he had been forbidden to take a wife until their goal was accomplished. Judging from his youthful face, Monique guessed him to be a few years her junior. For some reason, though, his youth put her more at ease around him than around other men. Even so, she never dropped her guard when he stopped by to chat or offer a hand with the plowing.

On a June day in 1996, Aloys knocked on Monique's door. The sun was high in the sky when Monique answered. Aloys had two bottles of soda in hand. "Sit with me a while?" he asked.

Monique came out into the sunlight, and Aloys took a seat on the stoop outside her house. Monique did likewise, leaving a generous space between them. Pulling a bottle opener from his pocket, Aloys popped the top from the glass bottle before handing her the drink. The young soldier cleared his throat before he began. "Monique, I'm not a wealthy man, you know." He cracked open the cap of his own bottle and took a swig. When he finished, he sat flipping the metal cap over in his hand using his thumb and forefinger. The repetitive action held his gaze for some moments. Monique too watched his nervous motion.

"But I'm a hard worker," he suddenly continued. "That I know is true." He breathed in. "You've seen that, I hope?"

Monique nodded.

"And I think, even though I don't have much, I can make your life better, and you mine." The lid turned more quickly now in his hand

and then suddenly stopped. "I guess what I'm trying to say—what I want to know—is whether or not you will be my wife."

Monique was stunned. Without looking up, she could feel Aloys' gaze on her as surely as she could feel the heat of the sun without looking into its direct light. She sat for some minutes collecting her thoughts before taking a deep breath. "Aloys, I ... I can't marry you."

Aloys dropped his eyes back to the ground, his elbows pressing into his knees, his fingers laced together around the soda bottle.

"You will understand, when you know my story," she said. Monique breathed deeply, gathering strength. She had not yet told another living soul, for she had never imagined telling anyone the horrors that had befallen her over those one hundred days. But Aloys' calm, gentle presence opened her up. Not once did he interrupt her as she spoke; he sat still, listening, nodding, or shaking his head.

When she had at last finished, only then did he look her square in the eyes. She could see that his eyes, like hers, were wet. He looked at her for a long time before he finally told her in slow, deliberate words, "You did not deserve that. I am so sorry this happened to you."

It wasn't until then that Monique lost her composure and began to weep. She excused herself, but Aloys sat still, watching the sun until it had dropped below the horizon. He then rose and walked home.

The next day he came again. When Monique opened the door this time, he could see she had been weeping. "I want to ask you a question," said the young man.

"Aloys, as I told you yesterday, my answer is no."

"You haven't yet heard the question," he said.

"I'm sorry. Tell me then. What is the question?"

"I want you to get tested for AIDS."

"Was that a question?"

"Monique, I'm serious. You need to get tested. You know it's the truth."

"Where would I go?"

"Kanobi Hospital has a clinic that does the testing."

"But that is far from here and I have no money."

"I will pay for you," he said.

"But ..."

"I will even go with you and be tested myself. I just think you should. You should know."

"I'm still waiting for the question."

Aloys smiled. "Will you go?"

IT WAS A FAIRY-TALE ENDING TURNED UPSIDE DOWN. A MAN MEETS A woman, they fall in love, and then they both discover they have a terminal illness. But upside down or not, this ending was what Monique and Aloys had, and they determined to make the most of it.

Monique and Aloys married later that July, once the one hundred days of remembrance had passed. The ceremony was brief. Monique had not seen her parents or her younger siblings since 1992 when they went to Burundi. Her older siblings had died in 1994 in Kigali. None of her immediate family was present, nor did she have a dowry. Indeed, there would have been little to give. But from the smile on Aloys' face that day, no one would have guessed the grim circumstances of their union. He was a beaming groom, his smile like the breaking sun after the season of rains. Less than a year later, he was also a beaming father. Aloys lavished love on that child and the two children who followed.

The fact that Monique found it in her heart to trust and love a man again was itself a miracle. But even so, and even as she held her son, Deo, in her arms, still there was a deep sadness in her eyes.

Sometimes when Aloys spoke to her, it was as if Monique looked somehow beyond him and through him at the same time. Over time, he came to conclude that suffering creates chasms between people who know pain and those who do not. It was as if no matter how far he reached, pain had removed her farther still.

Aloys did not live long enough to see that faraway look removed completely, but he did live long enough to see Monique find a sense of purpose and a measure of the peace that had evaded her for years.

In 2004 a cousin of her first husband knocked on her door. It had been years since Monique had seen Pascal, and in the interim he had matured into a man of quiet dignity. Word had reached her already that Pascal had returned to the area and had begun teaching on forgiveness and reconciliation. So it didn't surprise Monique when Pascal asked if she would attend some meetings of survivors and ex-prisoners in order to begin a dialogue. Had Pascal not been so dear to her first husband, Auguste, perhaps she would have refused. As it was, she agreed to go.

At the meeting, she was startled to find ex-prisoners who openly asked survivors for forgiveness — even those, like her, whom they had not directly wronged. She could tell that many of them were sincere and deeply broken men. In the course of the talks, she also learned of the benefits of forgiveness. She heard how forgiveness can bring a sense of release for those who have carried with them pain and grief, how releasing the debt to God frees them to focus more fully on the life before them instead of continually living in the past. And finally, she learned how forgiveness frees people to live again in a community where Hutu and Tutsi must find a way to coexist.

At the workshops, they read stories of forgiveness from the Bible. Monique remembered the stories from childhood, but the words came alive to her again as she heard how Jesus Christ had taken our sins and our sorrows to the cross. Pascal explained how this meant that Christ had taken both the sins of the genocidaires and the sorrows of the victims and carried those with him to the cross. As an innocent victim, Christ identified with those like Monique who suffered wrongfully. But by laying upon him the sins of the world, Christ also took away the reproach of sinners who would look to him in faith. He forgives.

Monique also learned that Christ would come again to judge the living and the dead. This meant that she could trust that justice would one day be accomplished for those who did not repent and turn to him by faith. This too helped her to forgive: knowing that those who sought mercy from Christ would receive it, and those who refused to believe they had done evil would one day stand before a perfect judge.

Little by little, Monique felt that she too could extend forgiveness to the people who had wronged her.

IN LATE AUGUST OF 2004 MONIQUE FINALLY WORKED UP THE courage to make the journey. By that time Aloys was too weak to travel with her, so she walked alone.

Even though she had not ventured that way in more than ten years, she remembered the route. She stayed on the main road until she reached the district headquarters. The hair rose on the back of her neck as she passed by the place where she had heard gunshots end the lives of perhaps fifty Tutsi. The feeling of claustrophobia in that back room where the colonel had held her as his "wife" for nearly a week clamped icy fingers around her throat as she walked past.

From the district headquarters, she stepped off the main road out into the bush that had been both cover and terror to her for so many nights in that long season of evil. Somehow that particular area brought back the sensations and memories more keenly. She could sense the sting of the rain, taste the mud, and feel the throbbing of fear clearly as she walked those paths. Soon she found the footpath to the house where Hakizimana lived. Along the way, she passed the crumbling remains of the abandoned house where she waited for the RPF to reach the village. There, each night, Hakizimana brought her food and took the last shreds of her dignity. He was the only one of the many men who raped her who had returned to the village.

As she approached the small home where Hakizimana lived with his wife, she could see a bicycle propped outside the door and some chickens pecking at the earth. She breathed a prayer to God for the strength to do what she had come to do.

She held her breath and knocked. A few moments later, Hakizimana answered. He stepped back in fright as if he had seen someone return from the dead. For several moments the two of them stood blinking at one another, neither knowing quite what to say. Finally, Monique spoke.

"I've traveled some distance to see you," she said. "I have something important to tell you."

Hakizimana lifted a hand to his forehead and rubbed his temple as if he were trying to make the apparition disappear.

"First of all, I am here to ask you to go to the hospital. Eight years ago, I found out that I am HIV positive. I have already lost two children to AIDS and my husband now is near to death also. Chances are that you too are infected."

Hakizimana still couldn't formulate a sentence. He just nodded dumbly.

"Second, I am here to tell you that God has helped me to forgive you for how you sinned against me. I want to tell you that I forgive you."

Hakizimana lurched back, catching himself from a near collapse. "I should have come to you," he admitted. "I wronged you. I could have simply helped you and instead, I betrayed you. I'm sorry. I have often wanted to come to you and ask your forgiveness, but I have been afraid. I have been a wretched coward."

"I forgive you," repeated Monique. "I must go now," she said, feeling she had reached the end of her strength. She turned and began the long journey home.

SOON AFTER MONIQUE FINISHED THE WORKSHOPS WITH PASCAL, SHE took on the responsibility of leading the work group closest to her home. It was over one hundred strong, composed of survivors, ex-prisoners, and the wives of prisoners, especially those whose husbands were still incarcerated. In her group was also Yvette, the woman who had betrayed her own children.

Perhaps of all the people who had sinned against her in 1994, Monique had the most difficult time forgiving Yvette. Others had violated her physically, but Yvette had taken from her something more precious to her than even her own body—her children. To make matters worse, after the genocide she had come to her with money. Her request for forgiveness had felt like little more than a bribe. Monique had rejected her outright. Only after the workshop did she go back to her. She explained that she had come to her on her own terms. "What you did when you asked for my forgiveness before was wrong," she told her. "I could never accept money to purge your conscience. But I'm here today because God has forgiven me and he asks me to forgive you also. I hope that God will work in your heart for you to feel true sorrow for what you have done. But even if you never do, by the grace of God, he has given me the strength to offer you forgiveness."

It was the hardest thing Monique had ever done or had to say. The result, though, exceeded her imagination. In the months that would follow she saw Yvette truly change. Soon she came to properly beg Monique's forgiveness and to pledge her help to the work group. From that point on, she never missed a Monday meeting and never complained, even if the work was difficult.

The group built fences to hold the cows that had been given to the villagers in Rwanda's One Family, One Cow policy. They also built homes for the returning prisoners. Between them they pooled a bit of money for the emergency needs that arose among them. Perhaps the greatest accomplishment was that the wives of the prisoners took the stories of the reconciliation that they saw happening back to their husbands in prison. They personally urged their guilty husbands to seek out forgiveness from the families they had injured, whether by letter or in person once they returned home.

Monique also began meeting with a smaller group of widows: those who, like her, had been raped or who had tested positive for HIV. They grieved together and found in one another someone else who could understand them in that chasm of pain that separated them from the rest of the world.

Aloys died soon after Monique returned from her journey to see Hakizimana. He would join their two oldest children in heaven. He would leave Monique and young Ruzindana Seth behind. Ruzindana Seth had been named first for Ruzindana Aloys and then for that child given to Adam and Eve after Cain killed Abel. When he was born, it was the first time that antiretroviral drugs were available, which can reduce the chances of a child of a parent with AIDS from becoming HIV positive himself. In that way, Monique and Aloys hoped that Seth would outlive them both and would grow up into the name that they had given him, "God has granted me another."

Despite the pain Monique still carried with her, she believed that God had granted her gifts she never imagined she would see again after the genocide: faith, hope, and love.

facing
the darkness

The past is not dead.
In fact, it is not even past.
William Faulkner

IN JOSEPH CONRAD'S HEART OF DARKNESS, THE SAILOR KURTZ peers into the void of evil on his deathbed, and all he can say is, "The horror! The horror!" Most of us will not peer so directly into the very heart of darkness, but if, like Monique, we do, we discover that darkness—evil in its purest form—has no heart.

It's no wonder then that our tendency when it comes to the evil that others have done to us is to try to bury it, to banish it to the furthest reaches of memory. The trouble with this is that wrong that hasn't been dealt with has a way of pushing its head up to the surface in our lives at the times we least expect or want it to reemerge. Part of the reason is biological, another part is theological. As we come to terms with the past, through grieving, forgiving, and reorganizing, we free ourselves to live well in the present.

Pain, whether psychological or physical, conditions our response system. Classically, behaviorists call this fear conditioning. Scientists have illustrated the process in laboratories with rats. A scientist sounds a tone, a conditioned stimulus. At the end of the tone, the rat receives a painful shock—an unconditioned stimulus. If the shock is strong enough, it will only take the rat one time to associate fear with the sound of the tone.

The next time the rat hears the tone, its body will respond. The rat freezes. Inside the rat, "corticosteroid releasing factor is excreted and signals the hypothalamus to stimulate the pituitary to turn on the stress system,"[1] releasing more stress signals to the body. If it can, the rat will try to escape. If it can't, the rat will try to attack.

Of course, this system is biologically in place to protect us from harm. Fear is a learned response that helps us to live safely. But often what happens is that painful experiences in our past may "trigger" the conditioned response in new relationships. The result is "we'll meet the situations in our current life, bracing ourselves with our fight/flight/freeze apparatus in full gear, assuming at some unconscious level, that a crisis is at hand."[2] Stress chemicals flood the body. And suddenly we find that the "line between the present and the past blurs, and we feel as if we're being hurt all over again, even though it may be mostly yesterday's pain that is being triggered."[3]

But then there is also the power of a thought, or of a pattern of thinking, to affect us physically. Scientists conducted a study to explore the relationship between thinking patterns and health. They divided their test group into two. To one group, they showed a film of violent acts from the Holocaust. To the other group, they showed a film about the life of Mother Teresa. Both groups were asked to reflect on the films throughout the day. At the end of the film and then again at the end of the day, doctors tested the blood of each group. They found that the group that had recalled the "Nazi war acts experienced a *depressed* immune function *throughout* the day, while the group imaging Mother Teresa showed *elevated* immune functions *throughout* their day."[4]

Unforgiveness is a powerful emotional cocktail. It can be defined as "delayed emotions involving resentment, bitterness, residual anger, residual fear, hatred, hostility, and stress."[5] Like all emotions, it is experienced not only mentally, but bodily as well. Muscles throughout the body and face may tense, teeth may grind, the stomach may churn, and the pulse may rise. As the study on thought pattern shows, our immune functions may actually be lowered as a result. What's more, the negative emotions may inhibit our ability to experience positive ones.

> Because emotions are whole-body experiences, they often blend if they are relatively similar. For instance, anger, fear, and sadness are all perceived negatively, especially if they are experienced intensely. Joy, happiness, and satisfaction are also relatively similar and are perceived positively ... However, when emotional states are very different, they don't blend. They compete. For instance, when our facial muscles are set in a grimace of anger, the grimace edges out a soft smile of happiness and peace or even a frown of distress. The patterns of hormones in the blood or neurochemicals in the brain also compete ... That is why we can be in a sad mood and laugh at a joke but return immediately to feeling sad.[6]

This is one reason why it is so important to deal with the emotions of unforgiveness. Not only do they condition us, but if we are ruminating on them they may actually affect our health and our ability to experience positive emotions or emotional well-being.

Understanding the nature of evil can also help us to understand its damaging effects on those who stare into its heartless darkness and why it's so important to deal with the evil that has been done to us. As a counselor who deals extensively with cases of sexual abuse, Dr. Dan Allender has had to examine evil closely. He points out that evil is "working to destroy hope through powerlessness, faith through betrayal, and love through ambivalence."[7] If evil can damage these core aspects of a person, it can shatter selfhood, connection to others, and connection to God. In essence, it can shatter life.

Evil attacks hope by creating a sense of powerlessness— nothing one does can alter the future. After repeatedly losing control, a person may lose the capacity to imagine a future in which anything good may occur. Instead, the future resembles the present torment of evil continued without end. Without hope, a person can plummet into despair.

If powerlessness severs the cord between a victim and a future devoid of hope, then betrayal severs the cord between a person and any other person who might help them out of goodwill. Betrayal destroys trust, and in so doing it colors not only the relationship with the offender but taints other relationships as well. While hope is primarily future oriented, faith is anchored in the past. When betrayal undermines faith, it uproots what we have believed to be true about intimacy and relationships in general. That threatens not only physical relationships, but spiritual ones as well. The victim begins to doubt whether God is trustworthy.

After uprooting the hope of the future and the security of the past, evil's final act is to destroy even innocence and pleasure.

As evil delights in the cruelty of holding out false tenderness and false notions of safety, it creates a feeling of ambivalence, or a feeling of being ripped in two. As Allender writes, "he or she feels shame or hatred from having trusted someone who used intimacy to gain access to do harm."[8]

If evil had the final say, then it would, indeed, be a most pitiable world in which we live. But it does not. Faith called into question leads to doubt. But doubt can drive us to seek God. Allender notes that nearly every prophet mentioned in the Old Testament must wrestle with doubt. Doubt doesn't have to drive us from faith, but can push us to grapple deeply with the core questions of existence.

Likewise, the loss of hope may lead to despair, but even despair may serve a higher purpose. When we despair of the things we have trusted in the past—even good things—we may be led to search for something or someone more reliable. When we come face-to-face with despair, we may find a hope no evil can shatter.

Finally, as one regains faith and hope, love can grow. Allender says it best:

> Love is the primary weapon against evil. Evil is committed to devouring, to absorbing others in an attempt to fill an insatiable emptiness. It despises both light and the invitation to humbly receive forgiveness. Therefore, the nature of true love involves revelation and invitation. Godly love exposes darkness with a strength that reveals God's righteousness and a tender mercy that invites the heart to repent and receive forgiveness.[9]

Only through repentance can evil be transfigured. Only through love can such a transfiguration occur.

Whether looking at past trauma from a biological, ground-up

point of view, or from a theological, top-down point of view, it is evident that past wrong will have present ramifications. Forgiving is only one aspect of dealing with the evil in our lives. Grieving the loss, accepting the loss, struggling through doubt, reorganizing our view of the world based upon our experiences, and integrating those experiences into our new developed sense of self are all vital aspects of the process. Though the story can end with an increased freedom to live in the present without the entanglement of the bonds of the past, it must begin with facing the darkness.

Questions for Reflection and Discussion

How have you been conditioned through fear? Can you identify any "triggers" that may be causing you to react negatively in today's relationships that are really left over from yesterday's wrongs?

How often do you find yourself brooding or ruminating over events of the past?

Which effect of evil have you felt most in your life: powerlessness, loss of trust, or ambivalence?

snakes
in the grass

*As I've learned, human beings are strangely easy
and strangely hard to kill.*
**Gary Haugen, president,
International Justice Mission**

ABOUT A KILOMETER NORTH OF NYAMATA, DEVOTA MUHANGERE
took her three-year-old daughter, Claudina, and eight-year-old son,
Claude, one by each hand, and set out for church. Perhaps she was
overly protective, but she almost always took them by the hand, even
though Claude was already a young man. That day he didn't resist,
though on some days he would pull away from her and run ahead,
eager to assert his independence.

Devota, newly divorced, lived an isolated life, save for her weekly
Sunday jaunts to church. A new Christian and a member of the
choir, Devota sang a few bars of a chorus as she walked along. *"Uru
wera wera, Imana nyiringabo, Isi yose yuzuyemo, Icyubahiro Cyawe."*
Her voice rose and fell along with the footpath. She had a gentle,
pleasant voice, and it soothed both her and the children as they
walked along.

People outside seemed more harried than usual. Clumps of adults stood talking nervously, children were hauling water with a quickened step, and some women were even outside gathering beans or manioc, an unusual sight for a Sunday.

It was Sunday, April 10, 1994, and just four days earlier, President Habyarimana's plane had been shot down. The killings had not yet erupted—though all that was to change quickly.

When they arrived at the church, Devota immediately realized that something was wrong. No one had yet taken their seats, and the usual smiling faces did not greet her and the children. Only a few had gathered there, and she could hear snippets of conversation as she approached. "I think it could be very bad this time," said one. Standing a little farther off, a deacon spoke to another man, "They are saying that all Tutsi must die."

Devota's throat tightened as she listened, and so did her grip on the children.

"They say that the killings have already begun in Nyamata, and houses are being burned and looted," said the man talking to the deacon.

Devota turned, swinging the children with her.

"Why aren't we staying for church, Mama?" asked Claude.

"It isn't safe today, Son. We've got to get home." Devota processed what she had overheard as she walked. In the past, when raiding bands had entered the area, she and others had always fled to the center in Nyamata. But if those people who lived closest to the center were coming their direction, it must be bad. She recalled the phrase "all Tutsi must die." Things had taken a turn for the worse. She quickened her step and said a prayer for protection as she walked.

THE VERY NEXT DAY, HUTU SOLDIERS FROM NEAR THE BASE AT GAKO systematically began to slaughter Tutsi in the streets of Nyamata. At the command of the local authorities and with the encouragement of the Interahamwe, local farmers brought their everyday tools, machetes, clubs, and sometimes spears and assembled on the nearby hills to map out their attack plan. Over the next three days, ordinary Hutu farmers and soldiers killed some ten thousand Tutsi refugees, first at the Catholic church in Nyamata, then at the Sainte-Marthe Maternity Hospital, and finally about thirty kilometers away at another church in Ntarama. In conflicts past, the churches had always been places of refuge and safety. This time they were the places of the most concentrated slaughter.

Surrounding the buildings, the attackers began by throwing grenades and using crowbars to pry open the heavy metal gates that swung over the doors. When they had broken through the exterior, they set to wielding their machetes at the masses of people gathered therein. They perforated the metal roof with bullet holes, bashed the skulls of newborns against the brick walls, and even raped women near the altar as others shot at a statue of the Virgin Mary, calling her a Tutsi. The men worked until four and then left the moaning and the dying for the next day, while a few stayed behind to guard the periphery.

The brave and relatively able-bodied crept out, evading the soldiers, and followed the steep paths down to the valleys and into the tenuous safety provided by the marshes. But many could not make it such distances, and perished in the valleys.

At first, Devota and her children stayed in their house during the day and fled into the valleys below at night. Some of the braver among her neighbors took stones, sticks, and whatever they could find to try and stave off the advance of the Hutu. But such courage did not last long as the news of the massacres spread.

Traveling with her sisters and brothers-in-law at night, Devota and her family headed many kilometers northeast to the valleys near the Butamwa marsh. At night they would tend to the wounded, but when the dawn began to break they would first cover the children and the weak with leaves and papyrus and then burrow their own hiding spots in the putrid-smelling mud. Around eight in the morning the killers would make their way into the marshes, fanning out in lines like search parties.

From their places covered deeply in mud and grass, it was difficult to see them, but their ears grew accustomed to their noises. Sometimes they would sing or hum, sounds so discordant to their barbarous tasks that it would make Devota seethe with rage. Other times they would try to lure the naive out of hiding, saying, "I have seen you. I know you are hiding in this marshland. Show yourself." But the sounds Devota dreaded most were the thumps of their clubs and machetes and the screams of women or children.

On one such morning, the killers found where Devota and her young daughter Claudina were hiding. Swinging their clubs and machetes, they hacked at her and the little girl. Devota lost consciousness at the third blow. When she awoke, she found Claudina mutilated almost beyond recognition. In the distance, she could hear the sounds of people moaning. She thought that the noise was coming from a house on the hill, and since the sun was already beginning to set, she decided to try to make it there to rest for the night away from the dank marshes. As she limped to the place where she had last seen Claude that morning, she could feel the lacerations on her back and thighs. She discovered a small footprint in the mud near where Claude had been hiding, but he was nowhere to be found. Devota hoped that her sister had taken him to a safer spot. Standing had already begun to make her light-headed and nauseous, so Devota moved in the direction of the moaning.

When she reached the abandoned house, she found two women tending to a young man. His eyes were rolled back into his head and he looked as if he were near death. Lurching into the doorway, Devota fell to her knees.

snakes in the grass

THE SUN PEERING THROUGH A SMALL WINDOW IN THE TINY MUD AND straw home pried open Devota's eyes. It was difficult to know for certain, but she thought that only one night had passed since she had made it to the abandoned home. She was lying on her stomach, and so she had to crane her neck to see if the young man that the two women had been tending to was still there. She could see a body behind her, but it was as still as a stone. Outside, she could hear birds calling to each other. She wondered if someone had disturbed them. No sooner had the question come into her mind than the door opened and a stocky farmer entered the room with his spiked club. She did not recognize him, but he cursed loudly, calling to others outside, "I thought we killed this one yesterday."

Another man entered the room. "Some snakes are hard to kill," he said, surveying her casually.

Soon Devota could hear three or four men in the room. Another one said in a deep, booming voice, "This kind you have to beat very well to make sure they are dead." He grunted, and she felt the weight of his machete come down on her back. She screamed—the last thing she felt was the sharp sting of a machete as it sliced her neck.

unquenchable

When you walk through the fire, you will not be burned;
the flames will not set you ablaze.
Isaiah 43:2

THE KILLERS HAD PLUNDERED THE ABANDONED HOUSE OF EVEN ITS metal roof, and so rain puddled on the floor where Devota lay facedown in a pool of her own blood. The rain continued to fall, and the porous clay floor slowly turned red.

No imagination should have to be pried open wide enough to see such an unsettling scene in full detail. It is enough to know that between the back of her skull and the top of her shoulder blades, Devota's skin hung in loose shreds. Could she have seen herself, she certainly would have walked by without checking for signs of life. No one would dream that a human being could live through such a vicious assault.

When Devota regained consciousness, she wondered if she had already passed into the second life. She could see the rain splattering on the ground around her, but she realized that she couldn't feel the rain on her skin. She concentrated harder, but still, she felt nothing.

That evening her brothers-in-law found her. They had heard her whereabouts from the women who were there when she had fainted two days before. When Devota heard the voices of her brothers-in-law, she tried to move. But when she tried to raise an arm, or move a leg, none of her muscles obeyed her. Her body felt as heavy and lifeless as if it were made of lead.

She could hear the men turning to go, so with one last effort, she forced all of her energy into a low moan. Startled, the men looked again more closely at the young man who was also still in the house, bending down to touch him, but his body was cold. A moment or so later one of them carefully squatted near Devota's body and groped for her wrist to try and find a pulse. When he found it, he jumped. "I think she's still alive," he said in a tone that sounded more like a question than a statement.

Both men stared at each other, saying nothing. Then finally, one called her name, "Devota! Can you hear me? Devota!"

She groaned again.

"What should we do?"

"We need to get her out of this rain."

"We passed a smaller hut. Did you see it? That one with the thatched roof."

"I saw it. Can we move her?"

"If we leave her, she will die."

"If we move her, she may die."

The larger of the two men squatted down and wedged his arms between the ground and her torso. "You will have to support her head," he grunted as he lifted her up. The other man did as he was told.

It was an awkward grip, but thankfully the hut was not far. And when they had gotten her settled, they called their wives, Devota's sisters, to do what they could to clean and bind her wounds. Devota's son, Claude, was with them, but they didn't let him come in. They thought it best that he not see his mother in such a state. Behind the house was an even smaller hut with a thatched roof where the owners had kept a goat. Claude slept inside, while the sisters stayed with Devota. But at first light, her sisters and their husbands left. This was the rule of the marshes, after all: survival dictated abandoning the badly wounded.

FOR NEARLY A WEEK DEVOTA LAY FACEDOWN IN THE SMALL HUT. EACH evening, when the sun had set, her sisters would come to care for her. When they could find it, they would bring a bit of manioc or beans. Always they would bring her a bit of muddy water from the marshes. But still they kept Claude from seeing her as best they could manage. As a boy of eight, though, his curiosity and desire to see his mother got the better of him. He would creep to the door and peer in, wondering if his mama would survive. After he had seen her, he refused to leave her in the daytime. Instead of going down into the marshes, he stayed in the small hut. But his aunties made him promise not to stir and certainly not to come out and check on her when the sun was high in the sky. Claude kept his promise.

In early May, the RPF had begun to make inroads into the Nyamata region. As they pushed in, Hutu began their flight toward the Congo. Had they not been distracted with looting or busy drinking their victims' beer and eating their cattle, it is likely they would have wiped out the Tutsi completely before being forced into exile.

Unlike other parts of Rwanda, where Tutsi were in the clear minority, in Nyamata the numbers of Hutu to Tutsi were almost equal. In the 1960s, the Rwandan government had forced many Tutsi to move into the region, largely because the area with its thick swarms of tsetse flies and large swaths of swampland was considered uninhabitable. But despite the obstacles, the Tutsi had managed to carve out an existence in the inhospitable hills. As Rwanda's population continued to swell and others saw that the Tutsi had settled the area successfully, more and more Hutu began to move into the region. When the genocide began in 1994, there were 60,000 Hutu and 59,000 Tutsi in the region. In just over a month, some 50,000 Tutsi were killed.

As the Hutu fled, they left destruction in their wake. If they could not have the land, they would not leave it for another. The hut where Devota lay recovering was one of many that the Hutu torched before making their way to the Gitarama road. Devota heard a band of men outside, yelling. But this time, no one came inside. Perhaps someone looked in a window and saw her and assumed she was dead. Perhaps there wasn't time for anything but burning. Either way, in a matter of minutes after they had passed she began to smell the smoke.

Soon she could see that the thatched roof was on fire. She tried to move, but she couldn't. Having not moved in nearly a week, she wasn't even sure if her limbs could still function. Closing her eyes, she began to do the only thing she knew she could do: she prayed. "Father God, I think it is time for me to leave. Let this fire take me from this world." But as Devota prayed, she felt a strong wind blowing against her face. And then she slept.

In her sleep, she began to dream. She could see a man, well-built but doubled nearly in half, his arms outstretched. He was leading a little child, helping it to walk. The toddler took faltering steps, but each time its legs would give way, the man would raise the babe up and help it to take a few steps more. How long this went on, she couldn't say. What the man's face looked like, she didn't know. She only knew that the man led the child, and that the child walked.

When Devota regained consciousness, she found herself not on a brushed mud floor, but in the tall grasses. The hut was perhaps two and half meters from her, and it was burnt to the ground. Looking at her body, she couldn't see any burn marks. Immediately, Devota surmised that the man she had seen in her dream had been an angel, and that the baby he had helped to walk was her.

Suddenly, Devota felt an unexplained surge of energy. On her feet, and supporting her torn skin with a free hand, she began to look for Claude. With some relief, she could see that the smaller hut where Claude had hidden, the goat's hut, had not yet caught on fire. She opened the door and found Claude with his chin resting on his chest. "Claude," she said. But he did not respond. "Claude," she said again, shaking him. He did not respond; as instructed, he had stayed put because it was still daylight out. The smoke had suffocated the little boy.

Distraught, Devota headed for the marshes, holding her head with her hand as she descended the hill. She did not know where she had found the strength to stand, but she didn't stop to wonder. She just ran.

IT WASN'T UNTIL AFTER SUNSET THAT DEVOTA MANAGED TO FIND HER sisters in the marsh. Pus had begun to ooze from the wounds at the back of her neck and her sisters helped to clean them, if using muddy swamp water could be called cleaning. Wherever Devota's strength had come from, it quickly vanished when she was back in the marshes with her sisters.

In the valley, several hundred people were hidden. They came out at night, huddling under the stars. That night, they spoke of the rumor that the RPF were close at hand, perhaps even already in the area. When another two days of hiding in the marsh had gone by and no killers came, those who were fit decided that it was time to see if they could move by cover of night and find the liberation troops.

Devota's sisters told her that they were leaving, but that they would come back for her. They just couldn't risk trying to move someone so badly injured. As they explained, Devota felt like she was about to lose consciousness. Already, she had lost the only thing dear to her, her two precious children. Her strength was gone; her wounds seemed irreparable. And now, the only family she had left was abandoning her.

That next day that Devota spent utterly alone in the marsh was the most desolate day she had ever spent on earth. Feeling completely abandoned, she prayed to God that he would let her die. Her mind wandered to her two children. She had not even been able to bury them.

That night, as Devota's strength ebbed to its lowest possible limit, the Tutsis' hope materialized. The RPF arrived, and it was making its way through the swamps searching for survivors. When they came across Devota, they cut two long sticks and stretched cloth around them to create a makeshift stretcher. They may not have been angels, but to Devota they were saviors nonetheless.

CHAPTER 15

the pain bearer

Forgiveness is the giving,
and so the receiving, of life.
George MacDonald

THE RPF SOLDIERS BROUGHT DEVOTA ON A MAKESHIFT STRETCHER TO
a temporary hospital at a secondary school in Nyamata. There, with
lack of medical personnel, RPF soldiers did what they could to play
doctor for the next three months. But it was not much. Finally, in
mid-August, a month or so after the RPF had secured Kigali and established victory, one soldier suggested that Devota's relatives try to
get her to King Faisal Hospital in Kigali. Certainly there the doctors
could heal her, he told them. So with the help of the local authority and one of her sisters, Devota traveled from Nyamata to Kigali,
sustained by the hope that she would finally receive help.

King Faisal Hospital, a large modern building on the east side of
Kigali, built by the Saudi government, had been completed a year
before the genocide. It had been one of the best-equipped hospitals
in Africa. But many of the nation's doctors were Tutsi, and they
had either fled or been killed. In July of 1994, there were only four
doctors working: two international volunteers from Doctors Without
Borders, and two local doctors. The only power the hospital had at

that time came from generators that had to be shut off during the day, and could only run for four hours in the evening.

The hospital was treating around four hundred patients a day, nearly twice its capacity, and sometimes held as many as two thousand patients. Maimed children, dying women, and the putrid smell of rotting flesh filled the hallways. In one locked ward were those wounded who the RPF had identified as having participated in the massacres; they were being kept alive to face trial. The doctors had to contend with machete wounds, limbs blown off by land mines, bullet wounds, malaria, tuberculosis, and cholera.

In August, when Devota arrived, a contingent of Australian doctors from Doctors Without Borders had just arrived to provide urgently needed relief. It was one of these volunteers who examined Devota. Her wounds had gone far too long without proper treatment, and they were deep and pervasive. The young doctor shook his head and said, "There's nothing we can do to help you." The young man saw Devota's countenance fall, and she began to cry. Moved by her tears and her condition, he responded with a word of faith, "The God who helped you to survive—he is the same God who will help you now."

Although Devota had truly seen a miraculous intervention, the doctor's words crushed her. Without her children, without the use of her body, she started to pray, not to survive, but to leave this world. But God responded to Devota. From somewhere deep in her spirit, she felt God saying to her, "You have something left to do. You have a mission here." That was a message Devota wasn't yet ready to hear. Inside, she was arguing with God, saying, "But I don't have anything; I'm helpless."

Returning back to Nyamata to live with some relatives, Devota struggled to accept her own survival.

ALTHOUGH THE DOCTOR HAD TOLD DEVOTA THERE WAS NOTHING HE could do for her, slowly she did begin to heal. A year after the genocide, although the skin around the back of her neck sagged loosely and bore deep scars, she did regain her full range of motion. And although the scars on her back and legs would always tell a story, she began to walk and move again.

But while her body was healing, her heart was not. It wasn't until 1996, when Devota received an invitation to attend a three-day workshop sponsored by African Evangelistic Enterprises, that the process of binding the wounds of her heart began. The seminar was being led by a Welsh psychiatrist by the name of Dr. Rhiannon Lloyd.

Before beginning, Dr. Lloyd explained to them something of her own background with ethnic divisions; as a Welsh child, she had been brought up to hate the English for their mistreatment of her people in the past. "I come from a nation where two tribes have hurt each other," she said. "One day I was in a prayer meeting when an English Christian knelt at my feet. 'We have often made the Welsh our servants,' she said. 'Please forgive us.' And she proceeded to wash my feet. A deep healing took place in my heart that day because of the humility of one person who chose to identify with the sins of her people against my people."

Then, although the doctor could not in any official way represent the West, she turned to those present and asked forgiveness on behalf of the Belgian people who had such a long history of oppression in Rwanda, and on behalf of the West who had abandoned moderate Hutu and Tutsi Rwandans in their hour of greatest need.

By that point, the doctor had Devota's full attention, along with that of every other person in the room. But when she asked, "Where was God in April 1994?" Devota was riveted. Hardly a day went by that she didn't struggle with that question, so to hear someone say it out loud was a great relief. As the group discussed the question, they looked back at the story of Adam and Eve in the garden, and how God had not created robots, but had given humans the freedom to choose. As a result of Adam and Eve's sinful choices, all kinds of suffering and evil had entered the world.

But then they read in the Bible about God's grief when people turned from his ways and did evil. They saw how in the days of Noah, the wickedness of humankind had grieved God. They read of when Jesus Christ walked the earth and saw the wickedness of Jerusalem and how he had cried out, longing to gather them into his arms, but they had not been willing to change. These ideas eased Devota's mind, but it was the next words that brought her what she would call her "deliverance."

Dr. Lloyd read a passage from Isaiah, which said: "Surely he took up our infirmities and carried our sorrows" (53:4). Christians believe that this passage looks forward to what Jesus would accomplish on the cross, and Dr. Lloyd was pointing out something that Devota had never seen before. Not only had Jesus come to bear people's sins, he had also come to bear people's pain.

Dr. Lloyd explained to them, "It's not only our sins that are on the cross, but all the consequences of sin. The whole tragic human condition is there. Jesus invites us to offload our grief onto him, saying, 'Let me do the hurting instead of you.'"

To make the transfer of pain to Jesus more tangible, Dr. Lloyd encouraged every participant in the room to use a piece of paper to write down the worst experiences that they had had. They wrote key words on their papers, and then they were invited to get in small groups. With Tutsi as well as Hutu in the room, they listened to each other's experiences of pain. As they did, they began to feel compassion in their hearts for the pain of others.

Finally, Dr. Lloyd asked the group, "What does God feel about this?" At that point, she did something very unusual. She brought a big wooden cross into the room. She then gave Devota and the other participants nails. One at a time, as they were ready, they stepped forward and nailed their particular pains and sorrows to the cross of Christ.

For Devota, her life seemed to pivot on that moment. The weight of her grief and sorrow had been so great that in the months leading up to the workshop, she had been asking one question again and again: "Who can possibly carry such sorrow?" For her it was more lament than question. That day, though, she learned the answer. Jesus Christ was not only able to carry the full weight of human sorrow, but he was inviting her to lay her sorrows on him.

As these realizations came to Devota, all she could do was cry out, as if her pain was being relieved right then and there. When it was her turn, she took that piece of paper with the horrible deaths of her children, with the mutilation of her own body, with the loss of her dreams, her livelihood, and her home, and nailed it to the cross.

AFTER THE SEMINAR, IT BECAME CLEAR TO DEVOTA THAT THOUGH she had been praying to God to take her from the world, he had offered instead to carry her grief and her sorrow rather than carry her from the world. At that point, she began to understand the mission God had given her to share God's invitation with those who had killed her family and others like them.

She traveled to the headquarters of African Evangelistic Enterprises and trained as a reconciliation leader, and soon she was going with a small team into prisons around Rwanda to share her testimony, along with the news of God's forgiveness for those who would ask for it.

One day, after she had shared her story of survival, healing, and deliverance at a prison in Kyuma, a man stood up. She did not recognize him. But he confessed that he had been in the group of people who had cut her in the valley, and he asked for her forgiveness.

At first, she felt both frightened and ashamed. She had already taken her seat again after giving her testimony, and so she sat still and quiet for some minutes. But then, God reminded her of everything that had happened to her, and particularly of his words to her that he had given her a mission. As these things dawned on her, she stood up and told the man, "I am ready to forgive you."

The man began to cry. And Devota understood that God had been preparing her for that very moment, preparing her heart to forgive.

Devota continued to go with the group from AEE into various prisons across Rwanda. The experience of being asked for forgiveness would repeat itself, time and again, perhaps because the killers had worked in groups, or perhaps because they had come over a period of days to the same marshy area to hunt and kill. Each time, Devota would extend forgiveness.

Like Dr. Lloyd, Devota also acted as a proxy for other survivors. One day, she saw a group of prisoners on work release rebuilding a fence. Moved, she approached them and said, "I am a survivor. I want you to know that many of us are ready and willing to forgive. We are just waiting for you to confess and show us that you are truly sorry."

Several of the men began to cry. One asked, "How can this be, when we behaved like such animals?" Another asked, "Who are these people?" And still others just reached out to touch her hand as if an angel or a saint had stepped in to walk among them, saying, "Thank you, thank you. God is merciful."

A FEW YEARS AFTER THE GENOCIDE, DEVOTA CAME ACROSS A GROUP of six orphans living by themselves in a very small home. They were brothers and sisters and had lost both parents after the genocide. The oldest child, barely a teenager, was doing her best to care for the others. Although Devota did not have much money, she felt burdened to take in the children. Since she couldn't afford to take them all in, she went to two local pastors and asked if they would each be willing to take two children. They agreed. And so Devota took the two youngest of them in to live with her: Odette and Anamarie.

At the time she adopted them, Odette was just one and Anamarie was four. Like the angel in her dream, she stooped down and led Odette, teaching her to walk and picking her up each time she faltered. She took the children into her home and loved them as her own. But one thing she never asked them, nor ever cared to know, was whether they were Tutsi or Hutu. For Devota, they were her children and she was their mother, and that was all that mattered.

comfort my people

With the gift of listening comes the gift of healing,
because listening to your brothers or sisters until they
have said the last words in their hearts is healing and consoling.
Someone has said that it is possible
"to listen a person's soul into existence." I like that.
Catherine de Hueck Doherty

RUHUMULIZA WAS NOT HIS GIVEN NAME, NOT IN THE TRADITIONAL way. It was the name Rwandans gave John after spending a year and a half in Rwanda during the late 1990s as World Vision's manager of reconciliation and peace building.

John quickly found that nothing in his life had prepared him for this role. The native Australian and his wife arrived in Rwanda just as one and a half million Hutu refugees were swarming home to their country after being forced out of exile in the Congo. At the same time, moderate Hutu and Tutsi who had been exiled before the war also came flooding back, in many cases occupying the empty homes the Hutu had abandoned when they fled the country in 1994. In a country the size of

Maryland, millions of survivors, perpetrators, collaborators, and victims were on a collision course.

The other staff welcomed John warmly, but he caught the look in their eyes: "I'm glad I don't have your job. Best of luck, pal."

Wisely, John decided on a course of action that didn't include much action — at least not action as we typically consider it. He spent the first three months of his time in Rwanda simply listening to the painful stories of the people who visited him — staff, church leaders, youth, and prison workers. Before he had left Australia, he had read somewhere that listening is the greatest form of loving. It became the theme of his time in Rwanda. In a place where everyone has a story of horror to tell, people become so accustomed to it that few stop to ask or listen to the pain of someone else.

What John heard shook him to the core. From the woman who shook a bag of bones saying, "If I buried the bones of my parents, I'd be totally alone, wouldn't I?" to the man who said, "Every day I see the man who killed my wife, and his daughters wear the dresses which belonged to my daughters, whom he also killed." John had to learn to end his days by bringing the pain he had heard that day and placing it before God, who alone could comfort him.

Finally, after months of listening, John was ready to take the next step. They began to help people bring "their pain out into the open and grieve their losses" so that their wounds could begin to heal. They followed the words of Lincoln Ndogoni, a Kenyan psychologist, who said, "Everyone has a story to tell, a pain to bear, a grief to heal."

John had heard about a healing workshop, called the Personal Development Workshop (PDW), designed by a Dr. Gasibirege, a psychologist who, having lived in exile in Europe for over thirty years, had befriended Holocaust survivors who had experienced considerable measures of healing. The PDW consisted of five sessions, each one month apart, initially led by Dr. Gasibirege himself. On the first day of the first month, the participants—who came from all groups of Rwandans and all walks of life—committed to a process based on trust as they sought to better understand Rwanda's history. One month later they reconvened for three days, during which they shared their losses and grieved, particularly over departed family members. In the third month, they came together to confront a particularly unhealthy cultural way of thinking in Rwanda. As the Rwandan saying goes, "The tears of a man flow down the inside to his stomach." The point of the proverb is that emotions are private and better when suppressed, so the third session focused on valuing emotions and exploring feelings.

Not until three months had passed and trust was well established did the workshop turn to topics of forgiveness. By that time, people had exposed their grief in small groups where trust and compassion had been fostered. A month later, the participants returned for one final time to celebrate and share how the experience had changed them.[1]

When John's Rwandan work visa expired, he had to return home, but the workshops continued to spread across the country as Rwandans themselves took ownership of the healing process. Before John left, his Rwandan friends gave him a Rwandan name to express their gratitude and friendship. It was Ruhumuliza, which means "comforter." Today, John returns to Rwanda every six months to continue to nurture the relationships he began there and to encourage the healing process as he can.[2]

While few of us will face conditions as extreme as John's, many of us may find ourselves in situations where we too can play some role in facilitating the healing and forgiveness process of another. John's experience has several key lessons for all of us.

If a friend has recently experienced trauma or crime, one of the most important things we can do is to help that person feel safe. When it is true, it is helpful to say words like, "You are safe now."[3] If they are not safe, you can at least keep them informed about the extent of the existing threat.

You can also help with immediate physical needs. Be available to help with transportation, phone calls, a safe place to sleep, clothes, blankets, food, and the tasks of immediate decision making, since decision-making skills will be impaired in the immediate aftermath of a traumatic event. In some cases, a traumatized person may initially be more concerned about the safety of a child, spouse, or older family member. Caring for the immediate needs of others may be a way of caring for the victim.

If more time has passed since the event, understanding the symptoms of post-traumatic stress disorder (such as depression, isolation, rage, numbness to feelings, survival guilt, anxiety reactions, intrusive thoughts, or flashbacks) can also help us to know when to encourage that person to seek professional help.

Workers with the Red Cross—who frequently encounter people recently traumatized—talk about offering "the gift of presence," or simply being there.

Grief victims as well as trauma victims will benefit from what John discovered as the gift of listening. Allowing victims space to ventilate their emotions and thoughts is important, as well as validating their feelings of anger, grief, frustration, and insecurity.[4] Try to avoid saying, "I understand." Active listening skills such as maintaining eye contact, nodding, summarizing, clarifying, and allowing silence help the other feel valued.

Encouraging victims to tell their stories is also helpful. The process may not be as straightforward as it sounds, however:

Victims need to tell their story over and over again. The repetitive process is a way of putting the pieces together and cognitively organizing the event so that it can be integrated into the survivor's life. Their first memory of the event is likely to be narrowly focused on, say, a particular sensory perception or a particular activity that occurred during the event ... As time goes by, memory will reveal other parts of the event. These bits of memory will come back in dreams, intrusive thoughts, and simply during the storytelling process. The victimization story will probably change over time as they learn new things and use the new information to reorganize their memories ... It is perfectly normal for the process of ventilation to reveal a more complete story over time ... [which] helps them get control of the real story. The "real" story is not only the recitation of the event itself, but usually includes the story of various incidents in the immediate aftermath; the story of ongoing traumatic incidents related to the crime; the story of families' or friends' involvement in the event; and so forth. Each of these stories must be integrated into the victim's final mental recording of the event.[5]

For those who have lost a loved one, especially suddenly, the process of learning to tell their story of loss will be similar in many regards. Learning to talk about the loss and its effects helps in coming to terms with the emotions.

Since forgiveness begins with the process of recalling the hurt, and grieving the loss,[6] one of the greatest gifts a person can give to someone struggling toward forgiveness is to play the part of an active nonjudgmental listener. Helping them to face the offense and acknowledge the depth of the hurt is a first step. If a person is uncomfortable talking about the grief and hurt, they could also try writing a letter to someone who has hurt them and expressing the range of their feelings within it. The letter isn't for sending, but rather for facing their emotions.[7] Writing a journal entry as if your heart "had a voice" can also help put words to the feelings.[8]

In the Rwandan healing workshops, as Tutsi share their grief they are also exposed to the grief of other Hutu who may be offenders or who may simply have had association with the offenders. In many cases, empathy develops, or at least a recognition of the shared humanity of the other.

If you are helping another reach toward forgiveness or if you are working toward it yourself, it can be important to create similar opportunities for developing empathy. Throughout the United States and around the world, victim-offender dialogue groups can do just that. In some cases, it may be possible to talk to the person responsible for the crime, but in other cases simply hearing the stories of other victims and of offenders can help in the process of creating empathy.

But there are also less intense ways to facilitate empathy which apply to contexts beyond the scope of criminal or traumatic events. David Augsburger, a professor of pastoral care at Fuller Theological Seminary, suggests a process of guided visualization. In each of the four visualization exercises the intensity increases as does the difficulty in extending empathy:

1. Visualize a dear friend who through some blind choice has hurt another deeply. Think of listening until the story has been fully, freely told. Think of caring until the other feels cared for in spite of the wrongdoing done. Think of inviting the other to make a fresh start.

2. Visualize a dear friend who through some blind choice has hurt *you* deeply. Think of suspending your anger for a while seeking to understand the other's motives, choices,

actions from within. Think of setting yourself beside the other and helping him or her to make a new beginning.

3. Visualize an enemy, who through some malice has injured someone you love. Think of bracketing your anger for a period and choosing to hear what the enemy hears, see what he sees, feel what she feels, and make some degree of sense from within. Think of offering compassion for the other's confusion, distortion, or failure.

4. Visualize an enemy who through the worst of motives has injured you. Do not think of yourself reaching out as a friend; no, instead, visualize God as the most patient of friends, the most understanding of listeners, the most caring conversationalist before whom no evasion is possible or necessary, who, knowing the worst, yet takes a position firmly by the side of the enemy and invites a new beginning.[9]

Augsburg's techniques provide a powerful, growing level of empathy. Like a bodybuilder gradually increasing the weight, these increasingly difficult mental exercises can help build our empathetic stamina.

Writing a journal entry or letter from the point of view of the wrongdoer can also create empathy. Asking someone else for forgiveness for an unrelated situation can also help create immediate empathy for what it is like to be the wrongdoer.

It is unhelpful and unwise to make someone feel guilty about not being able to forgive. Forgiveness, especially of deep wrongs, is a long and difficult process. But we can help others who want to make this journey by traveling the road with them, being willing to listen, comfort, coach, and carry the burdens of another. In doing so, like John, we can come to carry the name Ruhumuliza, or comforter.

Questions for Reflection and Discussion

Which of the techniques for facing pain or creating empathy
appeal most to you? Which do not? Why? Try one of those that
you find intriguing.

John Steward states, "Healed people help others heal." From
what difficult circumstances have you successfully healed?
How could you use that experience to help others find healing?

Why is it so potentially damaging to make others feel guilty
about not being able to forgive? How can you help facilitate
healing and forgiveness rather than demand it?

bridges

Courage is not simply one of the virtues,
but the form of every virtue at the testing point.
C. S. Lewis

PHANUEL STUCK TO THE SHOULDER OF THE ROAD. THE NEVER-ENDING rise and fall of the hills made his legs ache, but he didn't mind—he was nearing home. If his legs hadn't told him, his other senses would have. The contours of these hills were as familiar to him as a beloved face. The undulating road, the luxuriant greens of the tea hills, the Iwuwa trees with their bright yellow flowers, and, of course, the river below, racing him homeward—these had all become more dear to him since he had been away at school. The road descended and each step raised a puff of red dust. As Phanuel reached the base of the descent, a weathered wood met his weary feet.

Phanuel recalled how as a child, he would bring his father's cows near this bridge sometimes. He would graze the cattle nearby just so he could watch and see how the water flowed. Phanuel watched it flowing now, seemingly as eager and restless as he was.

Growing up in the village of Giheke, near the town of Kamembe in the western province of Rwanda, Phanuel had become accustomed to bridges. He was surrounded by rivers—the Kirimbi, the

Mwogo, and the Ruzizi—and Lake Kivu, a body of water almost mythical in its beauty. Rivers marked boundary lines between countries, they were symbols of pride, and they were connections to life in seasons of drought. The bridges that spanned them were overlooked, and beautiful, necessities.

As he crossed, a loose plank conjured a scene in Phanuel's imagination. He was just five when the rains had washed the bridge away one year. If he closed his eyes, he could still feel his father's firm grip around his wrist as he helped him cross and the racing fear that the powerful current had sent through him.

As Phanuel reached the other side of the bridge and neared home, late that March of 1994, he had little notion how swiftly currents would carry his countrymen into violence and how soon he himself would be called upon to be trampled underfoot like a bridge.

The road rose again. Phanuel picked up his pace, beads of sweat forming on his brow. As he crested the next rise, he could see his father's farm stretching out before him. The dark green coffee plants were adorned with beans as red, and almost as valuable, as shimmering rubies. He scanned the fields, looking for his mother. He soon spotted her bright yellow headscarf and followed the color to the line of her back, bent over one of the waist-high bushes. She was presently twisting one of the red rubies into her hand. As she reached to deposit it in the satchel on her hip, Phanuel called out and waved. His mother straightened and waved back, smiling. When she stood, he suddenly saw Adeline, Theogene, and Jonathan straighten up as well.

Phanuel wove between the bushes in the direction of his mother as eleven-year-old Jonathan and thirteen-year-old Theogene raced toward him. Theogene tackled him a moment before Jonathan. Meanwhile, his mother stood, one hand shielding the sun from her eyes. As he approached, brothers trailing behind him, she shook her head in disbelief.

"Each time I see you, you are more man and less boy," she said with a smile.

Phanuel smiled and stretched out his arms to embrace her. He kissed her on the cheek. Her skin was hot with sun and work's exertion. He stooped to hug his sister, Adeline. "I'm not the only one growing up," he said as he looked at his youngest sister, thirteen going on twenty. "And Goretti and Flavien, have they arrived yet?"

"Not yet," said his mother as she turned back to the bushes. "I expect them before Sunday. They won't miss Easter."

Phanuel set his bag down and took a spot beside his mom, his siblings also turning back to the work in front of them. "And Father?"

"He's still at the school, closing things up for the holiday."

"The beans have ripened quickly this year."

"Just in time for your help." His mother smiled, putting another handful into her satchel.

Phanuel emptied a handful of ripened beans into his mother's bag. "Naturally," he said, "I wouldn't miss the harvest."

It was a little more than a week later, when the coffee plants had been almost completely harvested, and Easter Sunday had come and gone, that Phanuel's family of eight was lingering over a late dinner and the joy of being together again. The Africa Cup of Nations had been playing quietly in the background over the radio, but suddenly a voice interrupted the game. "At 8:25 this evening, a plane carrying President Juvenal Habyarimana and the Burundian president was shot down. They, the Tutsi, the rebels, have killed our beloved president."

His mother's eyes bulged. His father's forehead drew in at the brow and his sister began to cry, not knowing what it all meant. Phanuel's father, Faustin, although a prominent Hutu schoolteacher, had never had much of a stomach for politics. He generally kept his thoughts to himself. This time he did not. "God help us," he said, standing to his feet. "God help us."

IN A VILLAGE MANY MILES FROM PHANUEL, PRISCA, A GIRL ABOUT HIS age, also read her father's face. She knew the creases that had formed over his brow in the past few years as he worried about the cattle and the crops. She knew how his eyes gleamed when he had a special present for her, like the framed picture of Christ he had given her on her confirmation day. She knew the way he held his jaw when he was determined to get something done, like the time he had broken his shovel trying to remove a tree stump from the planting field. But she had never seen him look like this. His eyes shifted nervously and he looked from Prisca to her siblings to her mother.

"I don't want you to leave the house. Don't go to feed the cattle. Don't go to market. Don't go to cultivate." He paused, looking at each of them in turn, and then said deliberately, "I want you to understand. We no longer belong to this country."

"Can't we just flee to the church as we did years ago?" asked Prisca, whose naiveté afforded her courage that her father's experience denied him. Prisca had only recently come home from where she boarded at the secondary school. At the moment, she was more disappointed that this disruption would ruin her Easter holiday than she was afraid.

"No, even in the church they can find us," her father continued. "It would be better to go and hide at our relatives' house than at the church." He searched their eyes for some sign that they comprehended what was happening. Not seeing it, he spoke again, this time his voice dropping to a near whisper, "I don't think you yet understand. This is the end of the Tutsi." It was the seventh of April, and his family's peace had been shattered the night before when President Habyarimana's plane was destroyed. Prisca had not yet grasped that this was to be different than the unrest they'd experienced in the past. Her father, however, had a sense, and it had changed the face she loved to one that suddenly sent a chill through her.

By Sunday, Prisca had begun to wonder if her father was overreacting. After all, apart from people not going to the market as they usually did, she had seen very little change in their little village in the Kamonyi District. They had hardly left the house in three days, but on Sunday, the family dressed as usual and left for Mass. The crowd was smaller than normal at the cathedral, and before the service adults seemed to form small huddles where they whispered about the latest news they had heard. But otherwise things seemed much as Prisca remembered them. Her mind drifted more than usual during the service. She wondered whose house they would go to and wondered whether her cousins would be there too. She was presently wondering if all this would pass before it was time to return back to school to finish the semester, when suddenly she felt her sister's elbow in her side. She realized that the congregation was praying, and her lips moved to join in reciting the familiar words.

"And forgive us our trespasses as we forgive those who trespass against us. And lead us not into temptation, but deliver us from evil. For thine is the kingdom and the power and the glory forever and ever. Amen."

When the service was over, Prisca and her family headed for home, but almost as soon as they walked out the door they could sense something had changed. People moved about frantically. Some were carrying their possessions. Others were helping the old and the infirm to walk. In the distance, she could see smoke rising. Prisca saw her father quicken his pace, and she stepped more quickly to keep up.

When they reached their home, the door was standing wide open. Her father told them to wait. Stepping softly, he moved up to the side of the house and listened. After a few moments, when there was still no noise, he stepped through the open door. Finally, he returned. Again, she didn't recognize this look on her father's face. The light had drained from his eyes and his shoulders hunched. Her father had never looked so small.

"Gather what food and clothing you can find and let's leave quickly. Hurry!" he said.

The children stepped carefully over shattered clay pots as they walked into their home. What furniture they had—a few chairs, a table, and a bench—was turned over. The radio was gone, as was a large bag of rice and a bag of seed. The children grabbed a few articles of clothing, while their mother lugged a canvas bag of rice from a storeroom behind the house. Prisca's eyes followed her father as he walked to the framed picture of the crucified Christ that he had given her. He took it from the wall. She wondered if he were going to take it with them. Then she noticed behind the picture was a gap in the bricks. Her father reached in and grabbed a wad of francs. Stuffing it deep into his pocket, he turned and said, "We'll head back to the church and stay there until it is safe to travel to your aunt Esperance's house. Grab your things. We need to get a move on."

PHANUEL PACED THE ROOM. SINCE THE NEWS OF THE PRESIDENT'S assassination, his heart had felt weighed down, as if it were a satchel full of stones. He had a strong sense that whatever the evil was that had been unleashed two days ago, it would not be tamed easily. The way the announcers on the radio had spoken sent waves of fear through him. Having grown up in a Christian home, Phanuel had learned from his parents to love everyone. Never once could he remember a time when they had encouraged him to treat a Tutsi any differently. Mostly, they had ignored the political wrangling of the past few years, and focused on the things closer to hand, like the school where his father taught and the farm that was their livelihood. But now it seemed they couldn't avoid the conflict.

Phanuel stopped midstride. A strong pounding interrupted the steady monotony of the rain on the metal roof. It was coming from the front door. His pulse quickened. He moved cautiously out of his room to get a better look as his father walked to the front door. It had been two days since the radio's news had shattered the tranquility of their Easter holidays, and they had yet to have any visitors. Phanuel feared the worst—that perhaps there were men coming even now to pressure them into joining the hunt for the Tutsi. Phanuel tried to stay out of the line of sight as his father opened the door.

He felt a rush of moist air and could see a figure, a blanket wrapped over his head to shield from the rain, standing at the front door. His father hurried the covered figure in out of the rain and after looking carefully outside shut the door. The blanket fell to the ground and Phanuel saw Joel, his cousin, standing there, his eyes wide and frantic. In moments, Phanuel and his siblings had rushed to embrace him. Joel was exactly the same age as Phanuel, just seventeen, but because his mother had married a Tutsi, he was considered Tutsi also.

"Are you okay?" asked Phanuel's father.

"I—I think so," replied the boy, half sure of himself. "You would not believe what is happening out there. I barely made it here."

"Do you think anyone saw you?"

"If they'd seen me, they would have killed me. I have no doubt."

THE CHURCH WHERE PRISCA AND HER FAMILY FLED WENT FROM overcrowded to unbearable as people flooded in from Kigali and the Bugesera District. Word had traveled quickly that the chief of their sector, a man by the name of Caliste Ndagijimana, had put a line of Hutu soldiers at the perimeter of the church to protect the Tutsi hiding inside. As the killing spread from one end of Rwanda to the other, word of this leader's rare courage provided an example for others to do what they could to protect their neighbors. It also stirred some feeble embers of hope for the Tutsi who had gathered inside.

But soon the fire was quenched. The other chiefs grumbled,

"Why is it that this man should not kill?" His name was broadcast over the radio, and soon he had joined the list of targets. Nearly a week after Prisca's family had fled to the church, the chief was assassinated by the Interahamwe. The killers soon outnumbered the Hutu who had been protecting the church's perimeter. When that happened, the soldiers' ranks broke, some fleeing while others joined the killers' ranks.

Then the killers shut off the water supply to the church. Inside the church, the refugees barricaded the doors of the church and waited for the worst. The next morning the attackers returned with grenades. They worked systematically. In a few hours' time, they had gained entry. The killers targeted the men to insure that the strongest and the most able were the first to fall. The killers took them outside, forced them to lie down in the grass, and there they moved among them like farmers moving among their crops at harvest time, swinging blades left then right — but without the quick rhythm of the fields. This was a slower harvest. Around four, as the sun was already beginning to fall from the sky, the killers wiped blood-soaked blades on blood-soaked clothes and left.

A handful of militiamen stayed behind to stand watch.

Near midnight, Prisca and a few other children slipped past the militia into the hills. Prisca knew that her aunt's husband was Hutu, and that perhaps they would be safe if she could reach her. But she also knew that Calgui, where her aunt lived, was not close to the church. For three days, she hid in the bush. She could hear the killers as they moved through the bush and knew that if she so much as coughed, she would be dead. At night, Prisca would navigate the darkness, moving as fast as she dared in the direction of her aunt's home.

By no small miracle, Prisca managed to make it to her aunt's home safely. Within three more days, two of her brothers and a sister, who had also managed to escape in the night, made their way by different paths to the same place.

Hiding in a back bedroom, the siblings did what they could to comfort and reassure one another that everything would be okay. Having been separated from her mother in the confusion at the church, and having already lost her father, Prisca tried her best to keep her thoughts from wandering back to the church where her father had been killed and where as far as she knew her mother was still hiding. But each time such thoughts slipped past her, she felt a wave of nausea and helplessness wash over her. She bit her bottom lip to hold back the tears. She knew that if they hoped to survive, she had to be strong.

Almost a week and a half had passed when Prisca heard the sound of men outside the door. It was early morning and her uncle had gone to get water, a chore usually reserved for children and women, but that had fallen on him during these days of war. So it was that Esperance was alone when three Hutu men came to the door.

"Open up," one man shouted. "We know that you are hiding Tutsi inside."

Esperance hesitated, inhaled deeply, and moved to open the door.

She recognized two of the three men who stood before her. The man she didn't know was the one who spoke. "We know that you are hiding Tutsi inside," he repeated. Esperance knew better than to try to argue. If there was any argument that might convince them to leave, it was their own selfishness. Reaching into her pocket, she pulled out a tight wad of cash, counted out everything that was there, and gave it to the men. "Please," she said as she pressed the bills into the hand of the man she knew best.

WITHIN TWENTY-FOUR HOURS OF JOEL'S ARRIVAL, PHANUEL'S COUSIN Twagirayezu knocked on their door. Just one year Phanuel's senior, Twagirayezu had also been home from school on holiday when his neighbors busted down their gate and killed most of his family. Twagirayezu survived, but had traveled for days to reach his uncle's home, a place where he hoped to find safety. Phanuel's father had not disappointed Joel or Twagirayezu, hiding them in a back bedroom with Phanuel and his brothers.

Almost a week had passed since then with no other visitors. In the meantime, they had hardly stirred from their home. If they needed to use the bathroom, they waited until nightfall to venture outside. All of the children remained indoors and—for the most part—hidden in the back bedroom.

Early on the morning of April 17, the family had come together—as had become their habit in those days—to pray. Phanuel's father, Faustin, led them as they all crowded into the back room. Phanuel tried to pray silently as his father prayed aloud, but it was difficult. He had grown up learning the truths of the Christian faith, but now, like never before, that faith was being tested. Phanuel struggled to concentrate. Questions seemed to pound in his brain. Memories of his aunt and uncle and cousins, Twagirayezu's family, filled his mind. He struggled to understand where God was in the midst of their pain.

Just then, he heard the sound of men's voices as they approached the house. Faustin raised his bowed head and listened. He looked to his wife, then to Joel, and Twagirayezu. He didn't have to say a word. His look was clear: stay still, be quiet, your life depends on it.

Faustin rose, his hands reaching up to his eyes and cheeks as if to smooth the fear from his face. All the eyes in the room followed him as he walked to the door of the room and carefully closed it behind him.

Phanuel could feel his heart beating wildly in his chest. When he heard the knock at the door, his whole body tensed in fear. Closed into the back room, they could see nothing. In the minutes that followed, he could hear the rise and fall of voices, but couldn't hear the words being spoken. Phanuel cast a cautious look at his cousins, Joel and Twagirayezu—as the only Tutsi in the room, the danger was far greater for them. In that moment, he also knew that he would lay down his life to protect them if he had to.

With nothing else he could do, Phanuel mustered all his energy to pray. He couldn't form a complete thought, with the fear and the physical sickness he felt at the idea of anything happening to his family. But in his spirit he groaned for God to protect, for God to spare. As the moments dragged on, Phanuel strained to hear his father's voice. He could feel the sweat trickling down his back. He looked up at his mother; she had her hands clasped in front of her, her face taut with the fear that pulsed through them all.

The next thing Phanuel knew, the sound of the men's voices passed by the window and then grew fainter. Still, every muscle in him tensed, like a runner waiting for signal to spring into action. Several more minutes passed before the door opened revealing his father. "They've gone," he whispered. Phanuel did not know what his father had told the killers to satisfy them—all he knew was God had spared them.

THE MONEY KEPT THE KILLERS AWAY FROM ESPERANCE'S HOUSE FOR only one week. When they returned, they could no longer be bribed. The men were adamant. The Tutsi children that Esperance was hiding must die. They dragged Prisca, her younger sister, Liliane, and two brothers, Felix and Aimable, from the house while Esperance pleaded and invoked the name of her Hutu husband, Alfonz, as a reason that the children ought to be protected. The killers insisted that Prisca's brothers were old enough to join the RPF and therefore must be killed, and that Prisca, a secondary student, was old enough to have already been indoctrinated by the rebels. At last, Esperance managed to persuade them that Liliane, Prisca's younger sister, was no threat. As they dragged Prisca and her brothers to a place where they were gathering other Tutsi to be slaughtered, Prisca could see Liliane peeking out from behind her aunt's skirt, eyes full of tears.

By the time they reached the area where they were holding the other condemned Tutsi, night was already falling. The men led the other captives, whose hands were bound, out into the open and told them to lie down in the grass. But the killers had not bothered to tie Prisca and her siblings since they had marched the teens with machetes to their backs. Seizing the opportunity, Prisca's brother, Aimable, sprinted from his position in the grass into the bush. Darkness gave him the advantage, and as the killers dispersed to look for him, Prisca and her other brother ran as fast as they could in the opposite direction. As Prisca and Felix ran, they could hear Aimable's cry in the distance—her brother's choice to run spared the lives of Prisca and Felix.

Prisca could feel her eyes burning with tears as she ran with Felix deeper into the hills. She tried to concentrate on breathing and on the thud of her feet against the ground. Not knowing where else to turn, they ran for their aunt Esperance's home, hoping against hope that she could help them.

Esperance had not yet gone to sleep when she heard the knock at the door. She feared the killers had come again for Liliane. But when Esperance saw the children at her door, she stepped back as if the ghosts of her brother's children had come back from the dead to haunt her dreams. But the children's loud breathing recalled her to reality. Still panting, and choking back tears, Prisca explained how they had managed to escape and how Aimable had not.

Esperance knew well that when morning came the killers would be back again to see if the children were there, and this time they certainly wouldn't spare them. She had to get Prisca, Felix, and Liliane to a safer place. She called her son, Kwisone, who was currently in Kigali. He could be there in two to three hours, if all went well.

Kwisone Dehoneste was old enough to have a license, and was therefore old enough to be his cousins' salvation. And even though

Dehoneste's mother, Esperance, was a Tutsi, in Rwandan culture, blood flows from father's, not mother's veins. Dehoneste's identity card, not his mother, would be all that mattered traveling late at night across back roads.

In the early hours of the morning, Esperance kissed her son goodbye, knowing full well that the mission she was sending him on could cost him his life. If Dehoneste was afraid, his face didn't show it as he took the wheel of the four-by-four. Prisca, Felix, and Liliane lay on the back bed of the truck. Esperance and Dehoneste gathered up bags of fertilizer to put on top of them for cover. The smell was overwhelming, but the stench might prevent a careful search.

The rain had created deep potholes in the roads, and the truck lurched and jostled them painfully as it made its way on the country roads. Having just come from Kigali, Dehoneste knew where the biggest roadblock was and avoided it by driving cross-country with only his dimmers. If they were seen in the fields and the car was surrounded, it would mean certain death.

Almost an hour passed before Dehoneste reached the church in Gitarama where they thought they would find a refuge for the children. As the car approached, he could see fires lit on the ground outside it. Militia were sprawled about, some sleeping, some drinking. Anticipating the worst, Dehoneste didn't slow the car down, but kept driving on past. His mind raced through alternatives. Finally, he decided the safest place would be to take the children back to the Kamonyi District, near the children's home. He had heard rumors that the RPF had already begun to move into that territory around May 30. Perhaps if he could get them close enough to the RPF camp they might survive.

Two hours had never passed so slowly for Dehoneste and the children as they continued to skirt roadblocks and sentries. They were running out of darkness as they finally approached what looked like the RPF camp. In the distance, Dehoneste could see men in RPF uniforms holding rifles. He stopped the car about several hundred yards away. "I think we made it," he said, breathing for what felt like the first time in a hundred miles. "You'll have to walk it from here. I'm not sure if they'd trust a Hutu getting much closer than this."

Prisca kissed her cousin on the cheek as she grabbed Liliane by the hand. "Thank you," they echoed one after another as they climbed from the jeep. With Liliane between them, Prisca and Felix moved quickly in the direction of the soldiers. As they neared them they held their hands high in the air. Dehoneste turned the jeep around and drove away. As he did, he looked back, but the early morning sun reflected off the rearview mirror and he could only see light.

EIGHTY-NINE DAYS HAD PASSED SINCE PHANUEL AND HIS FAMILY heard the news of the president's assassination. Eighty-nine days of almost total confinement. Eighty-nine days of fear. Eighty-nine days of wrestling with God day and night in prayer. Eighty-nine days of not being able to tell the living world from a living hell.

The radio played quietly in the main living area as Phanuel and his family dozed or read. Although the authorities prohibited it, Phanuel's family had the radio tuned in to Radio Muhabura, the station run by the RPF from the National Park at the Rwanda–Uganda border. Phanuel put down the textbook he had been reading to listen as the radio announcers declared the RPF had taken control of Kigali, as well as Butare in the southern region. He shook his cousin Joel awake. "They've done it," he said. "They've pushed through. The war will be over soon."

Twagirayezu hugged Joel, who was just waking up, and Joel wondered if he were dreaming. "If this is a dream," he whispered, "I'm not going to try to wake from it."

"This isn't a dream, Cousin. The war will soon be over. You are safe."

you cry, I cry

Through compassion we also sense the hope of forgiveness in our friend's eyes and our hatred in their bitter mouths. When they kill, we know we could have done it; when they give life, we know we could do the same. For a compassionate man nothing human is alien.

Henri Nouwen

ALMOST EIGHT MONTHS HAD PASSED SINCE PRISCA AND HER SIBLINGS found refuge at the RPF camp. Life had hardly returned to normal, but life did have to go on, and so Prisca found herself jostling down the road in a van headed to a secondary school in Nyange—one of the few schools that was ready to accept students so soon after the end of the war. Not only was Prisca dreading being apart from her siblings and her mom, especially so soon after surviving such a horrendous ordeal, but she also feared the town of Nyange. The rumors of what had happened there in 1994 had spread far and wide.

Just as Prisca and her family had done, the Tutsi in Nyange had fled to the church for refuge when the genocide began. In fact, the local priest, Athanase Seromba, urged those who had come seeking refuge to let him know where there were others still "not in safety" so he could go and bid them to come. The mayor and the local police used the list to gather up other Tutsi in the surrounding area until almost two thousand huddled into the church. What happened next was more horrible than even Prisca—who had seen far too many horrors for her young age—could imagine. After depriving them of food for several days to weaken them, the mayor, the priest, and a number of killers drove a caterpillar bulldozer over the church, mercilessly slaughtering with machetes the few who survived. And after burying them in a mass grave, the priest, the mayor, the police inspector, and the killers shared congratulatory beers at a local cabaret.

The thought of this churned in Prisca's stomach, making her wish that the van would turn around. If the people in this city were capable of that kind of thing, she wondered to herself, what might happen at her school? The country had certainly stabilized significantly since July, but rebels still were crossing the border, making attacks. *Nyange*, Prisca thought, as she leaned her head against the window, *I wish I was going anywhere but there.*

PHANUEL LAY ON THE COT IN THE ROOM HE SHARED WITH SYLVESTE at the Nyange secondary school. His psychology textbook stood like a small tent on his chest; he crossed his arms behind his head, eyes wide open. In his mind, he was miles away. He couldn't help how his thoughts drifted back across the river, over the hills and coffee plantations, home to his family. With the frequent raids of militant Hutu across the border from the Congo, he feared constantly for the safety of his cousins and his family who were protecting them.

But the last year had added still more worries. One of his uncles had been arrested for participating in the genocide, and he faced the death penalty for his crimes. Phanuel tried to wrap his mind around the facts: his father's own brother, a murderer. Now with his uncle in prison, his cousin was also staying with Phanuel's parents. Orphans of genocide and a child of a genocidaire were living under the same roof, with the blood of the same grandparents running through their veins. His head ached as he tried to comprehend it.

Just then, Sylveste cracked open the door. "You asleep?"

"No," said Phanuel, realizing he must have closed his eyes for a moment. Sylveste opened the door and came in. Phanuel's eyes followed him as he sat down on the cot across from him. Sylveste had fast become one of Phanuel's best friends since arriving at the new secondary school. They were both in Senior Six, but Sylveste was one year older. He towered above Phanuel in height, though Phanuel guessed that, as skinny as Sylveste was, they were about the same weight.

"Let's go," said Sylveste, cocking his head toward the door.

"Now?"

"Why not now? Or would you rather stay here and study all weekend?" teased Sylveste, picking the book up off Phanuel's chest and dropping it on the bed.

"Alright," said Phanuel, swinging his legs off the bed and sitting up. He reached for his shoes. "But I do need to study sometime this weekend. We have that test next week. It's a big one, you know."

"It will still be here when we get back," said Sylveste as he grabbed a blanket from his bed, wrapped an extra shirt around a bunch of bananas, and tied the blanket around it. Phanuel tipped a yellow jerry can to fill his bottle of water and grabbed a blanket of his own and stuffed it into a satchel.

"Race you," said Sylveste without pausing to see if Phanuel agreed to the contest. Phanuel sprinted after him, but Sylveste already had a good lead on him. Phanuel concentrated on his stride, but even with a head start he'd never beat Sylveste. The boy had the legs of a gazelle. Between the thick trees around the school, and the steep terrain sloping down to the river, Phanuel had to use all his senses to avoid falling or running into something. He didn't see the men in uniform standing in a huddle as they passed into the wooded area on the other side of the schoolyard.

As Phanuel neared the river's edge, he found Sylveste doubled over with his hands resting on his bony knees.

"Beat you," Sylveste said with a smile.

"Next time," said Phanuel, wiping the sweat from his face and knowing very well that if they raced a thousand times, Sylveste would beat him every time.

For Sylveste, running was one of the few ways he'd found to escape from his thoughts after the genocide. Only when his heart thudded wildly and his lungs burned could he forget his parents' screams. Only when sweat stung his eyes and his mind navigated the maze of trees and hills did his eyes close on the looping reel of their final moments and the blood that pooled on the floor of their home in Kigali. If he could have run forever, he would have.

"The river's low," said Phanuel, stepping from one exposed rock to another.

"It won't be for long," responded Sylveste, still breathing heavily.

They fell into a contented silence as they made their way across the shallow water to the other side. As they reached the other side, the trees towered above them in a lush, green canopy. The way the light diffused through the branches reminded Phanuel of the soft yellows and greens of the light streaming through stained glass windows, while the stillness of the forest seemed to beckon them farther down the long aisles of trees. Soon they spread their blankets down on the ground.

Each boy lay contentedly on his own blanket, resting mind and body. They talked of girls in their class and who they thought was the prettiest. Phanuel maintained Seraphina was the clear victor. Before long the cool shade of the trees and the warmth of the afternoon was lulling Phanuel into an afternoon nap. He closed his eyes, enjoying one of the few remaining undefiled sanctuaries either of them had known.

Phanuel awoke in a sweat. He coughed. Thick smoke hovered above him. Eyes darting, Phanuel sat up trying to remember where he was. His heart slowed when he saw Sylveste bending over a fire he'd built. The canopy of leaves had been replaced by smoke and darkness, save for the light of the half moon.

"Wow, how long was I out?"

"A few hours," replied Sylveste, stoking the fire with a long branch.

"I guess the late nights studying are catching up to me."

"You're like an old man," needled Sylveste.

"You're the old one," retorted Phanuel good-naturedly.

"You mean the wise one." Sylveste peeled a banana and popped half of it in his mouth. Still chewing, he asked, "Have I ever told you the story my grandmother used to tell about the lion in the forest?"

"I don't think so," said Phanuel, sitting up.

"It's a good one. You might be old enough for it," he teased.

Phanuel smiled and shook his head. "Let's hear it then."

"Well, it all started when a cattleman got lost one night in the forest."

The room that Helena shared at the Nyange school with Prisca was dark except for the glint of moonlight through the window. Helena lay still, wondering about her father, arrested months earlier for crimes committed during the genocide. Did he have a cot to sleep on? And could it really be true? Could her own father have really done what they had accused him of doing? It haunted her. She turned over on her side, and as she did she heard Prisca. The quick breath—she knew the sound. She lay still. It came again. "You okay?" she asked finally.

Prisca didn't answer, but the sound of her crying became a bit louder. The nightmares had been coming more frequently recently.

Helena sat up. The concrete felt cool on her bare feet as she stepped across the room to Prisca's bed and sat down next to her. Helena paused a moment, then acted on impulse, stroking Prisca's head with one hand and laying her other hand on her shoulder. "It's alright," she cooed, her breath warm on Prisca's face.

Prisca's sobs came quicker. Helena searched her mind until it latched onto something she had recently memorized with the other Christian students who had begun gathering together for weekly prayer. "Who shall separate us from the love of Christ? Shall trouble or hardship or persecution or famine or nakedness or danger or sword?" (Romans 8:35). She felt Prisca's breathing calm a little. Helena continued, her voice growing in strength, "No, in all these things we are more than conquerors through him who loved us. For I am convinced that neither death nor life, neither angels nor demons, neither the present nor the future, nor any powers, neither height nor depth, nor anything else in all creation, will be able to separate us from the love of God that is in Christ Jesus our Lord" (Romans 8:37–39).

Helena heard Prisca breathe in deeply, but she didn't leave her side, not until she had fallen back to sleep.

SYLVESTE CAUGHT HIMSELF JUST BEFORE HIS CHIN REACHED HIS chest. He yawned and shifted position at his desk. Looking over at Phanuel in the desk adjacent to his, he saw a set of eyelids that looked as heavy as his felt. He smirked. They'd cut their camping trip short the night before when the sound of a wild animal woke them both out of a dead sleep. They'd abandoned the smoldering campfire and used the light of the moon to run back to the room they shared on campus. When they both caught their breath, they had laughed so hard they had thought they might pass out. Sylveste's mouth twisted in a wry smile even now as he thought about how his own story of the lion had frightened them nearly out of their wits.

Mr. Muringende raised his eyebrow at Sylveste as he lectured, noticing the faraway look of a boy whose mind is not on the lesson. He continued, "So, you all know that we have been dealing with the subjects of reconciliation and nonviolent protest recently, looking at the examples of leaders like Mahatma Gandhi, Nelson Mandela, and Martin Lurther King Jr. in their success in fighting injustice, finding forgiveness in their country, and bringing peace, unity, and love on a national level. We in Rwanda have a difficult history now, and generally we prefer not to talk about it. But as the next genera-tion it is imperative for us to talk about it. It is imperative that we find a way to deal with what has happened and find a way to move forward together."

Suddenly, Sylveste felt wide awake. Mr. Muringende had his full attention. He looked over at Phanuel. He was sitting up straight as well, focusing intently on the lecture.

"DO YOU WANT TO GO WITH US?" HELENA ASKED PRISCA, WHO WAS sitting in an empty classroom poring over her biology book. Seraph-ina's cousin had stopped by after school for a visit, and Helena and Seraphina were about to walk her home.

"That's alright," Prisca said. "I think I'm going to stay here and study a bit."

"Sounds good," Helena said with a smile. "I'll see you at dinner."

"Thanks," said Prisca with a grateful nod.

Outside the school, Valens, Emmanuel, and Jean-Baptiste passed around a basketball. The girls stopped a few minutes to watch and chat with Chantal, who was seated on the low wall, half-watching her boyfriend, Jean-Baptiste, and half-reading over her class notes.

Unsuccessful at convincing Chantal to walk with them, the three girls headed west into the glare of the afternoon sun. As they passed the edge of the school yard, they heard men's voices. Just ahead were three men in military uniforms. With the RPF military base so nearby, the girls thought little of it, but as they drew near, Helena blinked in recognition and disbelief. "Jean?"

The men turned, clearly caught off guard.

"Helena!" responded the young man, extending a hand in greeting. "I hardly recognize the young woman you've become." Helena blushed a little. "How are you?"

"Good, but how are you? It's been years since I've seen you."

The young man looked away and shifted his weight. "Yes—I've been gone, but I am back, at least for a little while."

Helena looked just then to see the other men standing with arms folded and eyes narrowed on her. One of them was whispering something to another as he eyed Seraphina and her cousin.

"Do you go to school here?" Jean asked.

"Yes. My friend, Seraphina, and I are in Senior Five, just one more year till graduation."

"Um—I see," said Jean, noticing her friend for the first time. "How are your parents?"

"They've been better. Mother's been sick and Father's ..." She hesitated and swallowed. "He's in prison—it's hard, of course."

"Certainly," said Jean, looking more and more uncomfortable.

"Well, we should be going. I'll see you around then?"

"Yes, see you around."

Helena tucked her arm in the crook of Seraphina's and the three girls hurried past. As the road dipped down the hillside, Seraphina looked back over her shoulder. It looked like the men were exchanging heated words.

"Who was that?" asked Seraphina when she was sure they were out of earshot.

"I just recognized Jean. He was a friend—a classmate in school."

"He's in the RPF?"

"That seems odd to me. I—I'm not sure."

"Let's get a move on."

PHANUEL SLIPPED INTO HIS CHAIR IN THE DINING HALL NEXT TO HIS buddies: Alohim, Sylveste, Emmanuel, and Valens. He'd just set his tray down when Helena and Seraphina walked through the door.

"There's your pick," said Sylveste, teasing Phanuel.

"Forget about it," said Phanuel. "I was just answering your question. I wasn't saying I'm interested."

"Right," nodded Sylveste. "Valens, you should have seen this boy run last night."

"You were running too," said Phanuel with a smile.

"True," laughed Sylveste. "It's not every day you hear a lion in the forest."

Seraphina and Helena took their place behind Prisca in line.

"What's for dinner?" asked Helena.

"The usual," shrugged Prisca. "How was your walk?"

"Helena bumped into an old friend," offered Seraphina.

"Really? From around here?"

"Yes, he's from this village, but it's been a while since I've seen him. How'd the studying go?"

"I'll feel better after preps tonight. I still feel so behind."

"It'll be alright," said Helena, offering that reassuring smile Prisca had come to depend on.

"I hate exams," pouted Seraphina. "I'll be glad when they're over."

AFTER DINNER, PHANUEL GRABBED HIS PSYCHOLOGY TEXTBOOK AND filed with his classmates into the classroom where they assembled for a nightly study hall. His mind was churning over how much read-ing he still had to finish, since their camping trip had derailed his study plans. Flipping through his textbook, he found the place where he'd last left off. He looked up at the clock to see how much time he had—that's how he knew that it was 8:15 when the gunshots rang through the air.

we are all Rwandan

On an altar of prejudice we crucify our own,
yet the blood of all children is the color of God.
Don Williams Jr.

EVEN THOUGH THE GUNSHOTS WERE DISTANT, THEY MADE PHANUEL'S
pulse race. Living near the RPF base, the students dismissed the
noise as RPF soldiers scaring away a thief somewhere nearby, but
Phanuel had a strange sense of foreboding.

He remembered how his father had called his family together to
pray during the genocide. Phanuel said to his classmates, about twenty-
four in Senior Six, "I think we should pray." Many of the students
followed Phanuel's lead and closed their eyes, saying short prayers to
God, but then, mostly unalarmed, went back to their studying.

Phanuel tried to concentrate on the words on the page of his psychology textbook, but couldn't. He scanned the heading of the section, "Attachment." Skimming, he could see that the section talked
about a mother's bond with her newborn child. Phanuel's mind
wandered to his home. He wondered if there had been more raids
recently, if everyone was okay. Several more minutes passed. Mostly
students were reading, taking notes, or reviewing flash cards for the
exam the following morning.

It was 8:30 p.m. when more shots rang out. This time they were much closer—they sounded like they had come from somewhere on the school grounds. Phanuel's heart raced faster. The other students looked at one another, eyes wide, bodies tensed. Sylveste looked at Phanuel, a sickening look of fear covering his face. Phanuel strained to listen for other noises. He heard footsteps in the corridor. Stepping to the window, he saw several men approaching their classroom and the Senior Five classroom farther down the hall. A few wore RPF uniforms, but others were wearing civilian clothes and carrying guns.

"Something's wrong," Phanuel whispered, looking at Sylveste. "I don't think those are RPF soldiers." Then turning back to the rest of his classmates, he said, "Get down on the floor!"

There was the noise of chairs scuffing against concrete as students ducked under their desks, covering their heads. Just then shots burst through the closed door and three men entered the classroom, two carrying guns and one a machete. No one had remembered to shut off the generator, so the students did not even have darkness to cover them, and the desks were a feeble shield.

"Do you know me?" asked one man in uniform, speaking French, the language spoken most commonly in the Congo.

"No," whispered several of the students.

"Well, you are going to see me," he continued, moving to the front of the classroom. "I am going to ask you one simple thing." Phanuel tried to get a better glimpse of the man. He looked young, perhaps twenty-two or twenty-three. "I want you to separate yourselves between Hutu and Tutsi."

Phanuel froze, returning his eyes to the ground. He listened; no one seemed to make a sound except he could hear one of the girls whimpering.

"Do you want me to repeat?" came the rebel's voice, louder, angrier. "I want those of you who are Hutu to go there and those of you who are Tutsi to go to the other side."

Phanuel felt like his heart would beat out of his chest. As a Hutu, he knew that he could say something and perhaps spare his life, but he couldn't imagine betraying his own friends. He knew also that as a Christian he didn't have that option. He prayed, "Lord, help us." It couldn't have been more than a few moments that the rebel waited for an answer, but to Phanuel it seemed like time had slowed. And then there was a voice. Phanuel winced.

"All of us are Rwandans here," said Chantal from the front of the classroom. A shot rang out in reply. The students gasped—the bullet hit Chantal squarely in the forehead.

"Hutu here! Tutsi there!" yelled the man.

"I don't want to die. Please help my classmates not to separate," Phanuel prayed again.

Then the rebels walked out of the room. Phanuel wondered what was happening—were they leaving? A moment later, an explosion shattered the soft sounds of crying and rapid breathing. Glass exploded and one of the walls crumbled. Excruciating pain shot through Phanuel as debris rained down on him. He could hear his other classmates wailing and groaning. When the smoke dissipated a bit, he heard the rebels move back in.

"This is your last chance," came the voice. "You will separate or you will all die."

Just then Emmanuel said in a steady low voice, "We are all Rwandans."

Shots punctuated Emmanuel's statement as the men moved their guns systematically across the room. Phanuel looked over at Sylveste lying beside him as bullets perforated his body. A moment later, he felt shots hit him, three in his shoulder and arm. He'd never felt such an intense pain, but he tried to lie still. Perhaps they would think that he was dead. He felt hot and near to passing out, but from somewhere in his spirit, he heard what sounded like a clear, calm voice. It said, "You will not die but will be a bridge to unite Rwandans." He breathed as quietly as he could. The pain shot through him again. Then everything went black.

IN THE CLASSROOM DOWN THE CORRIDOR, HELENA HAD JUST finished praying with her classmates in Senior Five when the shots rang out. Prisca and Seraphina exchanged frightened looks.

"What should we do?" asked Helena.

"We should go out and see what it is," said another classmate.

"No," replied Valens. "With the RPF camp so near, if anything is going on, they'll protect us. It's safer for us to stay here, together." Valens' word carried some authority. The other students knew that he had been in the RPF as a young boy. His job had just been to carry guns, but even so, the other students instinctively felt he knew best. They stayed still.

Prisca looked around the room. Everyone looked as tense as she felt. Suddenly, there were men's voices outside, some pounding, and then the door flew open. Three men entered the room as the students scrambled under desks and tables, girls huddling together. Prisca stole a look at the men. A few of them wore military dress, but she sensed immediately that these weren't soldiers there to protect them, but rebel militias.

One of the men yelled at them, "You are studying here while we are suffering in the forest. Stupid." He pushed over a desk. "You will listen to me and do what I say. I want Hutu here and Tutsi there."

The bravest of them, Valens, responded defiantly, "There are no Tutsi here."

The man replied by spraying bullets across the room. "Perhaps you don't understand our language," said the man, switching from French to Kinyarwanda. "Hutu here! Tutsi there!"

Prisca felt her body shaking uncontrollably. Then she heard one student say, "We are just Rwandans here."

Just then Seraphina, who was lying next to her, raised her head. She had recognized the men.

"You were parading around your beautiful face today," said one of the men, grabbing her and dragging her to her feet. "Now prepare for death. I do not want to kill you badly." As he said it, the noise of the gun firing made Prisca jump. Seraphina's body fell next to her on the floor.

Prisca breathed in deeply and then reached over to see if her friend was still alive. The man who had just shot Seraphina moved toward Prisca. "Who are you?" he shouted at her. Prisca could only see his legs; she didn't dare raise her eyes.

"I want to know," he yelled. Bracing her body, Prisca squeezed her eyes shut. "Maybe you are Tutsi because you are tall," said the man. She heard the blast of the gun and then an excruciating pain as three shots hit her: one in the shoulder, one lodging in her arm, and one glancing off her leg.

"Separate," another man demanded.

"We will not," said one student.

"You leave us no choice. We will kill all of you."

"Stop!" said Helena, standing to her feet.

Even though Prisca's whole body throbbed in pain, her senses were finely attuned to Helena as she stood. She knew her roommate was Hutu—that her father had even gone to prison for killing. Was she going to betray them? She felt sick. It had been Helena who had encouraged her to trust in God—who had calmed her fears with reassurances from the Scripture.

"Helena Benamina—don't be stupid. I know you are Hutu. Tell us who these cockroaches are." It was Jean, the boy Helena had recognized earlier that day.

"Why do you want to kill us?" she pleaded. "Forgive us." Prisca exhaled as she heard Helena plead for mercy.

"How can I help you now? If you want to save your friends, tell me which ones are Tutsi and which are Hutu," said Jean, grabbing her and shaking her.

"I—I can't," she said. "These are all my friends."

Prisca heard pounding and scuffling as the men began to beat Helena, trying to force her to talk.

"Tell us!" came the voice of the man who had shot Prisca.

"I can't," Helena repeated, her voice tortured. "We are all Rwandans." There was the sound of another shot and then a thud as Helena's body hit the floor. The men moved out of the room.

The students were confused, but Valens stood up and said, "In 1994, people were killed and they just kept quiet when there were people next door who could have helped. So stand up together and try to shout. Run—maybe they can just kill one of us." Those who could, followed Valens. He shouted and charged as a grenade detonated and the walls began to crumble. From beneath the debris, Prisca could tell that other classmates were screaming and running for the forest. She would have joined them, if she could have.

WHEN PHANUEL OPENED HIS EYES AGAIN HE WAS IN THE KING FAISAL Hospital in Kigali. He looked to his left where the pain was coming from and could see thick white bandages across his shoulder, chest, and arm. The rest of his body ached too, with bruises and cuts. "Where am I?" he mumbled.

"It's alright," said the familiar voice of a man bending over him.

"Dad?"

"Yes, Son. It's me. You're okay. I'm here. You're in the hospital. I'm so glad you're waking up."

"What about my classmates? Sylveste? Alohim? Are they okay?"

His father shook his head. "I'm sorry, Son. Sylveste made it to the hospital, but they weren't able to save him. He'd already lost too much blood. There were two others in your class who are dead—Chantal and Emmanuel—and three more from Senior Five who didn't make it. Alohim is okay. And the miracle is that so many of you did make it, and that you refused to let their hate separate you."

Phanuel turned his head away as tears welled up in his eyes. "Sylveste," he said, trying to understand his father's words.

"I'm so proud of you, Son," he said as he squeezed his good hand.

Just then a nurse entered the room. "Good, he's waking up," she said as she moved over to Phanuel's side. "Let's get some more fluids in you," she said, cradling his head with her arms and lifting him up a little as she put a cup to his lips.

As Phanuel sat up a little, he saw he wasn't alone in the room. To his right was another hospital bed, where Prisca lay sleeping.

"Is she okay?" Phanuel asked the nurse.

"Yes, I think her wounds are a little less severe than yours. She's just resting." Taking his chart, the nurse walked to the door.

Looking over at his dad, Phanuel asked, "Mom? The family? Is everyone okay?"

"Yes, Son. Everyone is okay. They are all praying for your speedy recovery."

"The last thing I remember was the grenade and then the shots. What happened to the rebels?"

"When you all didn't cooperate, and they had to fire and use the grenades, and then you all set to shouting and running away, they must have gotten scared that they would be discovered. When the RPF got there, they scoured the place and the forests, but couldn't find them. In fact, I understand that it took some coaxing on the RPF's part to convince your classmates who had fled into the forest to come out. They feared that it might be some kind of trick."

Phanuel winced as pain shot through his arm again.

"Listen, that's enough talking for now. I want you to lie back and rest. I'll be right here when you wake up."

AFTER THREE MONTHS IN THE HOSPITAL, PRISCA RETURNED HOME to convalesce. She'd had three bullets removed and a pin inserted to reconnect her shoulder. Physical therapy was helping, but still there were wounds that doctors couldn't help her overcome.

Her mother had moved back to the Kamonyi District after the genocide — her youngest sibling, Liliane, also still lived at home. While her home had survived the war, nothing of memory inside had been preserved. After the war, she never saw the picture of Christ her father had given her for her confirmation.

But since the shooting at the Nyange school, she'd carried another picture, tucked like a well-worn photograph in her memory. It reminded her of the same thing that the crucifixion scene had brought to mind. For months after the shooting, when she closed her eyes, she saw the scene: her roommate, Helena, standing up to the rebels, choosing to identify with her Tutsi classmates rather than to save her own life.

In Prisca's mind, she could still hear Helena's soothing voice, comforting her with words from the book of Romans: "For I am convinced that neither death nor life, neither angels nor demons, neither the present nor the future, nor any powers, neither height nor depth, nor anything else in all creation, will be able to separate us from the love of God" (Romans 8:38–39). Prisca knew that nothing — not even death — could separate Helena from the love of God. She also knew that she'd been given a new portrait to carry with her: this was of a Rwanda in which nothing could separate her people — not violence, not hate. They were one people, and Prisca knew that the best way she could honor Helena's memory was to share that message of hope.

PHANUEL SPENT NEARLY A YEAR IN AND OUT OF HOSPITALS RECOVERING from his significant wounds. Slowly, he adjusted to walking with a limp and not being able to raise his left arm above his waist. A year after the shooting, Phanuel passed his final exams and received a scholarship to the university in Butare to finish his studies. He accepted it, and just as he had always done, applied himself with steadfast vigor. Bit by bit, he mastered the necessary concepts in environmental sciences and land management, just as he'd relearned to walk after the shooting.

Phanuel had lost a year of his life, endured severe pain, and suffered with a permanent handicap, but he never regretted his decision to suffer along with his Tutsi classmates. Even so, in his heart, he struggled to forgive the men responsible. The bitterness had gone underground. It bubbled up from time to time, especially in moments of frustration at his new limitations, but mostly it lay dormant—that is, until 2004.

It was then that Phanuel had traveled home to visit his family. While at home, he was walking around the town center one day when he spotted a man in uniform. Without a doubt, he knew he'd seen the man before—he'd been one of the rebels who had infiltrated his classroom in 1997. Inquiring around, Phanuel soon discovered that this murderer had somehow joined the Rwandan army. Furious, Phanuel began to contemplate how he could exact revenge. How could this man go about freely when he had taken the life of his best friend and five other classmates?

The evening after making this discovery, Phanuel slept fitfully. His dreams were haunted. He felt a man beating him. The pain grew more and more intense and then suddenly he stopped. When Phanuel looked up, he saw the tormentor had moved on and was beating another man even more violently. The man receiving the lashes fell into a crumpled heap on the ground. Though he was bleeding profusely, the tormentor grabbed the man and turned him over. Phanuel tried to understand what he was seeing as the beaten man seemed to be raised up. It was dark, but soon Phanuel realized that the man who was being raised up was on a wooden cross. Phanuel stood looking up at the man who cried out in a loud voice, "Father, forgive them, for they know not what they do." Phanuel sat up in bed, shaking.

He prayed, "God, what does it mean?" In the moments that followed, he understood. "God, are you telling me that these people did this to your Son too?" Then Phanuel remembered the words he'd heard the night of the shooting. "You will not die, but you will be a bridge to unite the Rwandan people."

PHANUEL LOOKED OUT AT THE ASSEMBLED CROWD OF YOUNG PEOPLE. Their faces seemed young, but he knew they were no younger than he had been just a few short years ago. He'd spoken to countless people in the past few years, but this was his favorite age. Deep down, he knew that it was the young people who were the hope for his country's future.

He looked over at Prisca. She too seemed eager to share with the group.

Phanuel moved to the podium and cleared his throat. "Good morning, students," he said, looking at them intently. "Many of you have heard the story of the Nyange secondary school shooting. I'm here today to speak to you as a survivor and as a fellow Rwandan. You have all most likely heard how rebels infiltrated our compound in 1997 and ordered my classmates and me to separate according to Hutu and Tutsi.

"You have heard how my brave classmates refused. How they adamantly contended that day that there were only Rwandans in that classroom.

"Many of you here today have memories, memories like me of terrible things that happened to you. You've been told stories. Your parents, your grandparents, the ones who have survived genocide or exile or imprisonment—they've told you stories of the things they've seen, of the things they've suffered.

"I'm not here to deny those things or to tell you that they don't matter.

"I'm here today to tell you that if there is any hope for this country, we must find a way to speak truthfully about these things. We must find a way to listen to each other and to understand one another's pain. And we must find a way to forgive.

"I'm standing before you today as someone who has personally wrestled with this—as someone who has lost a year of my own life, who has lost family members to both sides of this horrible history we share. And I'm telling you, as our dear professor once told us, I'm pleading with you that it is imperative that we find a way forward.

"The only way that I've found, the only way I know to tell you, is through Jesus Christ. Beaten, mocked, despised, tortured, Christ in his final words here on earth called out, pleading for God to forgive the perpetrators. He was pleading for the forgiveness of you, of me, of the people who have hurt our families and our friends.

"And when he was on this earth, he taught us to do the same.

"I'm sure you've prayed these words before, that you learned them in school or from your mother or your grandmother. They've been passed down for centuries. They are simple: 'Forgive us our sins, as we forgive those who have sinned against us.'

"This is the way forward, my friends. Let us break down this chain of fear, of vengeance. If we break down this chain, we stand together. We stand together as brothers and sisters, as Rwandans."

Phanuel's eyes surveyed the crowd. His eyes locked on one student standing in the back. Tall, with a runner's frame, he reminded Phanuel of Sylveste. The resemblance shot through Phanuel with a pang—the kind that reminded him Sylveste wasn't coming back.

The young man before Phanuel looked at him with deep seriousness. As their eyes linked, the student nodded at him somberly, a motion that held both agreement and respect. Phanuel could see that his eyes were red and moist. Phanuel had no way of knowing the young man's experience. Was he a Tutsi who had lost family in the genocide? Was he a Hutu whose parents had participated in the killing or who had seen his own family members hurt in reprisal attacks? Phanuel couldn't know. But he could see that his message had penetrated his heart—not the heart of a Tutsi or of a Hutu, but of a fellow Rwandan.

reversing
the downward spiral

Love is being willing to value people
and unwilling to devalue them.
Everett Worthington Jr.

OLD HABITS DIE HARD. ALL OF US KNOW WHAT IT IS LIKE TO LET AN unkind word slip from our lips. The spark from that harsh remark ignites a response, and pretty soon flames leap back and forth until we find ourselves ablaze with anger. Ingrained patterns of thinking and relating can make us into powder kegs of volatile emotion needing little to cause the deadly chain reaction.

For those who have forgiven and reconciled, how can we keep this from happening? How do we maintain what we have worked so hard to build? How do we keep from falling back into the downward spiral?

Genocide is one of the most extreme examples of this kind of spiral. The International Campaign to End Genocide has identified eight stages of genocide: (1) classification, (2) symbolization, (3) dehumanization, (4) organization, (5) polarization, (6) preparation, (7) extermination, and (8) denial. In Rwanda today, the organization, preparation, and actual systematic killing of Tutsi has come to an end. Likewise, there is an acknowledgment that the genocide did happen.

But polarization, dehumanization, symbolization, and classification are harder to stop. These are the patterns of thinking that may make it easy for milder wrongs to ignite a chain reaction of events. Classification involves an us-versus-them mentality. In genocide, these categories develop along racial, ethnic, or religious lines. Such differences may be symbolized in the culture negatively. This may take on the form of a literal symbol, such as in Nazi Germany where homes and businesses of Jews were marked by the Star of David and targeted. Or symbolism can be a kind of stereotyping. In Rwanda, for example, as the RPF evaded the Rwandan government, their stealth in making night raids and surviving caused them to be labeled as cockroaches. This symbol became a derogatory word used to classify all Tutsi as conspirators against the government. Clearly, it also dehumanized them. As differences between groups are negatively characterized and classified, dehumanization increases, as does further polarization between the groups.

On a much less extreme scale, it is interesting to note the similarities between this downward spiral and what psychologist John Gottman has labeled as the four most likely predictors of divorce: criticism, defensiveness, contempt, and stonewalling.[1] Repeated criticism leads to defensiveness. Differences are classified and verbalized with absolute statements such as "You never" or "You always." Spouses become polarized. Contempt for the other solidifies. Contempt—an intense feeling or attitude of regarding someone or something as inferior, base, or worthless—is only a step away from dehumanization. The result is that spouses stonewall or deaden their feelings toward each other. They have closed out the other—a psychological exterminating of the other's presence.

We've seen how important empathy is in the process of forgiveness. Empathy rehumanizes the other. It removes feelings of contempt as we discover an emotional understanding of the other person's thoughts, actions, and motives.

But just as the offending person or group needs to be rehumanized, so too there is a need for the groups to be depolarized. That means moving away from "you always" or "they always" statements back into a more nuanced view of personhood or group culture. If this work of depolarization hasn't happened in the forgiveness process, it must happen before parties can move from neutral to positive ground in the reconciliation process. Empathy can be a first step. Humility is a second. And we must understand, as Aleksandr Solzhenitsyn wrote, that "the line of good and evil cuts through the heart of every human being." In other words, in all hearts there is a mixture of good and evil.

There can also be merit in learning, remembering, or rehearsing the positive aspects of the other person or group.

Everett Worthington Jr. describes the process as one of deconditioning. He had struggled for years with forgiving his father. But still when his dad came to mind, he would think negative, critical, and unforgiving thoughts. Then one day he decided to decondition himself. He began with staring at his father's picture. At first, each time he looked at the photo it brought up anger, hurt, and sometimes even fear. So each day, he took out the picture, and as the unforgiving thoughts came to mind, he would rehearse thoughts of forgiveness. Finally, through repeating the process again and again, he found that the negative thoughts were no longer the first to surface when he saw the image of his dad.

Similarly, he created a list of positive attributes of his dad. Each time when his dad came to mind, he practiced rehearsing the positive attributes. He had spent a lifetime dwelling on the negative ones. It took a lot of practicing, but gradually as his dad came to mind, thoughts of unforgiveness and negativity were not the first thoughts that came to him.[2]

Miroslav Volf talks about the same issue in how we remember rightly a person who has committed wrong against us. He asks, "Should I not try to remember his wrongdoing in the context of his whole life, which might exhibit a good deal of virtue? In memory, a wrongdoing often does not remain an isolated stain on the character of the one who committed it; it spreads over his entire character."[3] Putting the wrongdoer back into the context of an entire life can help reverse the trend of polarization and classification.

Where reconciliation has occurred, to maintain the health of the restored relationship, positive actions and thoughts need to replace the negative ones. Amends, restitution, and generosity on the part of the offender move the relationship back into the positive direction. But both parties need to practice positive interactions.

People who classify themselves in "good relationship," according to one study by John Gottman, usually have a ratio of five positive interactions to one negative interaction.[4] Increasing positive acts, such as words of affirmation or acts of service, and decreasing negative interactions, such as critical words or bringing up past wrongs, can dramatically improve the overall perception of a relationship.

We can also work on creating a culture or character of forgiveness. Americans were shocked when Charles Roberts opened fire in a small one-room schoolhouse in Nickel Mines, Pennsylvania, killing five and injuring five more before taking his own life. Certainly if violence could erupt in the idyllic rolling hills of Amish country, it could happen anywhere. But as startling as the shooting itself was, it was what followed that sent the real shock waves through the nation.

Within hours of the shooting, several members of the Amish community visited Mrs. Roberts and her family, to express their sorrow over her loss and to say they did not hold anything against them. Another Amish man visited the killer's father. A Roberts family spokesperson said, "He stood there for an hour, and he held [Mr. Roberts] in his arms and said, 'We forgive you.'" Four days later at the killer's burial, some seventy people in attendance were Amish. And when funds began pouring in for victims after the shooting, the Nickel Mine community established a fund for the shooter's wife and children.

But this response was not merely an aberration. In the Amish culture, forgiveness is a virtue that is cultivated. In a new book entitled *Amish Grace*, three Amish scholars explain, "Our actions are rarely random. We all embrace patterns of behavior and habits of mind that shape what we do in a given situation." As the scholars note, there are "habits of forgiveness" in the Amish culture, which come into clear focus.[5] For instance, the Amish only celebrate communion twice a year, but there is a month-long season of preparation. During that season of preparation, the Amish take seriously the admonition that if anyone holds a grudge against his brother he is not to partake until he has put it right. A council meeting two weeks prior to communion is a time of admonishment, then there is a season of fasting, and sometimes the communion service is even delayed for weeks if there is more widespread disharmony among the community.

Schoolbooks feature stories of Amish martyrs who practiced

forgiveness. And from an extremely early age, children are taught the Lord's Prayer, and in it the words, "forgive us our trespasses as we forgive those who trespass against us." This is the larger context which makes such a magnificent response to such a horrible tragedy possible.

Likewise, in our own lives we can cultivate a forgiving character. When a person cuts us off in traffic or makes us late or squeezes in front of us in the grocery store line, we can practice not taking offense at such minor wrongs. We can realize that much of the time people are not acting out of malice toward us, but with self-interest, a self-interest that we too often show in other circumstances. We can choose not to take offense.[6] We can tackle wounds from our past one by one and move through the process of forgiveness. Like the Amish schoolchildren, we can read about heroes of forgiveness. We can periodically take inventory of our relationships and practice confession and forgiveness. All of these activities can help to cultivate a more forgiving character, the kind of character that can maintain the health of a reconciled relationship over time.

Finally, making meaning of our pasts and building that meaning into our reconciled relationships can help maintain health over the long run. Many of the characters in these stories have done just that. Monique works with other survivors of rape; Devota goes into prisons to share her story; Prisca and Phanuel work with youth to help bring reconciliation. Those who can engage in such meaningful activities using their past experience to help others will find a renewed sense of purpose. If you can engage in such activities with the person or people with whom you have reconciled, this will have an even more powerful effect. The work groups made of survivors and ex-prisoners in Chantal's village who build homes and participate in various community-building activities are one example of this. The interdependence created in working together and the positive shared experience work to reinforce the reconciliation and feelings of goodwill within the group.

Growing in empathy, seeing another person in a larger context, rehearsing positive traits, increasing positive interactions and decreasing negative ones, cultivating cultures and characters of forgiveness, and making meaning together in restored relationships can all work to maintain the reconciled relationships we have worked so hard to build.

Questions for Reflection and Discussion

How have you dehumanized or falsely characterized someone that you have wronged or who has wronged you? How can you begin to see that person in light of a shared humanity once more? What characterizations do you need to release?

In what ways have you slipped into easy us-versus-them ways of thinking about people with whom you disagree? How have you let yourself fall into traps of polarized thinking?

Create a list of positive attributes of someone you find difficult to forgive or difficult to simply like. Try calling these attributes to mind when you think of that person.

In what ways could you help create a culture of forgiveness in your family, workplace, or church?

a killer called
me friend

In violence we forget who we are.
Mary McCarthy

CLAUDE'S IMAGINATION SOMETIMES FELT STRONGER THAN HE WAS. His thirteen-year-old legs wearied of grazing the cattle up and down the terraced hills of his remote village outside of Kibuye town. His arms ached when he carried heavy loads to market, and his feet blistered on the long walks home. But his mind never rested. In the lush green mountains rising up from behind the rippling waters of Lake Kivu he saw the arching back of a mythical sea monster. In the mist blanketing the glassy blue of the water, he felt the warm fog of the monster's breath. He reasoned that the red clay road twisted, dipped, and climbed in its effort to elude the slumbering giant.

Sometimes, while the cattle grazed, Claude would recall the Rwandan saying: "God roams the earth but comes to rest in Rwanda." Something about the luxuriant greens, soothing blues, and earthy reds that painted his world made him believe it. A hush would often come over him, especially as the sun dipped behind the mountains, and the world turned three shades of blue—water, mist, and sky. Such beauty lulled the senses and gave Claude things worth dreaming about at the close of the day. This was by far his favorite time of day.

On one such evening, Claude stepped lightly as he walked behind the long-horned Ankole cattle. Aside from their lowing, and the occasional shrill caw of a malachite kingfisher whose hunt he had disturbed, the journey home was a silent one. He crossed the small bridge at the base of the village and stepped into the familiar grooves of the footpath along with the cattle, forming an obedient single file that hugged the contoured hills.

In the distance, he could see the flickering glow of candles lighting the mud homes of his neighbors, and the brighter flare of outside cooking fires. The smell of smoke and cooking meat reached his nostrils, making him realize how long it had been since his last meal. The sound of his growling stomach interrupted the quiet reverie of paradise at dusk. He concentrated again on his step and soon had quickened his pace up the steep homeward path on Nyarunyinya Hill.

As the shadow of his family's home came into view, Claude saw another shadow move out into his path. He'd recognize the profile of his father, Thomas, anywhere. Each night he anticipated his father's quick nod of approval as Claude prodded the last cow up the sharp rise of the path home. With his father's help, Claude soon corralled the herd into the fence made of dried stalks strung together in a tight mesh. With the cattle safely secured for the evening, Claude felt the warmth of his father's strong hand on his shoulder as his father in turn guided his young calf into the house.

Inside, his sisters—Jeannette and Rode, ages ten and fifteen— stirred about with his mother, preparing the evening meal. Claude slipped off his sandals and poured water from the yellow jerry can into a basin, then dipped his dusty hands into the cool water.

THAT NIGHT, AS THE FAMILY SLEPT, CLAUDE'S CHILDHOOD ENDED with a loud explosion when a grenade flew through their window and detonated. If beauty stills the world, then violence, Claude discovered, wakens it.

Loud and irreverent, this violence entered breathing hard and shouting profanities. It left his mother Suzan's body tangled and twisted. It left the echo of his older sister's screams and moans as men did something to her that Claude would only later comprehend, long after her pain-wracked body had been dragged off toward the Congo. The crackling of the thatched roof in flame, the pounding footsteps following him and his younger sister as they ran deep into the brush, the final threats that the killers would find them in the morning's light — these were the sounds of violence that would reverberate in Claude's mind for years to come.

As sweat trickled down his face, Claude sheltered his younger sister with his body. Both breathed heavily, hearts thumping like warning drums as they waited for the world to grow quiet again. But long after the footsteps had faded, their fear spoke loudly in the darkness.

PERHAPS IT WAS AN INQUISITIVE MIND THAT SAVED CLAUDE AND Jeannette. Growing up amid the myriad inlets of Lake Kivu, surrounded by the Virunga volcanoes, the forest-fringed waterfalls, and roads tumbling through lush plantain fields and patches of misty rainforest, Claude had made a habit of exploring. So when his neighbors became hunters driven by blood lust, Claude did not flee with the ten thousand that would perish in a church in Kibuye. Instead, he guided his sister to the secret spots known only to his searching imagination. Their diminutive size made hiding easier; trees could be shimmied, mountain crags could be breached, and even harvest piles could be tunneled.

Finding food and water was harder. Claude became a nocturnal scavenger—snatching bananas, digging up roots, and sometimes even looting an abandoned house or field. But they had to be careful to choose what wouldn't be missed or tracked, and to move only while the killers slept.

Hiding in the day, and scavenging at night, Claude rested little. Even when he closed his eyes, fear kept him awake. In his tortured thoughts, his young mind tried to comprehend the things he had seen. It wasn't as if wandering thieves had penetrated his home. This was much more personal. Michel who lived down the road had thrown the grenade. Kanyenzi, also a man he'd known all his life, tracked him in the night. Edison—someone Claude passed every day on his way to graze the cattle—had dragged off his sister, Rode. The faces of these neighbors haunted his waking and his sleeping.

IT WASN'T UNTIL AFTER THE GENOCIDE ENDED THAT CLAUDE LEARNED how his father died. While Claude and Jeannette kept hidden in the hills near home, Thomas moved to Bisesero Hill to try and form some kind of resistance. Many of the Tutsi had fled there because it was high and they could see the attackers coming. A thick covering of trees also made it a spot where hiding was easier.

What Thomas did not realize was that in order to get to the hill, he would have to pass through a roadblock at Mugonero Center. There, drunken Hutu soldiers easily captured Thomas. As a well-known Tutsi, Thomas was a prize. The killers eagerly turned him over to their chief, a man by the name of Obed Ruzindana.

Claude would later be told that, for sport and spite, Obed ordered that Thomas be tied behind a car and dragged through the streets in a cruel caricature of Achilles and Hector. On the streets of Mugonero Center, the rage and madness of myth were made far too real.

CLAUDE HELD HIS SISTER'S HAND AS THEY MOVED CAREFULLY through the dark. He felt something hard underfoot and then heard a crack. He looked down and felt his stomach somersault—human bones. Two months had passed since the killing began; this corpse had been picked clean by birds or wild animals. Claude sucked in breath and pulled Jeannette to move along, hoping she was too sleepy to realize what had just happened. But still, Claude couldn't help but wonder whose body it might have been.

They weren't far now from what remained of their home. It was dangerous to move from their hiding spot, but they had heard killers close at hand that day and Claude feared staying put more than he did moving. Besides, they needed to find more food.

Claude knew that they were running out of hiding spots, and running out of strength as well. Once he circled back to one of the caves where they had gone for shelter early on, only to find that killers had started a fire at the cave's entrance. Claude did not venture in to see what he feared were the remains of Tutsi who had likewise sought refuge inside.

As they walked along Claude prayed silently, "God, help us to survive."

The moon illuminated a small home before them. Claude knew it well. The house belonged to Samuel, a longtime friend of their family. Part of him wanted to knock on the door, to ask for help, but even as he thought about it, images of neighbors like Michel and Edison flashed through his mind. They couldn't trust anyone.

Behind the house, a small, well-tilled field held sweet potatoes. Motioning to his sister to stay hidden in the nearby bushes, Claude moved out into the field and knelt in the cool red dirt. Some chickens pecked around in a pen. Catching sight of Claude, they clucked and cackled. Intent on finding some kind of food, Claude ignored them, using his hands to scoop away the dirt and search for the stringy roots. His fingers had just found a root system when a door creaked open. He looked up to see a set of eyes. Claude froze in fear. The figure stepped out into the moonlight. Immediately, Claude recognized the woman, who tilted her head to the side to examine the specimen before her—clothes muddied and tattered, kneeling, hands deep in dirt, looking at her like a treed animal.

"Nkundumukiza?" called out Samuel's aging mother, using Claude's given Rwandan name. "Is that you?"

Claude didn't know whether to stay or run, but his legs seemed paralyzed.

"I won't hurt you. Come here." She stepped closer. Heavyset, she seemed to waddle more than walk. He could have easily outrun her if his body would have only cooperated.

"I promise, child, I won't hurt you. But you need to come inside quickly, before you are seen."

Just then Claude heard a noise from the brush. Jeannette had stepped out into the clearing. Claude's heart sunk. He wished she had stayed put. But there wasn't any turning back now. They would have to take their chances and see if friendship still held.

SEVERAL WEEKS PASSED, AND SAMUEL'S MOTHER WAS GOOD TO HER word. She brought them food and water and hid them in a back bedroom of her small house.

One evening as the sky turned inky, Claude crept out from the back room. Hearing a noise outside, he stepped to a window to get a better look. He could see Samuel's silhouette as he returned from the hills. Just outside the house, Samuel stopped to wipe his machete on the tall grass. But as he turned to approach the house, Claude could see his clothes splattered a deep red.

Claude must have gasped because Samuel moved to the window. "Hello, little friend," he whispered with eyes full of sadness. Then he turned and walked into the house while Claude retreated back into his room. Claude slept fitfully that night and when he awoke in a cold sweat, he could not tell if it had been a dream or if he had been wide awake. So it is when living a nightmare. But whether from friendship or fear of his mother, Samuel never once threatened Claude or his sister.

One evening when the old woman brought in a plate of cooked potatoes for Claude and Jeannette to share, she whispered, "The war is over."

Already wolfing down the food, Claude froze midchew: Was this a sick joke? When he saw the seriousness in her eyes, his next thought was that the Hutu had succeeded in killing every last Tutsi—and somehow he and his sister were the only ones to have survived.

"Have they killed us all?" Claude asked, wide-eyed.

"No, the radio says the RPF has taken Kigali."

"Kigali? They've made it to Kigali?" asked Claude, half-choking on his food.

"Is it safe for us to leave then?" asked Jeannette.

"It isn't safe for any of us," replied the old woman. "We may have to flee to the Congo—and certainly, if you are seen before you find the RPF, the Interahamwe won't hesitate to finish the job they've started."

Even hearing her words of warning, Claude knew that at the first opportunity they would move. If they could find the RPF, certainly they would be safer with them than here in the house of Samuel, a killer who called them friend.

revenge's mirror

*What is most chilling when you meet a murderer
is that you meet yourself.*
Elizabeth Neuffer

WHEN CLAUDE AND JEANNETTE FOUND THE RPF, THEY WERE GIVEN food, clothing, and consolation. But soldiers' rations, a well-worn military jacket, and the well-intentioned words of men accustomed to death are little comfort for young orphans who have, in just one hundred days, lost their mother, father, grandparents, aunts, uncles, cousins, home, childhood, innocence, and trust.

Such heartache opens up inside like a bottomless pit. Claude felt himself tumbling ever further, ever faster. If the void could have swallowed him up, it would have been better than the chasm of ache. *Hopeless* was too light a word for what he felt. If there was a future out there for him and his sister, Claude could not imagine it.

The next three years were filled with wandering. For several months, Claude and his sister lived with a family of survivors on a hill near where he had been born. The father of the household encouraged Claude to go back to school, but the notion of school was unimaginable to him. For the man's sake, Claude tried, but he couldn't concentrate or think. Sometimes he couldn't even talk.

Unable to take school any longer, and not wanting to disappoint his host, Claude decided that he and his sister would take to the road.

They made their way to Kigali, where Claude found a job as a houseboy for another family of survivors. He fetched water and did household chores—no job was too menial. Sometimes the work helped him escape, but living with and working for a family who was as severely traumatized as him more often reminded him of his own pain. He felt like a ghost waiting on other members of the walking dead.

So Claude and Jeannette moved again. They lived for a month with another friend, another month with another family, and so the pattern grew. Without advocate, ally, home, or ties, Claude kept shifting, wandering. Finally in 1997 a friend he was living with at the time convinced him that he was foolish to not try and go back to school. If he ever wanted a job better than houseboy, he'd need to finish his education, the friend reasoned.

The future still didn't look any brighter to Claude, but facing it did seem more inevitable than it had even a few years before. By that time, Jeannette was also old enough to board at the secondary school. That made the decision a bit easier, since Claude didn't want to deprive her of the only future that she might have. Plus, he knew that he wouldn't have to leave her in someone else's home while he received his education. Going back to school would be difficult —but what in his life hadn't been?

IT TOOK SOME TIME, BUT GRADUALLY CLAUDE BEGAN TO ADJUST TO LIFE at the secondary school in the Kigali rural prefect. In every class, he felt hopelessly behind. It had been more than three years since he had been in school on a consistent basis, and no aspect of it came easily to Claude: not the sitting still, the concentrating, the note taking, or the studying. Claude blamed each of these frustrations on what had happened in 1994. If it weren't for the people who killed his family, he would have a secure future. If it weren't for those monsters, he wouldn't be facing all this alone. If it weren't for them, he wouldn't be struggling in school. If it weren't for them, his whole life wouldn't depend on whether he could make a way for himself—there would be others to lean on. There would have been a safety net. And he would not know the word *orphan* so intimately.

One thing that helped Claude, however, was something called the Survivors Club that the principal of his school founded. Each week those among them who had survived the genocide gathered together to support and encourage one another. Sometimes they also shared what they had seen, the sounds that still haunted them, and the hardships that faced them. Many of them, like Claude, had lost their parents and their families.

As the weeks turned to months, Claude learned that while the things he had faced had been horrific, they were by no means the worst of the violence. As he heard the stories of what other classmates had witnessed or endured, though, it began to increase his bitterness. These tales only fanned the embers of something that had begun to burn deep within him and haunt his waking and his sleeping: revenge.

His mind began to return to the thought more and more frequently. He'd close his eyes and imagine himself walking along the familiar paths leading out of Kibuye to his hill. Like the killers who had called him by name as they hunted, Claude knew the names of those he wished most desperately he could kill. Sometimes in his mind, as he retraced the pathways home, he'd say those names, repeating them again and again as a mantra of violence.

Beginning in April 1997, Claude's growing thirst for revenge increased. It was during that period that Obed Ruzindana, the man Claude had heard had so brutally killed his own father, was tried in the International Criminal Tribunal for Rwanda located in Arusha,

Tanzania. While this court was the highest court hearing serious genocide-related crimes, its proceedings were so painfully slow that to Claude the whole process seemed to make a mockery of justice.

It was around that time that Claude began to consider law as a career. Certainly, he thought, if he could become a lawyer, he could navigate the system to get revenge on evil men like those who had killed his family. There would at least be some satisfaction in prosecuting criminals.

And so with the man he believed to have killed his father on trial, and his newly imagined career path, Claude followed the trial of Obed Ruzindana and his coconspirator, Clement Kayishima, with intense interest. Between news articles and radio broadcasts, Claude put together a clearer picture of this monster that he had reason to think killed his father.

Obed, a prosperous businessman, living in Kigali until the president's assassination, had moved to the Bisesero region when the war began to stay with relatives. According to the testimony of witnesses, Ruzindana had played a lead role in the systematic killing of Tutsi in the Bisesero region, where tens of thousands were killed between April and June of 1994.

Over the months of proceedings, witnesses testified that Ruzindana had orchestrated transportation for killers and spurred them on to attack, especially at the hillside of Muyira, the Kigamara cave, and across the Bisesero region. He had even offered cash rewards for those who could bring him trophies of Tutsi heads or identity cards of the well-known Tutsi they had murdered.

What was worse, Claude learned that, however revolting the details of his own father's death were, Ruzindana had done still greater evil. Claude learned that Ruzindana had mutilated a sixteen-year-old Tutsi girl at a mine in the Nyiramurengo hillside. First he cut off her breasts, and then he disemboweled her by slicing her abdomen open with a machete. When Claude heard the details, he wept uncontrollably. He knew enough by now to know that his own older sister, Rode—about the same age as this girl—had been raped before being slaughtered. While Claude knew that Ruzindana was not the man who had perpetrated this crime against his sister, the story dredged up such hate—not only against Ruzindana, but also against the people of his own village that Claude knew—that there could be no turning back. Claude set his face toward Kibuye. Now it was only a question of when and how.

CLAUDE DIDN'T LOOK THE PART OF A KILLER — SQUISHED INTO A middle seat on a van bound for Kibuye. At seventeen, his face was still round like a boy much younger. Wearing the only clothes that still fit him—a school uniform—didn't exactly give him away either. But under the surface, rage boiled.

When the driver ran out of good road, Claude carried on the rest of the way by foot. Lake Kivu hadn't lost any of the beauty he remembered from childhood. But on this trek his imagination didn't busy itself with sea monsters in the lakeshore mist. On this trip, his imagination was otherwise employed.

He ran his thumb back and forth over the rough edges of the grenade in his coat pocket. So focused on how good it would feel to pull the pin and lob the exploding metal into the midst of the people responsible for his misery, Claude hardly noticed the labor of the climb or the landscape surrounding him.

Had his mind not been busy picturing faces and saying names, his thoughts might have gone to carbon dioxide and methane. After all, he had recently learned in school that lurking beneath the placid waters of Lake Kivu was something far more sinister than any sea monster. Because of the way the lake is situated in the Rift Valley not far from the churning activity of Mount Nyiragongo, the valley itself is being pulled apart by volcanic activity. An influx of heat into the lake, such as that caused by a volcanic eruption, could cause an overturn of the gases. Lava could cause gas-saturated waters to rise to the surface. The result would be the release of enough carbon dioxide and methane to kill untold numbers of the nearly two million people living in the surrounding regions. Like Claude, the surface of these waters seemed serene and predictable enough that no one would ever expect the potential destructive force bubbling just below.

This was an irony Claude missed that day, along with another much more important irony. Claude had become that which he despised.

His plan had not developed any good legs. The furthest Claude had gotten in his imagination was the grenade and returning to his village. He had no idea how he would find the specific people who had killed his family, or whether they were even there and not re-established in Goma, or further into the Congo. So far, Claude had decided that he would walk to the first house of Hutu he found, pull the pin, and lob all the built-up hatred, disgust, and hurt at the people inside.

He hadn't let his mind linger on what that would mean: on the family that perhaps lived inside; on the young boy who might lose both mother and father in the blast. He hadn't thought about how his own reasoning had come to look so similar to that of those who had first perpetrated violence against him. *There is a score to be settled here*, he reasoned. *How can these people enjoy life, when I must face a life of so much difficulty? The world will be safer, better without their kind.*

Claude crossed the small footbridge and stepped into the grooves of the footpath that hugged Nyarunyinya Hill. It didn't occur to him then that his sandaled feet now walked the well-worn path of the killers that had ventured here before him.

Eyes scanning the horizon, Claude quickly locked on the familiar mud form of a Hutu neighbor's house. Still hundreds of yards away, his pulse quickened and his palms grew wet with anticipation and fear. Even so, he was savoring the moment until he saw something that filled him with even more rage than what he had carried across the weary miles: men, women, and children were running. Warned somehow, they were sprinting headlong away from him, depriving him of the tantalizing satisfaction of revenge.

wake up and dream

In this way we differ from all animals.
It is not our capacity to think that makes us different,
but our capacity to repent and to forgive.
Only humans can perform that most unnatural act
and by doing so only they can develop relationships
that transcend the relentless laws of nature.
Aleksandr Solzhenitsyn

CLAUDE NEVER DID FIND OUT WHO WARNED THE PEOPLE OF HIS village the day he came carrying the weight of the world in the palm of his hand. Whether it was a child who caught a glimpse of him and ran back home to tell his parents, or whether someone had recognized him when he got out of the van at the center and sent word, he didn't know. By whatever means, the lives of Claude's neighbors were saved that day. It wasn't until seven years later that Claude was able to say that he was glad about it.

It was then, in 2005, a few months after graduating from secondary school, that Claude connected with a group called Solace. Like the Survivors Club at his school, this was a gathering of Tutsi who had managed to survive the genocide. The people who gathered were mainly divided into two groups: widows and orphans. But unlike the Survivors Club, this group sought consolation not simply from each other, but from God. Claude found that this wasn't like being a member of an organization or society. Solace was like family to him. When he gathered with the other orphans there each week and exchanged hugs, it felt like the embrace of his own kin. It was a feeling he had craved for so many years, and he simply could not get enough of it.

At Solace, Claude shared his story with people who empathized with him, who grieved with him, and who ultimately offered him physical and financial help. By that time, part of Claude's story of heartache was that he had not eked out a high enough grade point average for any college to even consider giving him a scholarship—the only way he could afford to go. Solace, however, through the support of several donors, helped orphans with educational costs. Without Solace, Claude never would have been able to go to the university.

Solace also offered counseling. Mama Lambert was one of the women who counseled Claude and other orphans who came to the weekly meetings. Having lost her husband and five children in the genocide, Mama Lambert knew well the grief Claude was suffering. She also knew what it meant to be an orphan. Killers hacked into pieces Mama Lambert's own aging father, eighty-two years old at the time of the genocide, and threw him into the river. They also forced her mother to witness the death of thirty-four children and grandchildren before they killed her.

After the genocide, the grief had driven Mama Lambert to kill herself. She had been on her way to drown herself in the river when she stepped into Solace's doors. There she found the first comfort she had experienced in years. She began to feel like a human being again and started to sleep for the first time since the genocide. Like Claude, Mama Lambert had found friends and a new family in the outstretched arms of the other survivors at Solace. She also found a relationship with Jesus Christ. As Mama Lambert told Claude and the other orphans, Christ became for her a refuge and took away her burdens. As she herself found comfort, she began to comfort and counsel other widows and orphans.

She was one of several who began teaching Claude how to pray. From Mama Lambert and others, Claude began to learn how to go to God for both comfort and his daily needs.

As Solace ministered to him, Claude also began to move out in compassion to others. The reality of those orphaned in the genocide — some three hundred thousand children — continued to be a burden on the recovering country. So at twenty-three years of age, Claude accepted a role as the head of a household of fifteen other orphaned children. Living in community helped ease his loneliness, but there was also the added burden of responsibility. Through part-time jobs, Claude began to earn a bit of money to pay for the housing, transportation, and some of the other needs of his household. During that time, Claude was deeply touched by the home visits he received from other survivors whom Solace had helped and who would come and check on those whom were new to the family.

It was during one of those night meetings when the world pivoted for Claude. Over the months since he had started attending the Solace meetings, Claude had developed a deeply personal relationship with God. He now prayed frequently and had begun to find hope in the new understanding he had of the meaning of Christ's death.

That night when Solace's founder, Jean Gakwandi, and two widows visited Claude, they talked for a while. Before they left, they asked Claude if he would like them to pray with him. Claude eagerly accepted. During that time of prayer, Claude laid before God the full story of what had happened to him during the genocide. As Claude listened, God began to speak to him, and Claude heard words of promise from the Bible. In particular, Claude heard that God had not left him as an orphan, but had given him the Holy Spirit. God also reminded Claude that he was a member of the household of God, adopted by a loving eternal Father.

During that time God reminded Claude that he too had been forgiven. The knowledge of that forgiveness began to work its way through Claude's heart and convict him. Claude knew that he needed to let go of the hatred in his heart for the people who had killed his family—he knew that he also needed to forgive.

ONE OF THE MOST HAUNTING THINGS ABOUT LIVING IN RWANDA AFTER the genocide is that killers still walk among survivors.

About a month after God had begun to convict Claude of his need to forgive, Claude went to visit a friend on the other side of Kigali. He had just gotten off the bus and had begun the walk to his friend's house. The streets bustled with people heading to the market, balancing baskets of vegetables on their heads and riding bicycles weighed down with banana bunches. Claude was lost in thought as faces of all shapes and sizes rushed by him.

Then, out of his peripheral vision, Claude saw a familiar profile. He felt the hair on the back of his neck rise and his skin prickle. In disbelief, he turned to get a better look at the man. Nothing could erase that face from Claude's memory. It was a face he had grown up seeing, a face that had haunted his dreams in the years since leaving Kibuye.

Kanyenzi hadn't noticed Claude. He was moving against the flow of foot traffic, walking a bicycle loaded down with bags of rice. One of the bags had begun to work its way loose, and Kanyenzi was presently stopped, trying to tighten the rope that held the rice.

Without even stopping to think, Claude began to move in the direction of Kanyenzi—the man who had hunted for him on the hillside, seeking to kill him, whose voice he heard calling his name as he cut through brush with his machete. By the time Claude reached him, Kanyenzi was kneeling with one knee to the ground, his head bowed as he fumbled with the rope and the heavy canvas bags of rice. His neck exposed, his body bent, Kayenzi tinkered, unaware of Claude's presence. As Claude took in the scene, the rage inside him began to boil. But then, even as he continued to watch Kanyenzi, Claude felt the calming presence of God come over him.

"Hello," said Claude to the man at his feet. Kanyenzi craned his neck around to see who had stopped to speak to him. When he recognized Claude, Kanyenzi almost knocked the bike over. He knew Claude's face immediately, but it was almost like seeing a ghost towering over him.

Claude noticed that Kanyenzi seemed to be shaking a little as he stood to his feet. He reached for the bicycle to steady him and nearly turned it over.

"Claude?"

"Yes," he said. "You're surprised to see me alive, aren't you?"

"Yes. What are you doing here?"

"I live here — not here exactly — but in Kigali. You?"

"Yes — I live here too now."

The men fell silent. Then, "I want to know something," said Claude.

Kanyenzi threw back his head to indicate that Claude could proceed.

"Why did you hunt me down in 1994?"

"That wasn't me, Claude. I — I was sick then, suffering from malaria."

"That's nonsense. You know it. You walked through the hills, calling out my name, searching for me. My sister was with me — she heard you. Why did you want to kill me?"

"I was searching for you, yes," he admitted. "But it wasn't to kill you. I wanted to hide you, to protect you from the killers."

"We both know that is foolishness."

Kanyenzi looked away.

"Listen," spoke Claude again, taking a deep breath as he did so, "I want you to know, if you approach me, and tell me the truth, I'm ready to forgive you. If you know God, you need to seek him. You need to ask him to forgive you. He knows, you know, and I know what you tried to do to me during the war. I'm ready to forgive you, but first you need to admit the truth—to yourself, to God, and to me."

Claude waited as Kanyenzi shifted nervously in front of him.

"I'll be waiting," said Claude after an awkward silence had passed. "I'm sure you can find me."

WHEN THE VAN BEGAN TO THUMP OVER THE DEEP POTHOLES AND gullies, Claude knew he was nearing the hill where he had grown up. It was only the second time for him to return there since the genocide. He felt almost as nervous this time as he had before, only now for quite a different reason.

He'd traveled back home for the dedication of a genocide memorial in his town. Bones of the dead had been gathered and buried in large crypts around one of the churches in that area that had been attacked. Inside, skulls and bones were spread out neatly on tables as reminders of the lives that had been lost. Large purple ribbons, the official color of mourning, looped around the outside fence.

Grief, anger, loneliness, and shame washed over Claude as he stood inside the church for the ceremony. Officials from the state were there for the dedication, as were many survivors, like Claude, who had traveled back to the area for the commemoration.

One of the dignitaries spoke, but Claude could scarcely listen —the raw emotions of genocide were too close at hand. Standing there, as his memories flooded back, Claude could feel the palms of his hands sweating and his heart thumping wildly. In some ways, he still felt like that thirteen-year-old boy hidden in the tall grasses; in other ways it felt like a lifetime ago.

Aside from the lump in his throat, a tight knot had formed in his stomach. As a survivor stood to share her grief and her hope for Rwanda's future, Claude's mind was miles away already. He knew that the commemoration wasn't the only reason he had come.

CLAUDE HAD MISSED THE COUNTRYSIDE. IN KIGALI, PEOPLE LIVED on top of each other. Only at nightfall, when the lights of the homes twinkled in the valley below, did Claude catch a glimpse that reminded him of the peace he had once known in his village. Even in those glimpses, it was a far cry from this.

As his feet kicked up the dust of the red dirt path below, he looked out across the familiar dark outline of the Virunga Mountains. The waters of Lake Kivu reflected the cloudless blue of the sky. Each square inch of land seemed neatly manicured in the well-tended terraces of meticulous farmers. Claude marveled again at the beauty lavished on this place.

Hugging the narrow path that led up the hill toward the remains of his home, Claude wondered about the lives of the children who still lived in these hills. He knew that many of the men had either been sent off to prison or had gone into hiding in the Congo, too afraid to face the consequences of their guilt.

As he walked along, looking out over the landscape of both his most cherished and most horrendous memories, Claude couldn't help but think how much had changed since he had last traveled these paths. He was making good headway in his college classes. He still wanted to study law, but his motives had changed from the vengeful ones that had driven him just a few years before. Nothing could replace his family, but Claude felt a deep satisfaction in helping to care for the other orphans. He'd even begun helping with the youth camps that Solace led, bringing Hutu and Tutsi youth together, and encouraging them to work together for a new peaceful future for Rwanda.

He loved teaching them. One of the stories he liked best was the biblical story of Joseph — mistreated, betrayed, and sold by his own fiercely jealous brothers. Life had bruised Joseph time and again — from his boss's wife who had falsely accused him of improper advances, to the long years in prison, to the neglect he felt even at the hands of those to whom he had shown kindness. But despite it all, God had shown favor to Joseph. He raised him from prison to the halls of power, where he served next to the most powerful leader of that day. Through Joseph, God had provided for the people in famine. And when at last Joseph's own brothers — the very ones who had betrayed him — came seeking help in the famine, Joseph chose to bless them rather than carry out the revenge he could have so easily arranged. He told them that the very things they had intended for evil, God had used for good.

As Claude taught that story, he would always see the young people nod in recognition. He knew how the story rippled through his audience with the same hope that had rippled through him when he had first heard it.

Already Claude had seen so many changes in the young people with whom he volunteered his time. There was Nadia, for example. When he had first begun interacting with her at the Solace youth meetings, she had been without direction and hope. Claude and others at Solace had comforted her and urged her to look at the fact that she had been given the gift of life. These days he had seen such a change in her. She had become the overseer of a hostel, and was finishing her second year in the university.

Nadia wasn't the only one he'd seen transformed. Claude had seen another boy named Kagame, like their president, come out of a deep depression. It felt like such a privilege to see God changing the lives of these young people. When he thought about it, he felt like a rich man.

In so many aspects of his life, Claude saw life beginning to bud again. As the homes of the killers rose up before him, he realized he was probably better off than the children of the men who had sought to kill him and who had succeeded in killing his family.

Perhaps it was because of the dedication of the memorial that the families who still lived in these hills did not scatter as Claude appeared, coming up the steep path. Perhaps it was because, like Joseph, he had changed so much that the people he had been born beside didn't even recognize him. Whatever the reason, when Claude knocked on the door of Innocent's home, he answered.

Recently released from prison, Innocent looked much older than Claude had remembered him. Malaria and residual guilt had bent his body like a strung bow. The old man's eyes widened as he saw Claude—he recognized the boy turned man. After all, he had been there when Claude was born. Claude's father, Thomas, had given Innocent the land he now lived on with his family.

In return for Thomas's kindness, Innocent had led a band of killers who murdered Claude's aunt, uncle, and grandmother. As Innocent stood there staring at Claude, he saw Thomas standing before him. Just seeing Claude, Innocent felt overwhelmed with guilt.

Guilt hadn't come immediately. In fact, he had spent nearly six years in prison before he began to feel remorse for his actions. But he remembered the day clearly—April 26, 2004—that he had turned to God and begged for forgiveness.

"Nkundumkiza?" asked the old man, calling Claude by his Rwandan name.

"Yes," said Claude, "it's me."

"Why have you come back to this place?"

"I'm here to tell you that if you confess, I'm ready to forgive you."

Innocent stepped back and tried to catch his breath. If Claude had hit him, he would have been less surprised.

"I'm the one who should have come to you," he said, still staggered. "Can you possibly forgive the man who killed your own grandmother, your aunt, and your uncle? Please, Nkundumkiza, I beg you to forgive me."

Tears streamed down the faces of both men by this time.

"With God's help, I forgive you," said Claude, choking back the pain and the relief of the moment.

CLAUDE MADE SEVERAL MORE STOPS IN THE VILLAGE THAT DAY BEFORE leaving to return to Kigali. Not all the people he met were as deeply repentant as Innocent. One family thought Claude had come to turn them over to the police for their actions in the genocide. They tried to bribe Claude with a cow, but he refused it. Others rejoiced to see Claude as if their husbands hadn't been among the men who had tracked Claude and his family down in 1994. Everywhere Claude went, he carried the same message. "You need to face the truth. I'm ready to forgive you, if you'll come to me and confess what you've done."

Returning back to Kigali and the children in his care, Claude felt changed. He tried to explain it to the others in his household, "I feel as though I'm free in my heart now. Before I forgave, I was small. Now I'm big."

Even so, the old feelings hadn't completely vanished. Claude found that even though he had forgiven Innocent, and had said he was ready to forgive others if they confessed, he still had to wrestle with the decision in his heart over and over again. Each day, he woke and prayed. Sometimes he prayed the Lord's Prayer. When he got to the lines, "forgive us our trespasses, as we forgive those who trespass against us," Claude would pray again for the strength to continue extending mercy.

Meanwhile, he continued with his studies, with his part-time jobs that helped provide for the household, and with encouraging the other children and young people, some of whom called him "Brother" and some "Daddy."

"How's your future?" he would ask them with a smile. "How are you preparing for your future? You're an orphan? That's true. But you must prepare for your future."

And so they would talk about the challenges that faced them. They'd talk through ideas, and sometimes Claude would see hope sparkle in their eyes. "Don't sleep. Wake up and dream," he'd say. And then he would pray with them.

ABOUT A YEAR AFTER THAT VISIT HOME, SOMETHING SEEMED TO beckon Claude back to the shores of Lake Kivu and to the sights and sounds of the hills he had loved as a boy, especially walking the cattle home at dusk.

Claude made his way to one of his favorite spots, a promontory overlooking the water and the mountains. He settled in while the descending sun reflected off the smooth surface of the water. The water, eager to be as beautiful as the mountains, the sun, and the sky, mirrored their palette with deep purple, warm gold, and pale rose hues.

Claude picked a blade of grass and slid it between his thumb and forefinger as he contemplated the morphing colors at the crowning of the day. He wondered at how God seemed to especially lavish such beauty at sunset and sunrise. And yet dawn and dusk, God squandered beauty on a world that is often at best oblivious, and at worst deeply antagonistic. Claude couldn't comprehend such generosity, such constancy, such goodness, but like the water he longed to reflect these hues. It was as if beauty gave us something worth dreaming about and something worth living for.

The imagination that had seen sleeping sea monsters in the shadows of mountains was rumbling again. Looking out at the horizon's edge, Claude's mind wandered to Rwanda's borders. He thought of Congo, wracked with violence of its own, of Burundi, suffering with many of the same dynamics that had torn Rwanda apart at the seams, and then beyond their borders to the Sudan. He longed for the healing that he had begun to see in his own heart and the reconciliation he had begun to see in many of his fellow Rwandans, to know no borders.

Claude's mind turned with possibilities, wondering what role he might play in that dream. He had seen how violence could startle a sleeping world. As never before, Claude was awake to the evil, the pain, and the suffering in the world around him. But having experienced his life both shattered and restored, he knew now that only hope could make the world wake up and dream. Only hope could offer the courage to carry the dream of beauty into the darkness of night and through the heat of the day. As the sun melted into the mountains, Claude stretched. He lingered for a moment in the twilight, before turning to go. It felt good to be awake and alive.

reconciliation as a transfiguration moment

WHEN I BEGAN RESEARCHING THE FORGIVENESS JOURNEYS OF Rosaria, Joy, Chantal, Monique, Devota, Phanuel, and Claude, I decided to explore the meanings of their names. I soon discovered that just as novelists carefully choose evocative names, so too do Rwandans, usually taking much more care in naming their children than their Western counterparts. For Rwandans, a naming ceremony for newborns is a much-anticipated rite. The ceremony generally occurs within the first four months after the birth of a child, and is marked with the sharing of banana beer amid community members. The mother or father will bring out the baby, and neighbors, friends, and family members will thoughtfully examine the child and offer suggested names replete with meaning. As the baby is held up to the sky, the father will choose the name he thinks most fitting, a name chosen not *before* the child is seen, but *after*, in the presence and with the collective wisdom of the community.

Had the people whose stories I tell here been my own fictional creations, sprung directly from my imagination, I could not have chosen better names for them. I am awestruck as I have learned how they have either lived toward or away from the meaning of their names.

There was Rosaria—a woman more given to prayer, Scripture memorization, and devotion than one may ever see. Rosaria's name means, quite simply, "rosary," and the name couldn't have been draped over a more prayerful woman. From her story you will remember that she named her daughter fittingly—Cadeaux, meaning "gift," and Byukusenge, meaning "wake up and pray."

Saveri, a derivative of Xavier, literally—and surprisingly —means "new house." This was Saveri, a killer who with the very same hands that killed Rosaria's family later smoothed bricks into a home for Rosaria and her family.

Then there was Joy. When I met Joy, I was amazed by the understated beauty of this young teenager: tall, slender, with eyes soft and brown like a deer, and a short boyish haircut. Her smile could warm an entire room, offering no clues about the horrors she had experienced. Yet, somehow, there now stands a girl—strong, dignified, and radiant—whose spirit of overcoming brings joy to all she knows.

My first look at Chantal came through Laura Waters Hinson's documentary film. Her eyes were red, her face sunken, with dark hollows beneath her eyes. She was full of rage, bitterness, and pain. I discovered the name Chantal means "stony place." The Chantal who had not yet forgiven John looked as desolate and lifeless as any stony place I could imagine.

John, the man who killed Chantal's father, ultimately found grace in God, and that grace was extended to him through Chantal. It was fitting then that this repentant murderer's name would mean, "Yahweh is gracious." Unmerited favor had certainly been extended to John.

When I interviewed Monique, she told me about the care she

had exercised in naming her son Seth, who was the "appointed" gift God gave to Eve after Cain killed Abel. I was familiar with that story, but had little familiarity with the story of Monica, the name from which Monique is derived. Scholars aren't sure what Monica means. Some think that it means perhaps "counselor," while others suggest "solitary."

What scholars do agree on is that the name gained prominence from the many women who named their children after St. Monica, the mother of St. Augustine. Monica was married to an alcoholic and abusive man. When she came to embrace the Christian faith, she eventually led, through her gentle spirit, this abusive man to repent of his ways and turn to God also. Monica's other children soon became Christians as well—all except for the dissolute Augustine, who continued to live a wild life. Monica prayed fervently for her son, even following him to Africa and pleading with him to change. One bishop who saw her weeping comforted her, saying, "The child of such tears shall never perish." Accordingly, Augustine eventually turned from the path of destruction. He is regarded as one of the key theologians of the Christian faith, while his mother is regarded as the patron saint of abused women.

When I first met Devota, I shook hands with a woman whose skin was softer than any I had felt before. When she unwrapped the beautiful scarf from around her head and turned to show me the machete gash at the back of her neck, it wasn't difficult to imagine how easily a machete could have severed such soft skin. What was difficult to imagine was how she could have survived—let alone be the encouraging woman she is. Devota's name means "devout," as the sound suggests. Like her name, this machete-scarred woman is so devoted that she follows God's leading into prisons, sharing with and teaching would-be enemies, offering peace and hope.

I'd never heard the name Phanuel before he spoke it to me. Phanuel is a biblical name that comes from the name given to the place where Jacob wrestled with the angel of God. It means "the face, the vision, or appearance of God." The Phanuel I met in Rwanda also told me that he saw a vision of God in a dream, and through wrestling with the meaning of that dream, he came to forgive.

It was Claude I interviewed last and with whom I would have perhaps the most deeply moving and personal experience. He agreed to take me to meet one of the men who had killed his family and to show me the place where he had survived the genocide. But when he told me the name of the man who killed his family, I had to ask Claude to repeat it. "His name is Innocent," replied Claude. And what does Claude's name mean? Going by his full name Jean Claude, it means "Yahweh is gracious to the weak."

As I struggled to understand this, Claude offered to pray for Innocent: "Almighty God, I am happy to pray to you. Thank you, God, for helping us travel from Kigali to this place and for your blessing, because we know Satan didn't want this to happen today. Thank you, God, that now you have joined me with this man today.

"God, you saw what happened in this country: we lost our families; we spent long days in the bush; it was raining very hard, but, God, you protected us. You had a purpose for us. This man, even though he killed a lot of people, today you want to forgive him and heal his heart. I thank you, God, that this man here, living here, is still alive, that he has changed his heart — has confessed. I ask you to bless this man. As you said, God, I am asking — I want to be blessed and for you to bless also this man.

"In Jesus' name, I ask that you remove all Satan's power in

this man and build a new heart in him. God, help the killers to pray and to change.

"God, I ask that you heal the sickness of this man if it is possible. Your will be done to this man. It is possible for him to be healed. This is not the only man who did wrong. We know, God, that you are the One who heals. Almighty God, please heal this man in Jesus' name.

"And for the survivors of this country, please help them. Please, God, you are the only one who can join the different people in this country, even throughout Africa. In the name of Jesus, we pray, amen."

Any person, regardless of faith or background, will glimpse the beauty of this moment. I couldn't close my eyes as we joined arms in this circle together. It was a moment of transfiguration for all of us. I felt like one of the three disciples who had been permitted to join Jesus on the mountain for a glimpse of his true glory. Here, for a moment, it felt as though the thin veil between heaven and earth was lifted to reveal a hint of true shalom.

In this transfiguration moment, I saw an orphan whose very name means "weak" standing in strength and extending forgiveness. I saw a man who was anything but innocent covered in the grace of the one who could accuse him — and covered in the grace of Christ who died so that Innocent could become exactly that.

Many people see forgiveness in a purely therapeutic light, an act that releases victims from the pain of bitterness and the prison of the past. This is true, but it is only part of the story. Forgiveness is also, as Dietrich Bonhoeffer so rightly said, a form of suffering. Miroslav Volf saw this in Christ's own passion, which he calls a prayer for the torturer. He wrote, "Under the foot of the cross we learn, however, that in a world of irreversible deeds and partisan judgments, redemption from the passive suffering of victimization cannot happen without the active suffering of forgiveness."[1] I know enough of Claude's own story to believe that he couldn't have offered that prayer except through the pain of his own experience. Forgiving is an active form of suffering offered on behalf of the victim to create a pathway of redemption, of peace, of shalom.

Transfigure is a fascinating word. *Metamorphosis* comes from a Greek word many of us know, meaning to change into another form, or for the outside to change to match the inside. In the transfiguration of Jesus, while the divine nature of Christ was still veiled (cf. Hebrews 10:20), his disciples glimpsed the glory of God. Reconciliation, likewise, offers us a glimpse of shalom, the peace that means the flourishing of humans and this world. True reconciliation shows the innocent extending love and grace in a way that is truly transformative, and that mirrors the divine nature of self-giving love. True reconciliation means evil humans turning from evil ways and walking in a way of goodness. It shows the brokenness of the world, like a fractured bone, being set back into its rightful position. True reconciliation lets us glimpse a world where both the victim and the offender desire that the other be blessed and flourish. In our world we only get glimpses of such true reconciliation, but I believe that such glimpses are all we need to take that vision back into the brokenness of our daily lives. That glimpse of shalom can change the way we act and react.

Like the names we are given, we have no control over the circumstances in our lives. We can choose, however, whether we will live into their meaning, or out of them. Chantal can choose to let her heart be a stony place or let it be transformed into rich, life-giving soil. Joy can choose whether the circumstances of her life will drown out the triumph of her name. Innocent can live in open rebellion to his name or embrace the God who can make his past as white as snow.

One of the names given to Jesus Christ was Emmanuel, or "God with us." Christ lived into his name. He was "with us" in that he took on human flesh and walked among us. He was "with us" in carrying both our sins and our sorrows to the cross. When God raised this man, Jesus Christ, from the dead, he didn't take away his scars. These scars testify to his pain, to his love, and to the extent to which God will go to conquer the evil of the world through the active suffering of forgiveness. Only through such active love can such scars of horror be transfigured into emblems of triumph.

Emmanuel was the seventeen-year-old whose scars began this story. Like a jagged boundary line, a scar juts across his face. It is a reminder of two realities: the human capacity for astonishing evil and the breathtaking human ability to heal. As much as I wanted to look away from Emmanuel's face, a face that came to symbolize to me the face of Rwanda, I couldn't. The scars of both of these Emmanuels are telling a story of pain, of healing, and of hope—a story I need to hear told and retold. Pain does not have to have the last word. Forgiveness can push out the borders of what we believe is possible. Reconciliation can offer us a glimpse of the transfigured world to come.

acknowledgments

A FEW YEARS AGO I HAD THE CHANCE TO STUDY ABOUT THE CLAPHAM Circle, a group of men and women with diverse occupations and gifts who came alongside William Wilberforce. Together they toppled the slave trade in England. I marveled at how the collaborative efforts of these friends and colleagues changed the face of England, and truly of the world. While I have no false pretensions of being a Wilberforce, I have nonetheless been deeply privileged to see that same spirit of collaboration alive and well in my small corner of the world. This book would not have been possible without the amazingly gifted individuals who aided every step of the way.

The creative vision for this project is really owed in large part to Laura Waters Hinson, whose documentary film *As We Forgive* inspired this book. Laura generously provided contact information for the people featured in her film (three of my seven stories), as well as the transcripts of her interviews and film footage. Laura was the trailblazer, and without her courage and vision, I might never have found the path.

Likewise, I am grateful to Debs Gardner-Patterson, whose short film *We Are All Rwandans*, tells the story of the Nyange school shooting. Debs also graciously shared the transcript of her screenplay and the film itself with me. The chapters on Prisca and Phanuel benefited greatly from the extensive research she did in meeting with

-265-

a large number of survivors of the Nyange incident and recreating their story in film.

There, of course, would not have been a book without the vulnerability and heart of the men and women whose stories I tell here. I can't begin to express my gratitude for how these men and women opened up the most deeply painful and sometimes shameful chapters of their lives and shared them with me and with the world. Time and again, I was humbled and amazed by the lessons I learned from these survivors, ex-offenders, and mediators. I thank them for their courage and their hope that their stories can help change the lives of others.

Zoe Sandvig, Greg Justice, and Livingston Sheats were the adventurous and giving souls who took me up on the wild idea of traveling to Rwanda to investigate a potential book. In a true act of faith they gave of their vacation, savings, and creative insight to make this project a reality. They waded through the grief of these Rwandan stories as we took turns interviewing survivors, ex-prisoners, and other Rwandans. And they undergirded my writing and research efforts through their faithful prayer support. Without their willing spirits, this project might never have lifted off the ground.

I can't mention them without also thanking our translator Chris Karasira, who helped us connect and build rapport with our interviewees. Chris also kept us laughing when the days grew long. Emmanuel Kwizera and Christophe Mbonyigabo were the wizards behind the curtain who helped connect us with so many people involved in reconciliation efforts on the ground in Rwanda. And Phil and Becca Smith of World Relief Rwanda graciously opened their home to us during our stay in Kigali. Experts John Steward and Meg Guillebaud also gave very good coaching on how to talk with and understand those who have been traumatized by genocide. The contacts they provided opened doors for us.

Zoe, Greg, Liv, and I never would have gotten to Rwanda in

the first place had it not been for the generous support of so many friends, our families, and our church, who supported our trip financially and who prayed for us continually. So many people prayed for this project and for me during the writing of it. I'm so appreciative and wish there was space to mention everyone by name.

I first came to learn about Rwanda's reconciliation efforts while interviewing for my current job with Prison Fellowship. My first story—in fact, my interview assignment—was to write about a man named John Rucyahana, the chairman of Prison Fellowship Rwanda. His story and the story of Prison Fellowship Rwanda's Umuvumu Tree Village made a lasting impact on me. My colleagues at Prison Fellowship have provided much encouragement and insight in this process as well. Conversations with Dan Van Ness, the director of the Center for Justice and Reconciliation at Prison Fellowship International, were formative in much of my thinking. His edits as well as those of David Carlson, vice president of communications, helped me refine and improve my message. Karen Strong provided helpful contacts and insight as well. And without the encouragement of my boss, Chuck Colson, I might not have had the audacity to write a book at all.

By nature, I have to talk before I write. (Perhaps if my elementary school teachers had understood that I would have gotten better grades in conduct.) But there were many sets of ears who served as a sounding board for this idea: my brother Dan Claire and his wife, Elise, who listened enthusiastically when the idea first came to me; my other brother David Claire and his wife, Amy, who fanned the idea's flame; Garrett Brown, Meredith Henne, Angela Wu, and Tom Walsh, who let me brainstorm with them; my dearest friends and writing buddies Lori Smith and Kristine Steakley, who offered of their publishing knowledge and encouragement at many points along the way; and the lunch bunch, Travis, Drew, Meaghan, Faith, Eric, and Zoe, who helped when I just needed to blow off steam and get my mind off the book. And finally, my agent Beth Jusino listened to my passion for this project and believed in it enough to help me refine the original proposal to find the right publisher.

While many ears listened to my ideas, many eyes proofed and examined early drafts of this book. In addition to many of the people listed above, I'm grateful to Bishop Alexis Bilidingbago, who read and offered feedback on the manuscript. As a genocide survivor and reconciliation leader, Alexis' encouragement and critique meant so much. My editor, Angela Scheff at Zondervan, also took this manuscript to the next level with her on-target suggestions for improvement and edits.

Finally, I'm grateful to the people closest to me. My parents, Earl and Sally Claire, listened, gave, read, encouraged, prayed, and walked this journey with me. They've been my number one fans for three decades now, and their encouragement and faith in me, I hope, has paid off in this manuscript.

And last, to the man who will be my husband by the time this book hits shelves: Mark, God used you to bring this book to life. Your daily prayers, your steadfast confidence in me, and your faith that this book can make a difference in the lives of those who read it sustained me through the emotionally exhausting writing process. I couldn't have done it without you.

resources

If you are interested in helping to further reconciliation in Rwanda, here is a list of ministries to contact or support.

AEE, African Evangelistic Enterprise

AEE/Rwanda is a Christian interdenominational, multicultural ministry of evangelism, reconciliation, leadership development training, relief, and community development that works under national leadership in Rwanda. AEE/Rwanda works closely with local church and parachurch leaders in Rwanda to mobilize congregations in outreach to key cities in Rwanda. AEE was influential in conducting the healing workshops that helped Devota learn to forgive.

AEE/Rwanda
P.O. Box 1435
Kigali, Rwanda
aee@rwanda1.com
www.africanenterprise.org

CARSA, Christian Action for Reconciliation and Social Assistance

CARSA Ministries—Christian Action for Reconciliation and Social Assistance (CARSA)—is a nonprofit organization formed in 2002 for the purpose of promoting reconciliation, reconstruction, and the restoration of a peaceful society. The healing workshops conducted through CARSA helped people like Chantal, John, and Monique to find healing.

CARSA Ministries
P.O. Box 3408
Kigali, Rwanda
carsa_ministry@yahoo.fr
www.carsa.org.rw/carsa/english.htm

Center for Justice and Reconciliation

Prison Fellowship International's Center for Justice and Reconciliation promotes restorative justice initiatives that work to heal broken relationships, repair the damage done by crime, and restore the offender to a meaningful role in society. The research and training provided by this center have helped to equip countries like Rwanda to engage in restorative justice efforts such as the Umuvumu Tree Project.

Center for Justice and Reconciliation
Prison Fellowship International
P.O. Box 17434
Washington, DC 20041
1-703-481-0000
rjonline@pfi.org
www.restorativejustice.org

MOUCECORE

MOUCECORE (Mouvement Chretien pour l'Evengelisation, le Counselling et la Reconciliation or The Christian Movement for Evangelism, Counseling, and Reconciliation) is a nongovernmental organization based in Kigali, Rwanda. The organization focuses on discipleship, peace-building, healing, reconciliation, sustainable community development, and HIV/AIDS care and prevention.

> **MOUCECORE**
> P.O. Box 2540
> Kigali, Rwanda
> mouce@rwanda1.com
> http://www.moucecore.org.rw/index.htm

PHARP, Peace-building, Healing, and Reconciliation Programme

PHARP Rwanda began in 1998 to facilitate healing and reconciliation by focusing on training leaders from groups of youth, women, and pastors, who in turn reach out to many people in their own churches and communities. The main purpose was to create opportunity for dialogue where people from different ethnic groups and religious backgrounds could begin to share experiences and sufferings and create an understanding. This led to confessions and the offering of forgiveness between the participants as well as the transformation of attitudes people previously held toward one another.

> **PHARP**
> P.O. Box 2425
> Kigali, Rwanda
> pharp@rwanda1.com
> www.pharp.org

Prison Fellowship International

Prison Fellowship International (PFI) is the world's largest and most extensive criminal justice ministry with over one hundred national Prison Fellowship organizations worldwide. It is active in every region of the world with a network of more than one hundred thousand volunteers working for the spiritual, moral, social, and physical well-being of prisoners, ex-prisoners, their families, and victims of crime. The national Prison Fellowship organizations are indigenous, volunteer-based, and transdenominational. Prison Fellowship Rwanda has been actively involved in developing victim-offender reconciliation programs through the Umuvumu Tree Workshops and the house-building project which was featured in the story of Rosaria and Saveri.

Prison Fellowship (U.S. headquarters)
P.O. Box 17434
Washington, D.C. 20041
1-703-481-0000
info@pfi.org
www.pfi.org

Prison Fellowship Rwanda
P.O. Box 2098
Kigali, Rwanda
bpjohnr@rwanda1.com
nyirakaberuka@yahoo.fr
http://www.pfi.org/news/regionaltop/pf-rwanda/

Rwandan Partners

Since 2004, Rwanda Partners has been working directly with the Rwandan people as they seek to rebuild, reconcile, and restore their lives and their nation. They do this through developing projects to care for the needs of Rwanda's vulnerable poor, and by partnering with Rwandan men and women that are seeking to make a tangible difference in their country in the area of healing, reconciliation, and restoration but who need help to do this. Rwanda Partners provides these individuals or organizations with financial support, training, encouragement, personnel, and any other necessary support to help them carry out their God-given call to care for Rwanda's hurting people. Rwanda Partners supports AEE, CARSA, and other reconciliation groups.

> **Rwanda Partners**
> 12420 NE 7th Place
> Bellevue, WA 98005
> 888-342-4999
> info@rwandapartners.org
> www.rwandapartners.org

Solace Ministries

Solace Ministries is a Christian nonprofit organization primarily devoted to bringing healing and hope to the widows and orphans of Rwanda. Through the outreach and care of Solace, Claude learned to forgive and seek reconciliation with the people who killed his family.

> **Solace USA, Inc.**
> W164 N9703 Water St.
> Germantown, WI 53022
> 262-251-0598
> info@solaceusa.org
> www.solaceusa.org

> **Solace Rwanda**
> P.O. Box 6090
> Kigali, Rwanda
> mucyo@rwanda1.com
> www.solacem.org

Sonrise School and Orphanage

Bishop John founded the Sonrise School to be a "light on a hill" and a demonstration to everyone in Rwanda as to what is possible. The school's mission is to set the standard for academic excellence and servant leadership. The majority of the Sonrise School's students, like Joy, are genocide/AIDS orphans chosen because they were the neediest children in their villages. Because the majority of the Sonrise School's students are orphans, the Mustard Seed Project launched a student sponsorship program to fund the annual operating costs of boarding and educating each of the school's orphaned students. To support the program contact:

> **Sonrise Orphans Ministry**
> P.O. Box 1337
> Moon Township, PA 15108
> www.mustardseedproject.org

World Relief Rwanda

The Mission of World Relief, as originated within the National Association of Evangelicals, is to work with, for, and from the church to relieve human suffering, poverty, and hunger worldwide in the name of Jesus Christ. Many of the economic development projects in Rwanda are microenterprise efforts that help further practical reconciliation.

> **World Relief Rwanda**
> 7 East Baltimore St.
> Baltimore, MD 21202
> 443-451-1900 or 800-535-5433
> worldrelief@wr.org
> www.rwanda.wr.org

World Vision

World Vision is a Christian humanitarian organization dedicated to working with children, families, and their communities worldwide to reach their full potential by tackling the causes of poverty and injustice. John Steward worked with World Vision Rwanda in developing and facilitating healing and reconciliation workshops.

World Vision
P.O. Box 9716, Dept. W
Federal Way, WA 98063-9716
1-888-511-6548
www.worldvision.org

choices on the way to peace

Steps to Forgiveness

The Victim

Step 1

- I face my truth.
- I move from denial to grieving the loss.
- I open my wounds and begin to heal my pain and shame.
- I forgive myself and cease blaming.
- I accept God's forgiveness

Step 2

The first hand of forgiveness ...
I let go of my bitterness and the right to revenge.

Step 3

The second hand of forgiveness ...
I confront the offender with a request to uphold my dignity by restoring something of what was lost.

Step 4

I become open to accepting the humanity and dignity of the offender—and even the possibility of restoring the relationship

Moving toward Justice

The Offender

Step 1

- I face my truth.
- I move from rationalizing to grieving my losses.
- I open my wounds and begin to heal my pain and shame.
- I forgive myself and cease running away.
- I accept God's forgiveness.

Step 2

The first foot of justice ...
I repent and turn to face the victim.

Step 3

The second foot of justice ...
I step toward the victim, apologize, and make an offer of restitution.

Step 4

I become open to accepting the humanity and dignity of the victim—and even the possibility of restoring the relationship.

bibliography

Augsburger, David. *Helping People Forgive.* Louisville: Westminster, 1996.

Cartensen, Laura, John Gottman, and Robert Levenson. "Emotional Behavior in Long-term Marriage." *Psychology and Aging* 10, no. 1 (March 1995): 140–49.

Dayton, Tian. *The Magic of Forgiveness: Emotional Freedom and Transformation at Mid-life.* Deerfield Beach, Fla.: Health, 2003.

DeMoss, Nancy Leigh. *Choosing Forgiveness: Your Journey to Freedom.* Chicago: Moody Press, 2006.

Huyse, Luc, and Mark Salter. *Traditional Justice and Reconciliation after Violent Conflict: Learning from African Experiences.* Stockholm: International Institute for Democracy and Electoral Assistance, 2008. Available online at www.idea.int/publications/traditional_justice/upload/Traditional_Justice_and_Reconciliation_after_Violent_Conflict.pdf.

Kraybill, Donald, Steven Nolt, and David Weaver-Zercher. *Amish Grace: How Forgiveness Transcended Tragedy.* San Francisco: Jossey-Bass, 2007.

Luskin, Fred. *Forgive for Good: A Proven Prescription for Health and Happiness.* San Francisco: HarperCollins, 2002.

———. *Forgive for Love.* San Francisco: HarperOne, 2007.

Philpott, Daniel, ed. *The Politics of Past Evil: Religion, Reconciliation,*

bibliography

and the Dilemmas of Transitional Justice. Notre Dame, Ind.:
University of Notre Dame Press, 2006.

Sande, Ken. *The Peacemaker: A Biblical Guide to Resolving Conflict*.
Grand Rapids, Mich.: Baker, 2004.

Tiemessen, Alana Erin. "After Arusha: Gacaca Justice in Post-Genocide
Rwanda." *African Studies Quarterly* 8, no. 1 (Fall 2004).

Tutu, Desmond. *No Future without Forgiveness*. New York: Image, 2000.

Umbreit, Mark S. *Victim-Offender Mediation Training Manual*. Center
for Restorative Justice and Peacemaking, School of Social Work,
University of Minnesota, 1998.

Van Ness, Daniel E., and Karen Strong. *Restoring Justice*. Second edition.
Cincinnati: Anderson, 2002.

Volf, Miroslav. *The End of Memory*. Grand Rapids, Mich.: Eerdmans,
2006.

———. *Exclusion and Embrace*. Nashville: Abingdon, 1996.

———. *Free of Charge: Giving and Forgiving in a Culture Stripped of
Grace*. Grand Rapids, Mich.: Zondervan, 2005.

Worthington, Everett L. Jr., ed. *Dimensions of Forgiveness: Psychological
Research & Theological Perspectives*. Philadelphia and London: The
Templeton Foundation Press, 1998.

———. *Five Steps to Forgiveness: The Art and Science of Forgiving*. New
York: Crown, 2001.

Zehr, Howard. "Restoring Justice." In *God and the Victim*. Edited by Lisa
Barnes Lampman. Grand Rapids, Mich.: Eerdmans, 1999.

For Further Reading

Bilindabagabo, Alexis. *Rescued by Angels*. Lancaster, Pa.: Acorn, 2001.

Colson, Charles. *Justice That Restores*. Wheaton, Ill.: Tyndale, 2001.

Cose, Ellis. *Bone to Pick*. New York: Atria, 2004.

Dallaire, Romeo. *Shake Hands with the Devil*. New York: Carroll and
Graf, 2003.

Des Forges, Alison. *Leave None to Tell the Story.* New York: Human Rights Watch, 1999.

Gourevitch, Philip. *We Wish to Inform You That Tomorrow We Will Be Killed with Our Families.* London: Picador, 1999.

Guillebaud, Meg. *After the Locusts: How Costly Forgiveness Is Restoring Rwanda's Stolen Years.* Oxford, U.K.: Monarch, 2005.

Hatzfield, Jean. *Into the Quick of Life: The Rwandan Genocide—The Survivors Speak.* Paris: Editions du Seuil, 2000.

———. *Machete Season: The Killers in Rwanda Speak.* London: Picador, 2006.

Heitritter, Lynn, and Jeanette Vought. *Helping Victims of Sexual Abuse: A Sensitive Biblical Guide for Counselors, Victims, and Families.* Bloomington, Minn.: Bethany, 1989.

Ilibagiza, Immaculee. *Left to Tell: Discovering God amidst the Rwandan Holocaust.* Carlsbad, Ca.: Hay House, 2007.

Lampman, Lisa Barnes, ed. *Helping a Neighbor in Crisis.* Wheaton, Ill.: Tyndale, 1997.

Martin, Meredith. *The Fate of Africa: From the Hopes of Freedom to the Heart of Despair.* New York: Public Affairs, 2005.

Pakenham, Thomas. *The Scramble for Africa: White Man's Conquest of the Dark Continent from 1876 to 1912.* New York: Perennial, 2003.

Plantinga, Cornelius Jr. *A Breviary of Sin: Not the Way It's Supposed to Be.* Grand Rapids, Mich.: Eerdmans, 1995.

Rucyahana, John. *The Bishop of Rwanda: Finding Forgiveness amidst a Pile of Bones.* Nashville: Thomas Nelson, 2007.

Taylor, Christopher C. *Milk, Honey and Money: Changing Concepts in Rwandan Healing.* Washington, D.C.: Smithsonian Institution Press, 1992.

Van Ness, Daniel. *Crime and Its Victims: What Can We Do.* Downers Grove, Ill.: InterVarsity, 1986.

Wright, N. T. *Evil and the Justice of God.* Downers Grove, Ill.: InterVarsity Press, 2006.

notes

prelude: secrets of the Umuvumu's scars

1. Desmond Tutu, *No Future without Forgiveness* (New York: Doubleday, 1999), 272.

interlude: justice and human flourishing

1. Daniel E. Van Ness and Karen Strong, *Restoring Justice*, 2nd ed. (Cincinnati: Anderson, 2002), 8–9.

2. Howard Zehr, "Restoring Justice, " in *God and the Victim*, ed. Lisa Barnes Lampman (Grand Rapids, Mich.: Eerdmans, 1999), 132.

3. Books and dissertations have been written on the weaknesses and strengths of gacaca, and I commend them for further research: Luc Huyse and Mark Salter, *Traditional Justice and Reconciliation after Violent Conflict: Learning from African Experiences* (Stockholm: International Institute for Democracy and Electoral Assistance, 2008); available online at www.idea.int/publications/traditional_justice/upload/Traditional_Justice_and_Reconciliation_after_Violent_Conflict.pdf; Alana Erin Tiemessen, "After Arusha: Gacaca Justice in Post-Genocide Rwanda," *African Studies Quarterly* 8, vol. 1 (Fall 2004); available online at www.africa.ufl.edu/asq/v8/v8i1a4.pdf; Nicholas Wolterstorff, "The Contours of Justice: An Ancient Call for *Shalom*," in *God and the Victim*, 113.

4. Ibid., 121.

5. Daniel Philpott, ed., *The Politics of Past Evil: Religion, Reconciliation, and the Dilemmas of Transitional Justice* (Notre Dame, Ind.: University of Notre Dame Press, 2006), 14.

6. Ken Sande, *The Peacemaker: A Biblical Guide to Resolving Conflict* (Grand Rapids, Mich.: Baker, 2004), 22–26.

interlude: wrestling with forgiveness

1. As quoted in Miroslav Volf, *Free of Charge: Giving and Forgiving in a Culture Stripped of Grace* (Grand Rapids, Mich.: Zondervan, 2005), 168.

2. Ibid., 182.

3. Everett Worthington, *Five Steps to Forgiveness: The Art and Science of Forgiving* (New York: Crown, 2001), 10.

4. See Tian Dayton, *The Magic of Forgiveness: Emotional Freedom and Transformation at Mid-life* (Deerfield Beach, Fla.: Health Communications, 2003), or Fred Luskin, *Forgive for Good: A Proven Prescription for Health and Happiness* (San Francisco: HarperCollins, 2002).

5. Nancy Leigh DeMoss, *Choosing Forgiveness: Your Journey to Freedom* (Chicago: Moody, 2006).

interlude: journeying toward reconciliation

1. Before entering this discussion, it is helpful to note that reconciliation is not always possible or advisable, especially if one person has violated trust repeatedly or when it could put the victim in harm's way, either physically or psychologically. All movements toward reconciliation require risk, but the nature of that risk must be evaluated carefully. See Worthington, *Five Steps to Forgiveness*, 163.

2. As quoted in Roy Baumeister, Julie Exline, and Kristin Sommer, "The Victim Role, Grudge Theology, and Two Dimensions of Forgiveness," in *Dimensions of Forgiveness: Psychological Research & Theological Perspectives*, ed. Everett L. Worthington Jr. (Philadelphia and London: The Templeton Foundation Press, 1998), 85.

3. Ibid., 83.

4. Ibid.

5. Ibid., 84.

6. Worthington, *Five Steps to Forgiveness*, 162.

7. David Augsburger, *Helping People Forgive* (Louisville: Westminster John Knox, 1996), 35.

8. Worthington, *Five Steps to Forgiveness*, 199–203.

9. Baumeister, Exline, and Stillwell, "The Victim Role," 88.

10. Ibid.

11. Worthington, *Five Steps to Forgiveness*, 206.

12. Daniel Van Ness and Karen Strong, *Restoring Justice*, 77.

13. David Augsburger, *Helping People Forgive*, 43.

14. Elliot Dorff, "Forgiveness: A Jewish Approach," *Dimensions of Forgiveness*, 35.

interlude: facing the darkness

1. Everett Worthington, "The Pyramid Model of Forgiveness," in *Dimensions of Forgiveness*, 113.

2. Tian Dayton, *The Magic of Forgiveness*, 26.

3. Ibid.

4. Ibid., 33.

5. Worthington, *Five Steps to Forgiveness*, 26.

6. Ibid., 29.

7. Dan Allender, "The Mark of Evil," in *God and the Victim*, 40.

8. Ibid., 44.

9. Ibid., 45.

interlude: comfort my people

1. John Steward, "Drinking from the Waterfall," *Presence* 10, no. 1 (February 2004): 20–27.

2. See Appendix for several helpful handouts from John Steward on the forgiveness process.

3. Mark S. Umbreit, *Victim-Offender Mediation Training Manual* (Center for Restorative Justice and Peacemaking, School of Social Work, University of Minnesota, 1998), 50.

4. Ibid., 17.

5. Ibid., 53.

6. See, for example, Mary White, "Every Knee Shall Bow," in *God and the Victim*, 195; Dayton, *The Magic of Forgiveness*, 59–65; or Worthington, *Five Steps of Forgiveness*, 38–39.

7. Dayton, *The Magic of Forgiveness*, 248.

8. Ibid., 263.

9. David Augsburger, *Helping People Forgive*, 170.

interlude: reversing the downward spiral

1. Laura Cartensen, John Gottman, and Robert Levenson, "Emotional Behavior in Long-term Marriage," *Psychology and Aging* 10, no. 1 (March 1995): 140–49.

2. Worthington, *Five Steps to Forgiveness*, 115–16.

3. Miroslav Volf, *The End of Memory* (Grand Rapids, Mich.: Eerdmans, 2006), 15.

4. Worthington, *Five Steps to Forgiveness*, 256.

5. Donald Kraybill, Steven Nolt, and David Weaver-Zercher, *Amish Grace: How Forgiveness Transcended Tragedy* (San Francisco: Jossey-Bass, 2007).

6. Dr. Fred Luskin, *Forgive for Love* (San Francisco: HarperOne, 2007), 57.

postlude: reconciliation as a transfiguration moment

1. Miroslav Volf, *Exclusion and Embrace* (Nashville: Abingdon, 1996), 125.

If you enjoyed this book, you should see the movie!

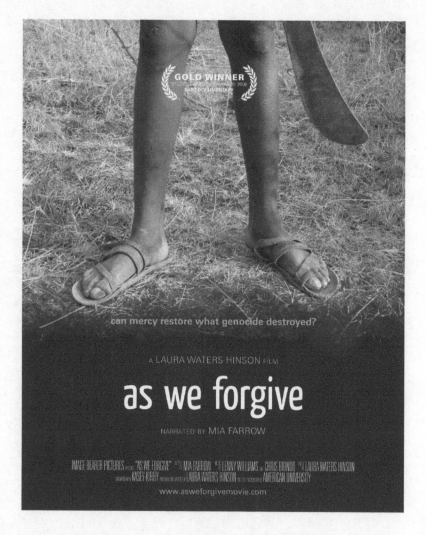

can mercy restore what genocide destroyed?

A LAURA WATERS HINSON FILM

as we forgive

NARRATED BY MIA FARROW

IMAGE BEARER PICTURES PRESENTS "AS WE FORGIVE" A FILM BY MIA FARROW MUSIC BY LENNY WILLIAMS AND CHRIS BIONDO PRODUCED BY LAURA WATERS HINSON
SCREENWRITER KASEY KIRBY PRODUCED AND WRITTEN BY LAURA WATERS HINSON DEVELOPED IN PARTNERSHIP WITH AMERICAN UNIVERSITY

www.asforgivemovie.com

"It's hard for me to talk about this film without getting emotional ...
a very powerful film, but also uplifting at the same time."

— CALEB DESCHANEL, five-time Oscar nominated cinematographer,
The Passion of the Christ

as we forgive

Gold Winner, Best Documentary,
2008 Student Academy Awards

A film by Laura Waters Hinson,
narrated by Mia Farrow

The book you have in your hands was inspired by the subjects of *As We Forgive*, an acclaimed documentary on the lives of Rosaria and Chantale — two Rwandan women coming face to face with the men who slaughtered their families during the 1994 genocide, and their incredible journeys from death to life through reconciliation.

The characters of Rosaria, Saveri, Chantale, Yohana (aka John), Pastor Gahigi, and Joy originally appeared in *As We Forgive* the movie, and now their incredible stories of forgiveness are explored in depth in Catherine Larson's captivating book. In *As We Forgive*, viewers join Chantale and Yohana during their momentous first encounter in fourteen years since the murder of Chantale's father. Viewers also witness the incredible act of practical reconciliation as Saveri, the killer of Rosaria's sister, rallies the community of survivors and ex-prisoners to help Rosaria move into the new house he helped build for her.

Winner of the 2008 Student Academy Award for best documentary, *As We Forgive* has been featured in the National Geographic All Roads Film Festival, and has been presented to the U.S. Congress, to the World Bank, and at numerous churches and universities across the country.

As We Forgive the movie is a perfect complement to small groups that are discussing Catherine Larson's book, or for readers wanting to put faces to the stories of faith and forgiveness of the courageous Rwandans profiled in these pages. If you are interested in purchasing a copy of *As We Forgive* the movie, or would like to host a screening in your community, please visit our website:

www.asweforgivemovie.com

LiViNG BRiCKS

Rebuilding Rwanda.
Brick by brick.

Would you like to get involved in Rwanda's reconciliation movement? Join filmmaker Laura Waters Hinson and Prison Fellowship International to support the Living Bricks campaign. Choose to be a Living Brick!

Living Bricks helps repentant ex-prisoners build desperately needed homes for genocide survivors, creating villages where former enemies live together in peace and reconciliation.

Will you give a brick today? Visit:

www.LivingBricksCampaign.org

CPSIA information can be obtained
at www.ICGtesting.com
Printed in the USA
LVHW040449180519
618300LV00007B/122